Jane Campion

Jane Campion

Authorship and Personal Cinema

ALISTAIR FOX

INDIANA UNIVERSITY PRESS

Bloomington & Indianapolis

This book is a publication of

Indiana University Press
601 North Morton Street
Bloomington, Indiana 47404-3797 USA

iupress.indiana.edu

Telephone orders   800-842-6796
Fax orders   812-855-7931
Orders by e-mail   iuporder@indiana.edu

Manufactured in the United
States of America

Library of Congress Cataloging-
in-Publication Data

Fox, Alistair.
  Jane Campion : authorship and
personal cinema / Alistair Fox.
    p. cm.
  Includes bibliographical
references and index.
  ISBN 978-0-253-35618-5 (cloth : alk.
paper) — ISBN 978-0-253-22301-2
(pbk. : alk. paper) 1. Campion,
Jane, 1954—Criticism and
interpretation. I. Title.
  PN1998.3.C3545F69 2011
  791.4302'33092—dc22
  [B]
                          2010037827

1 2 3 4 5   16 15 14 13 12 11

FRONTISPIECE Jane Campion and her daughter, Alice. Courtesy of
Jane Campion, with permission from the photographer, Patrick Swirc.

For Ashleigh and Hannah Fox

I'm here for one reason only, to find out who I am. . . . It is
not as easy as it sounds for a lady to find out who she is.

VOICEOVER OF THE LADYBUG
in Jane Campion's segment of *Chacun son cinéma* (2007)

Contents

Acknowledgments

My greatest debt, as always, is owed to Hilary Radner Fox, my wife and intellectual partner, whose formidable expertise and interest in cinema exerted the gravitational pull that ensured that sooner or later (and not unwillingly) I would be drawn to assay a study of the sort presented in this book. Her insights, particularly with respect to psychoanalysis and women's cinema, set me thinking along lines that I hope have borne fruit.

Thanks are due to friends and colleagues in Paris, where most of this book was written during a period of sabbatical leave in 2008. I would like to acknowledge my debts to Raphaëlle Moine, who made available to me the extensive collection of interviews that Jane Campion has given in France, which remain largely unknown in the English-speaking world; to Michel Marie and Huguette Dorelli, who, apart from offering us matchless hospitality and introducing us to the sights and delights of Burgundy, also drew my attention to the work of French film scholars such as Francis Vanoye and psychoanalytic theorists such as Danièle Flaumenbaum and Françoise Dolto, all of whom helped to shape my thinking; to Raymond Bellour and Christa Blümlinger, not only for their hospitality, but for insights shared in the course of many convivial discussions and for alerting me to the importance of the work of Daniel N. Stern; to Irène Bessière for triggering my interest in Campion in the first place; to Jean Bessière for including me in the network of the Centre d'études et de recherches comparatistes (CERC) at Paris 3 and for helping to liberate me from an Anglo-Saxon reserve about theorizing; and to Laurent Jullier for his invitation to attend the seminar conducted by Francesco Casetti at Université de Paris 3 in February 2008. The influence of these French film scholars and of the vitalizing intellectual atmosphere that surrounds cinema studies in Paris generally will be everywhere apparent in this book. Other scholars whose assistance I would like to acknowledge include Kathleen McHugh, who generously shared with me information that she gathered during her own research on Jane Campion, and Barry Keith Grant, who provided comments on an early draft of the theoretical sections of this book and supplied me with some of his own work on authorship. Special thanks are also owed to the staff of the Margaret Herrick Library in Los Angeles, who facilitated my access to the wealth of material on Campion's films held at that archive.

Closer to home, I would like to thank Jane Campion for time spent with me in amicable conversation; for giving me an advance glimpse of *Bright Star* while it was still in the process of being edited; for providing me with photographs of herself, her daughter, Alice, and her mother, Edith, and a poem written by Edith; and for supplying me with a DVD of her little-known short film, *The Water Diary*—all of which helped to consolidate and deepen the view of her work that is presented in this book. I would also like to thank Pamela Gordon for allowing me to read correspondence between Janet Frame and Jane Campion concerning the latter's plans to film *An Angel at My Table*.

The writing of this book would not have been possible without the sabbatical leave I was granted after a lengthy period spent in senior administration. For this, I would like to record my sincere thanks to the vice chancellor of the University of Otago, Professor David Skegg, whose enlightened view of the humanities in general, and whose support for my scholarship in particular, I have greatly appreciated. As far as the preparation of the manuscript for publication is concerned, I would like to acknowledge the invaluable assistance of Lisa Marr, especially with helping me to check the proofs, compile the list of works cited, and construct the index.

Jane Campion

Introduction: Authorship, Creativity, and Personal Cinema

1 Several decades after the idea of the author as the prime source of meaning was pronounced "dead," authorship has once again resurged as a focus of scholarly interest. This renewed preoccupation is apparent in the reprinting of foundational texts in the authorship debate, together with the publication of a volume of essays that revisits key issues that have been a source of contention.[1] Indeed, despite the widespread currency of the belief that the individual creative genius of the author is an outdated concept, such a supposition has failed to exert a lasting influence on the practices of those who engage academically with cinema: even though many poststructuralist and postmodernist theorists have denounced the idea of authorship, the majority of exegeses of films or bodies of films, and almost all critical biographies, have worked with it, rather than against it, and auteurism remains a standard approach in many university film studies programs.[2] A notion of authorship in cinema remains important for a number of reasons. First, at some level, viewers are interested to know why they—in instances where it occurs—are so powerfully affected by what is shown on the screen; from where does this affective impact originate, and how is it produced? It is not sufficient to say simply that a film's impact is produced by the operation of discursive interplay. What discourses are selected? By whom? Why? For what purpose? To what effect? What is the role of the director in this regard relative to the input of other members of the production team (the cinematographer, scriptwriter, producer, and so on)? To what extent has the director had a determining influence? Second, prospective authors are curious as to what contributes to a film that is recognized as "good,"

and in this respect the nature of the creativity that is at work becomes a central issue. Third, why is the auteur-director celebrated at film festivals and accorded such an esteemed status in prize ceremonies? Despite theoretical attempts to downplay his or her significance, the crucial input of the auteur-director continues to be recognized and remains a source of curiosity, not only at an intuitive level by those who love the cinema, but also formally by those who control or influence its cultural economy, and intellectually by academics.

This ongoing interest in auteurism has been accompanied by a re-conceptualization of authorship, which now takes into account the influences of historical, industrial, and ideological contexts as intersecting determinants of meaning. Despite this modification, the effect of which is to correct the simplicities and dogmatism of the critics who originally propounded the auteur theory, the theory of authorship remains incomplete because of its evasion of questions like those I listed above. Moreover, the whole issue of creativity in filmmaking remains under-theorized.[3] Notably absent is a theoretical account, backed up by a fully developed example, of the creative mediation that occurs in the process whereby a filmmaker responds to elements of his or her real-life experience by transmuting it, through symbolic condensation and displacement, into a work of art.

A foundational beginning was made in this respect by Christian Metz in his collection of essays *The Imaginary Signifier: Psychoanalysis and the Cinema,* originally published in French in 1977, in which he explores the operation of meaning in the film text. Driven primarily by his concern with spectatorial positioning and identification, however, Metz did not proceed as far with the other side of the equation—that is, with the relationship of the filmmaker to his or her filmic representations—as we might have wished. Metz expressed frustration at the lack of studies of whole films and major filmmakers upon which could be based a "nosographic" exploration of cinema (that is, one that aimed to identify the traces of psychological symptoms), which he had become interested in pursuing at that time.[4] In the absence of such evidence, he was restricted to describing the importance of condensation and displacement in cinematic representation, but without being able to attach these processes to specific states of mind in the filmmaker. Unfortunately, subsequent theorists, preoccupied with Metz's semiotic theory of cinematic language, have largely ignored the nosographic approach he was contemplating, with the notable exception of Anne Gillain, whose studies of Truffaut's films, interpreted through the lens of D. W. Winnicott's theory of transitional space, might have supplied Metz with precisely what he felt was lacking.[5]

A number of subsequent theorists have sought to identify alternative ways in which authorial presence is inscribed in filmic texts. One of the most cogent of these is Kaja Silverman, whose essay "The Female Authorial Voice" in *The Acoustic Mirror: The Female Voice in Psychoanalysis and Cinema* has become a locus classicus in the study of cinematic authorship. Silverman, however, as is characteristic of many scholars writing under the sign of poststructuralism during the 1980s and 1990s, assumed that all that could be known of an author was necessarily derived from "inside" the text—that is, from the impression of the author generated by the discourses at play. Hence, the author that Silverman has in mind is one

> who would be subordinate to all the discursive constraints emphasized by [Émile] Benveniste, who would in fact *be nothing* outside cinema—an author "outside" the text who would come into existence as a dreaming, desiring, self-affirming subject only through the inscription of an author "inside" the text, and not one who could ever lay claim to a radical and self-present exteriority, even though he or she might masquerade in such a guise.[6]

To bracket the referent in this way, even though it has informed some fine studies of the enunciative practices of individual auteurs,[7] strikes me as unnecessarily limiting, not only because it detaches art from personal, social, and historical contexts,[8] but also because, in doing so, it forecloses the possibility of identifying the formative roles of projection, identification, and evocation in cinematic creation—especially in instances where, as in the case of Jane Campion, a great wealth of pertinent biographical information is available from sources "outside" the text. "Projection" in the psychoanalytic sense, as Laplanche and Pontalis have suggested, occurs when "the subject sends out into the external world an image of something that exists in him [or her] in an unconscious way," and it is motivated by "the subject's ability to recognize in others precisely what he [or she] refuses to acknowledge in himself [or herself]."[9]

Similarly, "identification" is a process whereby one subject adopts as her own one or more attributes of another subject. "Evocation" involves the creation of a mental representation that is capable of eliciting awareness of prior or current states of being, or desired potential future states, with the aim of making the external environment "symmetrical to human need" through the creation or identification of a symbolic equivalent.[10] In cinema, I will argue, all three processes can be seen at work when sufficient information is available about the circumstances of the author's life outside the filmic text for correspondences between the external and fictive worlds to be identified. In this way, the contributions of projection, identification, and evocation to the determination of the filmic text can be ascertained. Equally, those aspects of the filmic text that are likely to elicit a parallel process of identification on the part of the viewer, and the reasons that they have the power to do so, become more readily apparent.

My aim in this book is to pursue the nosographic line of investigation that Metz felt unable to complete. To do so, I will conduct a detailed examination of the films of a major filmmaker, Jane Campion, of the sort he felt was lacking. My aim is to explore a crucial aspect of authorship that tends to be missing from most studies: the process of fictive invention whereby an author constructs a representation that serves to address concerns arising from his or her extratextual life. In this way, I hope to demonstrate the close relationship between filmic textual systems and the biographical circumstances that, in my view, constitute an important dimension of authorship that has been underestimated in film studies. Without a sense of the dynamics that characterize this relationship, it is impossible to understand fully the nature of the creativity that invests many of the films that are most admired with the qualities that make them distinctive.

2 The debate over authorship was triggered in the first place by the provocative claims made in the late 1950s by a group of young French critics and directors who were reacting against the preceding school known as the *cinéma de qualité*—big production films, often involving literary adaptations, that this group considered clichéd, lacking in conviction, remote from the reality of contemporary life, overburdened by convention, and offering the public "its habitual dose of smut, nonconformity and facile audacity."[11] Against the conventional practices of

the "tradition of quality," this group of young turks (mostly associated with the journal *Cahiers du cinéma*) promoted André Bazin's view that a film should represent a director's personal vision, particularly through its mise-en-scène.[12] As Fereydoun Hoveyda, one of the critics writing for the journal, put it:

> The originality of the auteur lies not in the subject matter he chooses, but in the technique he employs, i.e., the *mise en scène*, through which everything on the screen is expressed. . . . the thought of a *cinéaste* appears through his *mise en scène*. What matters in a film is the desire for order, composition, harmony, the placing of actors and objects, the movements within the frame, the capturing of a moment or a look; in short, the intellectual operation which has put an initial emotion and a general idea to work.[13]

Accordingly, the quality of a film was to be measured by the distinctiveness of the auteur's enunciation and cinematographic technique: "a work is good to the degree that it expresses the man who created it," insisted François Truffaut, quoting a view expressed by Orson Welles.[14]

The idea, originally formulated by Alexandre Astruc, that the filmmaker is an artist who wields his camera in the same way a writer uses a pen or a painter his brush,[15] eventuated in a very elevated view of the director, especially after it had crossed the Atlantic, where it was elaborated into a fully-fledged theory of film authorship by Andrew Sarris, who emphasized the director's "distinguishable personality" as a criterion of value.[16] Auteur theory, however, was strongly contested almost as soon as it appeared. In America, for instance, the critic Pauline Kael was provoked to indignation by Sarris's views, scathingly observing that "often the works in which we are most aware of the personality of the director are his worst films—when he falls back on the devices he has already done to death."[17]

An even more serious challenge to the elevation of the director as auteur came in the form of the poststructuralist assault on the idea of authorship itself. By the end of the 1960s, Roland Barthes had proclaimed the author as the originator of meaning in any kind of text "dead," while Michel Foucault had replaced the idea of an actual author with that of an "author function."[18] Rather than an individual originating genius, "the author" was, in this view, the product of a network of relationships and discourses. For the followers of Barthes and Foucault, any text (a film included) is a discursive construction—the site of intersecting discourses and perspectives in which the relation between the enunciating and the spectating subjects is constantly shifting.[19] Accordingly, a film (like language itself) becomes a multivalent place of "play," an indeterminate field of slippages and substitutions that render meaningless both the idea of the auteur and the idea of analyzing the text to find the author's meaning. As Barthes puts it:

> [T]he modern [poststructuralist] scriptor is born simultaneously with the text, is in no way equipped with a being preceding or exceeding the writing, is not the subject with the book [or film] as predicate; there is no other time than that of the enunciation and every text is eternally written *here and now*.[20]

Furthermore, Barthes continues, "Once the Author is removed, the claim to decipher a text becomes quite futile. To give a text an Author is to impose a limit on that text, to furnish it with a final signified, to close the writing."[21] Self-evidently, these assumptions, if allowed, would render any conception of the author—especially in the terms proposed by Truffaut and Sarris—impossible.

Despite the challenge posed by poststructuralist theory, the idea that the filmmaker could be a prime source of meaning in a film refused to die.[22] During the 1970s, certain scholars sought to reinstate the director as author by revising auteur theory to accommodate the objections of the poststructuralists. Peter Wollen, for example, propounded a theory of "auteur structuralism," in which the individual author is reconceived as the orchestrator of trans-individual codes and binary structures (such as the contrasts between culture/nature, civilization/wilderness, settler/nomad, and so on) that are broadly disseminated in the culture at large.[23] The job of the critic, according to this approach, is to peel off the superficial layers of an author's work to reveal these underlying patterns, as is apparent in Wollen's concluding view of Howard Hawks, whose films he had analyzed as a case study:

> Hawks first attracted attention because he was regarded naïvely as an action director. Later, the thematic content which I have outlined was detected and revealed. Beyond the stylemes, semantemes were found to exist; the films were anchored in an objective stratum of meaning, a plerematic stratum, as the Danish linguist [Louis] Hjelmslev would put it.[24]

In this approach, the author is viewed as "something more like an unconscious catalyst for elements and influences beyond his or her conscious control"—a supposition signaled by the placing of the name of the director within quotation marks (for example, "Hitchcock" rather than Hitchcock, "Ford" rather than Ford, "Hawks" rather than Hawks).[25] While allowing for the auteur's existence, auteur structuralism thus responds to the objections to the romantic idea of the director as creative genius by depersonalizing the auteur in order to render his or her role that of an unconscious facilitator.

Other commentators have similarly sought to modify auteur theory for the sake of admitting other influences on the production of meaning, such as financiers, producers, scriptwriters, and cinematographers.[26] In comparing films by Frank Capra and Alfred Hitchcock, for example, Robin Wood emphasized the importance of ideological and generic determinants, while nevertheless according the director an ability to make a decisive intervention through his "artistic personality."[27] As a result of such modifications, the terms in which authorship is now being conceptualized have become less dogmatic and more inclusive than used to be the case: "auteur studies now tend to see a director's work not as the expression of individual genius but rather as the site of encounter of a biography, an intertext, an institutional context, and a historical moment."[28] Using Campion as an example, Deb Verhoeven has accommodated these developments within a theory she labels "post-auteurism"—which strikes me as throwing the baby out with the bathwater. To recognize that filmmaking is a collaborative venture is different from eliminating the formative influence of the auteur-director altogether.[29]

According to Janet Staiger's useful summary, seven main approaches to authorship as practiced since the Second World War can be identified:

(1) Authorship as *origin*
(2) Authorship as *personality*
(3) Authorship as a *sociology of production*
(4) Authorship as *signature*
(5) Authorship as a *reading strategy*
(6) Authorship as a *site of discourses*
(7) Authorship as a *technique of the self*[30]

Among the approaches enumerated in this list, two acknowledge the director's direct input into the process of authorship: authorship-as-personality and authorship-as-signature. Authorship-as-personality refers to the assumption that meaning is produced by the director's aesthetic choices regarding the organization of her materials, the use of cinema as a language for the expression of ideas, and the view that a unified personal vision should be expressed in the films of a director.[31] Authorship-as-signature refers to the idea that "the author is known by repetition among the various texts 'signed' by a historical person" through motifs and habits that are traceable across a set of films.[32]

Neither of these approaches, in the absence of other considerations pertaining to the actual mindset of the director, is entirely satisfactory as an explanation of the role of personality in authorship. This is because such approaches focus exclusively on *symptoms* of the director's personal engagement, rather than on the causes and overall consequences of that engagement, which, as I will show, are inseparable from the nature of the whole work as a symbolic representation. Studies of this kind limit themselves to identifying the presence of recurrent themes, characters, and situations in successive films or on the "enunciative presence" of the director as revealed in her cinematic style.[33] It is dangerous, however, to make assumptions about personal authorship on the basis of thematic and stylistic attributes alone. In the absence of further corroboration, neither can be confidently taken as an expression of personality, for as Graham Petrie has pointed out, "continuity may be the result of working within a certain genre, or for a particular studio, or in habitual collaboration with a favorite scriptwriter or actor," and few filmmakers have a visual style so distinctive that it persists "no matter with whom they are collaborating or for whom they are making the film."[34] Because of this, critics have sometimes been forced to resort to impressionistic or mystical language to describe the personal element they detect in a film. Andrew Sarris, for example, in attempting to explain the "interior meaning" he believed could be extrapolated from "the tension between a director's personality and his material," could find no way of describing it other than as "an *élan* of the soul" or "that intangible difference between one personality and another, all other things being equal."[35]

In my view, none of the approaches that have been adopted to date has paid sufficient attention to one of the most important aspects of "personality," for want of a better word, which concerns the psychic structure that is generated by the filmmaker's actual experience of the world and how that experience conditions the way in which the director decides upon, and executes, his or her artistic intentions. Without a sense of these linkages, there is no way of ascertaining the personal nature of an auteur's relationship with his own work, which is one of the main determinants of meaning. Peter Wollen's insistence that "[a]uteur analysis does not consist of a re-tracing [of] a film to its origins, to its creative source," but rather seeks "a structure (not a message) within the work, which can then *post factum* be assigned to an individual, the director, on empirical grounds,"[36] is one with which I fundamentally disagree. It is only by retracing a film to its origins that the nature of the creative process that brought it into being can be fully understood. This book, therefore, will outline a theory and a method that are capable of illuminating the motives and effects of this creative process. To do so in no way precludes diverse viewers from deriving whatever types of meaning they wish from the experience of watching a film when it is finished, but such interpretations will be distinct from the authoring process of the auteur-director, and should not be confused or equated with it.

3 As I develop a theory of the personal element in authorship, I will explore the films of Jane Campion as a body of work that exemplifies the nature of what I will call—adopting a term proposed by the French film scholar Francis Vanoye—"personal cinema." I have chosen Campion as the subject of this investigation because many of the issues concerning the question of authorship have been raised by the scholars who have written on her.

In the first major exploration of Campion's oeuvre, Dana Polan was struck by its apparent incoherence: "Campion's career bears no unity of theme and style but is marked rather by shifts of direction and changes of emphasis." Polan's perplexity at the disturbances he found in her work— "the divergences; the dispersions; the tensions"—was nevertheless accompanied by a recognition that "she is one of very few women directors who could be considered within the framework of auteurism." (Indeed, much of his analysis of Campion's output is auteurist, even though he seems reluctant to acknowledge this.) The apparent incompatibility between these two perceptions led Polan to conclude that the case of Campion gave good cause to rethink the very nature of authorship.[37] He even went so far as to suggest, following Foucault, that it is best "to treat the

name 'Jane Campion' as signaling . . . a space of 'dispersion'—the name
of the author as a shorthand for all the forces that work against unity,
against the career as a coherent unfolding of a vision."[38]

Other scholars will have none of this, discovering in Campion's work
precisely the kind of unity that Polan denies. Kathleen McHugh, in a
2007 monograph on Campion, offers a corrective:

> Despite the endless critiques of auteur theory, some of which have explicitly
> cited the example of Jane Campion, this director's films demonstrate a remark-
> able if complex consistency of narrative, thematic, and stylistic concerns that
> run from her student films up to her most recently released feature. . . . The early
> shorts, edgy and explicit, focus on power, violence, and emotional pain in dys-
> functional sexual, familial, and social relationships.[39]

Among the continuities McHugh detects are "cinematic techniques that
both represent and blur the differences between objective and subjective
narrative states"; the use of often surreal cinematic modes to "convey a
sense of astute psychological realism"; a focus on "relationships between
siblings, parents and children, and friends"; and "the importance of wom-
en's work, their creative expression, and of sexual desire as a powerful,
necessary, and compelling *threat* to that expression."[40] McHugh admits,
however, that frequently the filmmaker appears to have a habit, as in *A
Girl's Own Story,* of inviting spectators to "experience perceptually the effects of traumas whose nature or exact causes the films frequently with-
hold from us."[41] Similarly, McHugh sees *Sweetie* as presenting "a puzzle
from which some of the pieces have been permanently lost," meaning
that the viewer has no option other than to follow Carlo Ginzburg's ad-
age: "when causes cannot be reproduced, there is nothing to do but to
deduce them from their effects."[42]

McHugh's concession that, despite the continuities she detects,
there are lacunae in Campion's films for which she can find no explanation, indicates the persistence of questions that still need to be answered.
The negative reactions of certain critics to Campion's later films also
invite one to look for the missing pieces of the puzzle. Feminist critics, for
example, have highlighted the contradiction of a director who has been
associated with a feminist vision of the female right to self-determination
allowing her heroine in *The Piano* to be subjected to the indignity of being patriarchally disempowered and treated like a possession.[43] Others

have alleged a progressive decline, in which they see Campion as losing any sense of unity between form and content after *Sweetie*,[44] while some have suggested that, with *The Portrait of a Lady*, she sold out her talents on a money-laden, middlebrow project in "a cheap bid at a larger audience."[45] The persistence of such perplexities and allegations suggests that the deeper source of the unity of Campion's work—the preoccupations that motivate her migrations between diverse modes, genres, and styles—has still not been adequately identified. It is the purpose of the discussion that follows to show how an understanding of the autobiographical subtext of Campion's movie-making reveals not merely the symptoms that indicate the presence of a coherent personal vision, but the causes that inform it. When Campion's personal motivations are understood, one can say of her films, as Robert McKee has observed about films by masters such as Robert Altman, John Cassavetes, Preston Sturges, François Truffaut, and Ingmar Bergman: they are so idiosyncratic "that a three-page synopsis identifies the artist as surely as his DNA."[46]

The anti-auteurist tendencies evident in Polan's approach to Campion's films reached an extreme expression in Deb Verhoeven's *Jane Campion* (2009). Not only does Verhoeven endorse Timothy Corrigan's conclusion that auteurism has come "to constitute a form of film consumption which no longer involves the viewing of a film,"[47] but she espouses the view that auteurism is merely "an intricate set of industrial processes."[48] Consequently, in Verhoeven's account of Campion, there is no discussion of any particularities of content in her movies at all; it is as if the author as a living, thinking, feeling individual capable of exercising personal agency and choice in the making of her films has disappeared altogether, to be replaced simply by an impersonal nexus of economic and marketing forces aimed at ensuring that the consumption of the film-as-product will deliver a profit to its producers and financiers. The position of "auteur" as a dimension of self-fashioning on the director's part and marketing on the part of the industry emerges out of ancillary textual materials such as interviews, press releases, festival appearances, and even scholarly responses, which are not necessarily tied to intrinsic elements of the film itself.

While no one would deny that industrial considerations exert an important influence on a filmmaker's choices nor that the complexity of a film's reception cannot be understood as exclusively a product of its own innate qualities, it is perverse to conclude that this is the be-all and end-all of filmmaking itself. If it were that simple, Hollywood would produce only hit movies. A useful analogy might be drawn with the practices of Shakespeare and other Elizabethan and Jacobean dramatists, who were highly aware of the different echelons in their audiences: the "unskilful" standing in the "yard," who were looking for blood, gore, and sensational action in tragedy ("when the bad bleed, then is the tragedy good," as one of Tourneur's characters in *The Revenger's Tragedy* puts it) and for belly laughs and knock-about farce in comedy, and the "judicious," who were looking for thematic depth on matters of political, social, and psychological importance.[49] Dramatists of this period catered to these audiences to ensure the success of their plays, and Shakespeare, who was a share-holder in the theatrical company that was mounting his plays, hoped to make a profit no less than anyone else; however, no one these days would claim that the plays Shakespeare wrote under these conditions do not display the indelible signs of his authorship, which are manifest in their recurrent thematic concerns, choice of subjects, and verbal style (equivalent to a filmmaker's techniques of enunciation). Nor can we explain the continued success of Shakespeare's work, that his name remains a synonym for literary greatness, while Tourneur is relatively unknown, without reference to the texts to which their names are affixed.

As I will argue in this book, it is exactly the same with the films of Jane Campion. Campion undoubtedly has an acute sense of her own persona as an auteur and its importance to her ability to operate within an industry that is largely indifferent, if not overtly hostile, to the kinds of projects she wishes to pursue. She clearly cultivates and encourages a view of her work that highlights its personal and artistic singularity, knowing that even the success of *The Piano* is unremarkable in comparison to films like *Pretty Woman* (Garry Marshall, 1990) or *Sex and the City: The Movie* (Michael Patrick King, 2008), each of which had international box office takes of over $450 million. Her efforts would be in vain if her films did not bear the marks of a personal vision that resonates with female audiences, in particular with women seeking validation for experiences not encompassed by typical Hollywood "femme fare." While her films demonstrate the influences of her collaborators, they nevertheless contain a wealth of detail in the mise-en-scène and enunciation that cannot be accounted for merely by consideration of the industrial and cultural circumstances of each film's production, nor the consumerist circumstances of each film's reception, as valid as studies of these phenomena might be in their own right. Studies of the industrial and cultural contexts, the topics of economics and the sociology of culture, offer valuable insights into why and how certain larger trends emerge in a given period, yet they tell us little about the origins and trajectories of the individual creative process as it responds to the emergent possibilities offered at a particular period in history. The position I will be maintaining in the analysis that follows is that, without further consideration of the personal motivations and concerns of the filmmaker-director, a large part of the overall signification of a film will go unrecognized, and hence unappreciated—in particular, in terms of the way that individual works respond to, and resonate with, their audiences as shared experience, an experience shared not only with other audience members, but also with the creator of that work. A "thick description," to borrow from the anthropologist Clifford Geertz, of a work of art includes an understanding of its maker and her relations with that work, as well as its social and cultural uses and circulation.[50]

At the other end of the spectrum from Verhoeven are scholars such as Sue Gillett, who take Campion's films themselves as their exclusive topic, without venturing beyond the film-as-text.[51] Gillett, pointing to the centrality of the mother-child relationship in generating Campion's narratives, calls upon a psychoanalytic paradigm to interpret the films as symptoms, not of a particular individual, but of the psyche as a generalized phenomenon that, if not universal, at the very least characterizes subjectivity within contemporary culture. The limitation of this approach, however, is that without recourse to the origins and biographical specificities of the filmmaker's own experiences, it is not possible to illuminate the particularities of the creative process that mark Campion's films nor to comment more fully on the creative process and the relations between art and psyche with regard to the individual artist and her work. Further, Gillett, in particular, is limited by her desire to explore the films within a typology defined by Lacanian theory, which at times seems to take precedence over the films themselves. Just as the analyst cannot understand the analysand without the process of analysis, the individual psyche and the work that it produces cannot be fully encompassed through the evocation of a particular theoretical model (even though these may provide useful guides). It is only through a painstaking recreation of the individual itineraries that were brought to bear upon the work, and which are constitutive to its genesis, that we can come to develop insights into the creation of art. Because of the personal nature of Campion's films and the copious material available about her early life and family, Jane Campion's oeuvre offers a unique opportunity to gain an insight into the relations between the individual psyche of an artist and her work.

My second reason for choosing Campion as a case study is that she has professed her sense of vocation as an auteur. She will not read Hollywood scripts and has no interest in mainstream cinema, finding its way of trying to please all the time "nauseating." Instead, she desires "to understand the world through stories," through ideas, and in an ideal world "would make only films of which she was the author."[52] Given these predispositions, Campion's films provide a fertile field for an exploration of the mechanisms of authorship.

Finally, Campion is an ideal subject for this investigation because of the frequency with which she has drawn attention to autobiographical elements in each of her movies. For example, in her director's commentary on *Sweetie* (1989), she affirms that Kay, the sister whose superstition and pathological anxieties cause her to withdraw into sexual aversion, is "a very extreme version of a part of me" and that she herself has had problems with intimacy.[53] Similarly, in the commentary on *An Angel at My Table* (1990), she reveals that her depiction of Janet Frame, a New Zealand novelist who was institutionalized for schizophrenia, was deeply personal, owing to the fact that it mirrored her own mother's struggle with depression and with electric shock treatment.[54] Campion's personal investment in her fictions extends even to small details in the costuming and props. In an interview with Marie Colmant, for example, she reveals that the reason she depicts Janet Frame wearing "gumboots" was not only because everyone in New Zealand wears them in the country on account of the mud, but also because when she was thirteen years old, her own parents moved the family to the country. Whenever she puts on gumboots, Campion declares, "it is like a physical memory, an extraordinary sensation," emphasizing the power of these objects to evoke her childhood past. "When I am very old," she muses, "I can see myself very clearly on a farm wearing gumboots. I don't know whether Janet actually had them, but I wanted her to wear them."[55] Similarly, one of the reasons she ended *An Angel at My Table* with a shot of Janet Frame writing in a caravan (a trailer), Campion reveals, was also a personal one because her father had won a caravan in a raffle.[56] Her passion for caravans, which are associated with her father, extends to a comparable enthusiasm for huts, or "baches," as they are known in New Zealand, and it is not coincidental that when she was working on the screenplay for *In the Cut* (2003)—a film deeply concerned with issues relating to her father—she spent several months in her writer's hut near Glenorchy, located deep within the Southern Alps.[57]

Indeed, Campion's personal investment in every film she has made is so ubiquitous and sustained that it truly can be said to inform every aspect of the work, in terms of both content and the mise-en-scène. The readiness with which Campion has revealed the presence of autobiographical elements in her work means that the process of creative transformation of the real-life elements that is entailed in authorship is easier to ascertain than is the case with many filmmakers. Drawing inferences from what a director says in interviews can be a perilous business, given that, as Deb Verhoeven has emphasized, "Campion" has become the name of "a constellation of cultural and individual investments of varying intensities," including the manner in which the director chooses to represent herself and "the commercial creation and circulation of the 'auteur-name.'"[58] Moreover, as Verhoeven points out, Campion herself is uneasy about some aspects of the interviews she has given: "I'm an idiot," Campion says, "because as soon as I say something I think I can stick with, I immediately realize the opposite is true."[59]

Campion is not the first director to contradict herself in interviews when issues of a deeply personal nature have been at stake. When François Truffaut's *Les 400 coups* (*The 400 Blows*) was released, the director oscillated between adamantly claiming, on one hand, that nothing in the film was an exaggeration and that he had personally experienced as a child all the hardships endured by Antoine Doinel, and, on the other hand, flatly denying that *Les 400 coups* was autobiographical. Anne Gillain ascribes this inconsistency, in part, to Truffaut's desire to spare the feelings of his mother and father (at that time, they were still alive), who could have felt mercilessly attacked through their fictive surrogates in the film.[60] On occasion, one senses that Campion is similarly caught between a concern to spare the feelings of family members and a desire to highlight the origins in her personal life of details that appear in her films. As with Truffaut, this tension between revealing and concealing can, from time to time, produce inconsistencies. She can also appear to change her mind—for example, on the question of whether or not she projects in her films. Nevertheless, despite Campion's warning about her propensity to contradict herself, there is such a consistency and unity in the impulses, perspectives, and significant biographical events she describes in her interviews and director's commentaries across the whole course of her career that one can build a fairly accurate picture of what is reliable, especially when it can be corroborated from other sources, such as the independent statements of her sister, Anna, and facts concerning her family that are known from the public record.

4 The frequency and density of autobiographical allusions in Jane Campion's films, many of which can be associated to circumstances in her childhood involving her parents, confirm that Campion's oeuvre belongs to what Vanoye has termed *cinéma personnel,* or "personal cinema."[61] Among filmmakers whose work can be described as constituting a personal cinema, Vanoye includes Woody Allen, François Truffaut, Federico Fellini, Raymond Depardon, Chantal Akerman, and Andrei Tarkovski, to cite just a few, all of whom have an autobiographical or personal element that "extends implicitly, to various degrees, through the entirety of their works, in the eyes of the spectator."[62]

Films displaying the traits of personal cinema reveal a number of strategies that filmmakers use to project the autobiographical subtext (or *scénario autobiographique,* as Vanoye calls it) that is always present in this kind of cinema. At the simplest level, a director can use the mediation of an actor matched with a particular character—such as Jean-Pierre Léaud and Antoine Doinel for Truffaut in *Les 400 coups, Antoine et Colette, Baisers volés (Stolen Kisses), Domicile conjugal (Bed and Board),* and *L'Amour en fuite* (*Love on the Run*); Marcello Mastroianni and his avatars for Fellini; or Lee Kang-sheng as Hsiao-kang for Tsai Ming-liang in movies like *Ni na bian ji dian* (*What Time Is It over There?*) and *Tian bian yi duo yun* (*The Wayward Cloud*). In some instances, a director-actor will actually play some version of the self, as in the cases of Woody Allen, Charlie Chaplin, and Clint Eastwood.

At a more complicated level, the filmmaker can construct a more dispersed autobiographical recreation in which the "I" is diffused through various elements of the film, such as the use of narration, a first-person voice (*voix-je*); the introduction of a character, temporarily or for more extended lengths of time, who serves as a mouthpiece for the author; manipulation of point of view, etc. Examples of this kind of strategy can be found in Fellini's *Amarcord* and in Woody Allen's *Annie Hall*.[63]

At the most complex level of all, the filmmaker can introduce an autobiographical dimension through a still more radical displacement in which one character in the film is made to carry the weight of a personal problematic, or this problematic may be distributed across several characters in successive movies—as in the case of Michelangelo Antonioni, who makes his various architects, writers, journalists, and photographers experience the conflicts and difficulties encountered by the contemporary creative artist. Another example can be found in Alfred Hitchcock, whose cinematic characters enact the indulgence and exorcism of troubling fantasies that the filmmaker recognized as emanating from deep divisions within his own personality.[64]

Jane Campion's films exhibit all of these strategies, sometimes within the same movie. In *Sweetie,* the character of Kay bears the same kind of relationship to Campion as Antoine Doinel does for Truffaut. Autobiographical references are also dispersed through all her films, as in the Bluebeard play-within-the movie in *The Piano* (1993), which alludes to and metaphorically recalls the outcome of the theatrical life of her parents. The reference to Isabel's dead son in *The Portrait of a Lady* (1996), which in the lingering close-up shot invites us to gaze with Isabel at the cast of her dead baby's hand, also evokes the loss of Jane Campion's own son, Jasper, who died twelve days after his birth—despite the fact that this episode is suggested in the source text by Henry James. Finally, different aspects of a multifaceted problematic are distributed across all the main characters in her successive movies. The fathers in *A Girl's Own Story* (1984) and *Holy Smoke* (1999) bear a shadowy resemblance to Richard Campion, Jane Campion's father, in their indulgence in extramarital affairs—which provoke a range of complex reactions in their daughters—while the depressed and symbolically mute mothers in *A Girl's Own Story* and *The Piano* bear a relationship to Edith Campion, Jane's mother, in their disempowerment and distress at the realization of it. The close relationship between Janet in *An Angel at My Table* and Edith, who had similarly undergone electric shock treatment just a few years before, is even more overt, and a comparable similarity to Edith can be discerned in Isabel in *The Portrait of a Lady*. Like Edith, Isabel inherited a large fortune which she allowed to let slip from her grasp because of her romantic attachment to an unfaithful man whose behavior left her equally miserable and disillusioned.[65] In Janet Frame, the great New Zealand novelist, Campion also found someone who could model how to use artistic creativity as a protective device to ward off the effects of existential terror—especially that which arises from narcissistic deprivation.

The list goes on. Dawn in *Sweetie* embodies aspects of a "certain wildness" that Jane Campion attributes to Anna, her sister, while Frannie and Pauline in *In the Cut* reproduce the sibling relationship between Jane and the half sister she discovered later in her life (the sister's name has not been made public, probably out of respect for her privacy). Similarly, Ruth's troubled relationship with a father figure, PJ, in *Holy Smoke* relates, one suspects, to Jane Campion's real-life father-daughter relationship insofar as it is informed by a fantasy of incest, which is replicated in *Sweetie* and in other episodes (for example, in *After Hours*, 1984) that depict the attempt of an older man to seduce a woman young enough to be his daughter, or vice versa (possibly recalling Richard Campion's relationships with the actresses in his theatrical company).[66] The full meaning of films in which this intensity of autobiographical reference is present can only be perceived, as Vanoye has argued, when the interrelations between the circumstances of the filmmaker's life and the constituents of the film are established through an approach that is *génético-biographique*—that is, one that traces the process whereby the form and substance of a film evolve from its origins in the family system of the artist who creates it.[67]

5 Jane Campion's characters, like all the main characters in films one can associate with personal cinema, tend to display psychological traits that are typical of individuals who have suffered some pathogenic circumstances or events in their family background. Drawing upon the work of the Gestalt therapist Noël Salathé, Vanoye has noted how these characters correspond to the main personality types encountered in psychotherapy. It is uncanny how closely Campion's characters can be matched to these fundamental types.

The first in Salathé's personality typology is the "sociopathic type," whose traits can be characterized thus:

> "Since no one has known, nor will know, how to love me, I seek to get even, I do what I like when I like, I use other people in whatever way I want, and for my own pleasure." Social instability, delinquency, aggression are the common behavioral traits—but also amiability, a needy dependence, immaturity, a refusal to accept responsibility for one's actions, an absence of ethical considerations and self-control, a weak imaginary, an oscillation between adopting the roles of persecutor and victim.[68]

Even though Salathé's characterization of this personality type was written without any reference to Jane Campion's *Sweetie,* its exactness as a description of Dawn in that movie is striking.

So, too, with the second of Salathé's personality types, the "masochistic type," to whom he imputes the following traits:

> "I am alone because I am worthless. I'm going to try to make myself loved and respected—but I'll never be able to succeed in doing that. No one can do anything for me." Recurrent failures, awkwardness in social and emotional relationships, a quest for approval and impulses to rebel, a futile effort to achieve perfection, a feeling of guilt and a desire to be punished, the invalidation of positive experiences.[69]

Just as his description of the sociopathic type matched Dawn in *Sweetie,* Salathé's description of the masochistic type could be applied in almost every respect to Kelly in *Two Friends,* to Janet in *An Angel at My Table,* and to both Frannie and Pauline in *In the Cut.*

Finally, the third of Salathé's personality types, the "tertiary narcissistic type," is equally relevant, being described thus:

> "I have been frustrated, humiliated, wounded. I shall get even by gaining the upper hand, by being above everyone else." Characterized by hyperactivity, success, vanity, a taste for power, a propensity to exploit others, a disturbed emotional life.[70]

This could serve as an exact description of Ruth in *Holy Smoke*. Ada in *The Piano* also displays many of the same traits.

The recurrence of these distinctive personality types in personal cinema points to the role that such cinematic creation can perform for the filmmaker as a vehicle for the expression of a response to earlier trauma. For authors of films that can be identified as manifesting a personal cinema, it would seem that the process involved in the creation of a film is a therapeutic one, usually involving a regressive "detour through the archaic," as one authority has put it.[71]

6 When one considers what is known about Jane Campion's earlier life, it is not difficult to detect the circumstances that fueled this kind of creativity, that prompted her to make films of an autobiographical cast that are designed to function as instruments of self-exploration and self-repair in response to the lingering effects of childhood trauma. The Campion parents, in addition to their emotional problems (which, as I will show, deeply affected their children), were intensely absorbed in theatrical careers—he as a director and she as an actress. Edith Campion also suffered severely from depression. These two factors combined to make Richard and Edith Campion, even though they were loving parents, relatively unavailable to their children in what Daniel Stern has called "the domain of intersubjective relatedness."[72] Consequently, Jane and her sister, Anna, by their own confessions, felt a desperate need to compete for their parents' love as children. They were also left alone for extensive periods while their parents were touring with their traveling drama company, with Anna and Jane being placed in the care of a series of nannies. Under the pressure of the psychosomatic stress this caused, first Anna and then Jane developed asthma.[73] As Anna recalls it, the impulse that eventually led her and Jane to make films began as a response to one particular woman who looked after them:

> "We were very rigorously controlled by this woman. There was a lot of discipline." Each of them dealt with this differently. "I went into my head into a fantasy haze where the real world didn't impinge. And that's when Jane got on to the idea of projects to save her. She was obsessed by the need to get everything right. She'd write these plays in which she took all the parts—king, servants, the lot. She'd control the projects to have the world appreciate her—which she still does, really."[74]

The imaginative creation of fictive worlds, in other words, sprang from a need in the girls to find a way of protecting themselves psychically from the otherwise unbearable pain of emotional deprivation. For Jane, the world she invented through art allowed her not only to place herself at the center of that world,[75] but it was also a way of gaining her parents' attention. By choosing to invent plays, Jane Campion was trying to join her parents in their theatrical world: her father by directing the piece, and her mother by acting all the parts. The young Jane also engaged in graphic art, and, once again, Anna Campion is astute in her remarks on this preoccupation in her sister: "Our parents believed that, if you wanted a child to do well, you'd just ignore them. So it's like Jane was always trying to make these drawings to get their attention and she's just moved on to more and more complicated and ambitious drawings. Our parents were fairly obsessed with themselves."[76]

We are presented, then, with a filmmaker who, from the beginning, turned to artistic creation in an attempt to repair psychic perturbations arising from a childhood in which she grew up feeling neglected and unloved. Even though the plays and drawings of her youth have turned into the more "complicated and ambitious" films she makes as an adult, they still serve the same purposes: to place Jane Campion at the center of her universe; to gain the attention of an audience who can compensate for the lack of interest shown in her earlier life by her parents; and, in the course of doing that, to work through the issues involved in a personal problematic that lingers as a result of the emotional starvation she suffered as a child.

7 Psychic perturbations have been very real for Campion in her personal life and that of her family, and she is unusually forthright in admitting this. Commenting on how "terrible" the disease of depression is for many people, and how badly her mother suffered from it, Campion adds, "And it's true enough for me, too."[77] For her, the fictive invention of art is a way of tackling the issues that lie behind these psychic disturbances. As she has said, "I can't let myself know things in a direct way, so I've always understood and known more than I can know directly through metaphor."[78] Filmmaking, then, is a vital necessity for Jane Campion; as she confesses in her director's commentary on *In the*

Cut, "one of the responsibilities of drama is working out the psychic fears."[79]

Indeed, phantasmal psychic fears abound in Campion's films, and they are recurrent from one film to another. They are visible in a fear of masculine sexuality (Ada in *The Piano*) that is nevertheless accompanied by an irresistible attraction to what is feared (Ruth in *Holy Smoke,* Frannie in *In the Cut*); in the sibling rivalry that could result from parental neglect (Kay and Dawn in *Sweetie*); in the repression that serves as a protection against anxiety (Kay in *Sweetie,* Janet in *An Angel at My Table*); in a generalized anxiety at the prospect of life that causes one to "feel the cold" (Pam in *A Girl's Own Story,* Janet and Isabel Archer in *The Portrait of a Lady*) and to seek compensation in eroticism for what is felt to be missing in one's inner psychic space (Ada, Ruth, Frannie); in the prospect of losing oneself as the result of patriarchal dominance (the sister in *Peel—An Exercise in Discipline* [1982], Ada, Isabel); in the fear of succumbing to madness (Dawn, Janet); and so on.

The depth, variety, and imaginative richness of Jane Campion's cinematic representations of these perturbed aspects of experience, combined with her extraordinary honesty in acknowledging their origins in the circumstances of her own family background, provide those who appreciate and study artistic creation with an almost unique opportunity to view and explore the wellsprings and processes of artistic creativity itself. An understanding of the dynamic processes taking place in a film by Jane Campion helps to explain the nature of her appeal to the wide range of audiences who respond to her work; as Freud recognized, if an artist is able to shape material into a form that embodies a particular image of his or her unconscious fantasy, then "he makes it possible for other people once more to derive consolation and alleviation from their own sources of pleasure in their unconscious which have become inaccessible to them."[80] Even more important, a recognition of the origins and nature of this process helps to illuminate an essential aspect of authorship itself: the motivating force that leads directors to load their films with their personal investments and identifications, irrespective of what genre they may be working with, what discourses they may be invoking, what audience tastes they may be trying to cater to, what socioeconomic dictates they may be compelled to observe. An understanding of what is involved in this kind of personal investment also explains why, no matter how major the input of other members of the production team, it cannot supplant the authoring influence of the filmmaker's psyche as the major source of meaning in situations where such an investment is present.

In this book, I will uncover the process whereby Campion engages with, and transforms, her personal life experiences through a strategy of radical symbolic condensation and displacement that has undergone a variety of permutations as her career has unfolded. In doing so, I will be building upon the work of scholars like Kathleen McHugh and Sue Gillett, who have already established the presence in Campion's films of preoccupations that indicate a deep psychological and emotional invest-ment on the part of the filmmaker, even though they have not attempted to explain it in terms that venture outside the filmic text. McHugh, in particular, has pointed to a nexus of concerns that invite speculation: Campion's recurrent fixation with "the pathological dynamics of dys-functional families, wherein children serve as translators, conduits, and targets for their parents' aggressions, desires, and ambivalence for one another"; her repeated interest in siblings; her recurrent presentation through the narration of "the structure of traumatized consciousness in the heroine"; her focus on the influence of "a lost or absent mother whose heartbreak and traumas are relived, repeated in their protagonist daughters' lives"; and the recurrent appearance of "seductive or inap-propriate fathers"—or father substitutes—in Campion's movies, with intimations of the enactment of a fantasized incestuous relationship.[81] My discussion will venture beyond the limits of these thematic studies in order to show the lines of connection between the diegetic world of the film and the real-life world of the filmmaker, so as to reveal the creative process whereby the former comes into being as an imaginative response to the latter.

In the course of this investigation, it will become apparent how Campion's personal investment in this inventive strategy, motivated by a desire to explore self-states through projection, identification, and evo-cation, has exerted a determining influence on the films' text. I will also show how the nature of her personal preoccupations impart a profound unity to her oeuvre, despite the apparent disparateness of her films as far as their mode, subject matter, and generically marked components are concerned. Finally, in the conclusion to this book, having demonstrated how Campion's oeuvre constitutes a unified personal cinema, I will speculate on the wider implications of what can be discerned in her practices for a theory of authorship at large. Specifically, I will suggest not only that the personal component is an attribute of authorship that it is unwise to ignore, but also that it is a powerful generator of meaning because of its ability to invest the work of art with the qualities of an "object" (in the psychoanalytic sense) capable of engaging the subjectivities of both the author and the viewer (or reader) in a negotiation that makes possible a shared experience that answers to the needs of their respective selves.

1 Origins of a Problematic: The Campion Family

1 Richard and Edith Campion, the parents of Jane Campion, came from very different backgrounds. Edith Hannah (whose "unpreferred name" was Beverley Georgette Hannah, according to the records of the Alexander Turnbull Library) was born in 1923, on the same day as Richard Campion, in the same town (Wellington, the capital of New Zealand). Edith was the only child of George and Jessie Hannah and the granddaughter of the industrialist Robert Hannah, the pioneer footwear manufacturer of Antrim House, whose shoe chain developed into one of the great dynasties of New Zealand retailing.[1] The fortunate circumstances of her birth, however, were not to be matched by equal felicity in the years that followed. Edith's early life was marred by acute insecurity, caused by the fact that she had to spend her early childhood with a mother who was addicted to alcohol and who dragged the young child along with her on drinking binges. Her father, too, succumbed to alcoholism; both parents suffered early deaths.

Having been orphaned in 1933 at the age of ten, Edith became uncontrollable. Parentless and an heiress, she was sent away to boarding school at Nga Tawa, the Wellington Diocese's school for girls, located outside the township of Marton in the Rangitikei district of the North Island of New Zealand. Founded in 1891, Nga Tawa housed girls in grades nine to eleven in rooms of two to six, and it boasted an equestrian center with stables for up to forty horses, a dressage arena, a full-sized show-jumping arena, a canter track, and a full cross-country course. The school, which still exists, was also notable for its cultural activities, which included productions of musicals, and performances of speeches and scenes from Shakespeare. Students were encouraged to take speech and drama lessons.

Edith hated being at boarding school and escaped at the first opportunity—on a pony sold previously to her English teacher.[2] Thereafter, she was put in the charge of governesses, which meant that she led a solitary childhood.[3] Two things remained with her from her brief time at Nga Tawa, however: a love of literature and theater and a lifelong love of horses and horse riding. In due course, Edith would become the most acclaimed actress in New Zealand, especially renowned for her performance as St. Joan of Arc in Shaw's play of that name. She would also develop into a significant, though minor, writer of fiction and poetry, establishing connections with several of the most prominent writers in the country, including Frank Sargeson, and publishing her work in the leading New Zealand literary journals.

Richard Campion, one of eight children, had more humble origins, growing up on Mount Victoria in Wellington, where his father ran a butcher shop. Although he became interested in theater at school, his parents were members of the Exclusive Brethren, an extreme branch of the Christian evangelical movement also known as the Plymouth Brethren. Predictably, Richard's parents disapproved of his involvement in theater, believing that it "belonged to Satan"—meaning that, in Richard's words, he had "to sneak it in."[4] According to Richard, he escaped religious confinement by becoming a paperboy for Wellington's *Evening Post* newspaper, buying a bicycle with the proceeds, and "seeing through the windows on his runs that not all non-Brethren houses were dens of iniquity."[5] Richard records that his family never had any books at home, so he "used to sneak into the library," which was located near the headquarters of the newspaper. The Exclusive Brethren, however, are notorious for the severity of their discipline. In order to maintain a "separation from evil," if a member of the sect breaks a serious rule, the dissident is first shunned and then "put out." If the dissident does not repent, he is then "disfellowshipped"—excommunicated. This usually entails the breaking off of all communication with members of the person's former congregation, even family members.[6]

According to Anna Campion, from the age of fourteen Richard Campion was no longer allowed to eat with his family, on account of his

Edith Campion as St. Joan. *Courtesy of Jane Campion.*

rebellion against the strictness of the Exclusive Brethren's rules, which had banned him from listening to the radio or reading books.[7] This punitive cut-off meant that Richard, like Edith, was turned into an emotional orphan.

Despite the contrasting circumstances of their respective families, it is not surprising that Edith and Richard were drawn together, not only because of their shared interest in drama—they met in acting classes conducted by the Jewish actress Maria Dronke, who had escaped from Nazi Germany to Wellington[8]—but also because of similarities in the formative experiences they had endured at a relatively young age. Both had suffered as the children of parents who had taken recourse to addictions as a means of self-soothing. In the case of Edith's parents, this had taken the form of addiction to alcohol; in the case of Richard's parents, it had taken the form of addiction to an extreme religion.[9] Even more damagingly, both Edith and Richard had suffered the trauma of parental desertion and abandonment at crucially formative stages in their development—literally, through the premature death of Edith's parents, and metaphorically, through the emotional and literal cut-off imposed by Richard's parents. The combined impact on the children of the addictive behaviors and the abandonment of their parents must have been severe indeed.

Modern psychoanalytic theory tells us that children who develop under such circumstances are likely to suffer acute damage to their sense of personal identity:

> Recognition of oneself as a separate and unique being is sought by the infant's avid gazing at his reflection in his mother's eyes—a reflection destined to give him not only his mirror image, but also what he represents for his mother. Only thus may he hope to recognize himself as having a privileged place and a personal value in the eyes of this Other who looks at him and talks to him.[10]

If anything occurs to impede the construction of a positive self-representation through this mirroring process—such as the diversion of the mother's intensity of feeling or attention away from the child—then the image of oneself is likely to be "a fragile and fleeting reflection," creating a narcissistic wound that needs to be repaired. The drive to attain a feeling of personal identity is "a primordial need in the individual's psychic life—equal in intensity and importance to the instinct of preservation in relation to biological life—an unending struggle against psychic death."[11]

In the case of Jane Campion's parents, the attempt to repair whatever wounds they might have suffered as a result of their family circumstances seems to have taken the form of an engagement with the theater so intense as to verge upon obsession. This is not surprising for, as many actors will confirm, to immerse oneself within the mindset of a dramatic character is a powerful way of gaining, and deepening, a sense of one's own personal identity. Empathic identification with a dramatized character also enables the vicarious release of feelings, thoughts, and emotions that palliate psychic pain which, in ordinary life, one dare not allow oneself to experience directly. Contemporary object-relations theory offers an explanation of this phenomenon. As Christopher Bollas puts it:

> We are forever finding objects that disperse the objectifying self into elaborating subjectivities, where the many "parts of the self" momentarily express discrete sexual urges, ideas, memories, and feelings in unconscious actions, before condensing into a transcendental dialectic, occasioned by a force of dissemination that moves us to places beyond thinking.[12]

Often, when a person suffers from painful affects, it is difficult for him or her even to admit their existence. The release of intense emotions through theatrical performance allows for the temporary evacuation of such affects and, in so doing, enables the actor to gain a fleeting sensation of actually existing as a coherent self. The search for such release and self-realization is what one can observe, I surmise, in the theatrical and literary careers pursued by the Campion parents.

Having married in 1945, Edith and Richard joined a circle of theater devotees, including Nola Millar, Margaret Turnbull, and Robert and Elizabeth Stead, all of whom were active in Wellington's Unity Theatre—originally an agitprop antifascist theater established in 1942, that had been inspired by the radical ideas of Group Theater in New York and Unity in London.[13] As members of Unity, Richard joined the executive committee, played opposite Nola Millar as a knight in T. S. Eliot's *Murder in the Cathedral,* and directed an "inspiring" production of *King Lear,*[14] while Edith performed in a number of roles, including Mary Boyle in Sean O'Casey's *Juno and the Paycock.* In 1949, the Campions left for London by flying boat to further their theatrical careers by study-

Richard Campion, c. 1953, from the Edith Campion Collection. *Courtesy of the Alexander Turnbull Library, Wellington, New Zealand (JA-578-01), used with permission.*

ing at the Old Vic Theatre School.[15] During this time, Richard took an advanced production course with Michel Saint-Denis and served as the stage director for the touring Young Vic in England and on the Continent. Sadly, the son that was born to the Campions in London in early 1949 died soon after birth.[16]

Following their return to New Zealand in 1951, using the money from Edith's inheritance, the two Campions approached Nola Millar, a local director, with a proposal to set up a national theater. As a result of this initiative, the first professional theater company in New Zealand, the New Zealand Players, was established. As Richard Campion later explained, drawing an analogy with the national rugby team, the All Blacks, this professional company was meant to be an "all black" theater by and for New Zealanders that would unify the country as the All Blacks did through rugby.[17] The new company was launched in 1953 (the year after Anna Campion's birth and the year before Jane's birth), supported by a sum of £20,000 sterling from Edith's legacy (a huge amount in those days), with two productions: *The Young Elizabeth* by Jeanette Dowling and Pinero's *Dandy Dick*. Thereafter, the company toured six plays around the country each year during its brief life, eventually offering thirty plays, five of them by New Zealand playwrights, to an average attendance of 50,000 per production, and giving employment to more than a hundred actors. Plays performed included *Saint Joan, A Unicorn for Christmas, Twelfth Night, The Solid Gold Cadillac,* and *The Mousetrap*.

By 1960, however, the New Zealand Players had collapsed. As Jane Campion recalls, "My parents lived an unreal life. For example, the need to make money was, for them, a complete mystery."[18] Even though the Players were given a tremendous welcome wherever they appeared, the cost of touring was inordinate, with the company incurring a huge loss of about £700 per week on its first national tour. Although this loss halved during the next season, the company proved not to be financially viable; it was a fantasy that not even Edith's inheritance could support.

Another factor may have contributed to its demise. In 1953, Nola Millar, who had played a crucial role in the formation of the company, had resigned—an event which enfeebled the Players by removing one of the company's most enthusiastic and experienced mainstays. The reason she offered to Richard Campion was her concern about the finances and particularly about the company's ability to support the costs of touring. For his part, Richard believed that she wanted to get back into directing. According to her biographer, however, the actual reason for Nola Millar's resignation was her disenchantment with the sexual conduct of Richard Campion himself:

> It was concerning Dick's personal conduct that Nola's regard had decidedly cooled by the end 1953, and he must have been in no doubt about how she felt. Some thought he was rather afraid of her; certainly he had reason to be wary, if

only of meeting her knowing eye. The daughter of Frank Millar was still the puritan regarding adultery, and his affairs, including one with Margaret Turnbull
(her marriage having finally disintegrated) and others with his players, appalled
her. Nola felt the betrayals professionally and personally, and her own loyalties
were compromised, especially her friendship with Edith.[19]

Here, then, was another major factor that would influence the emotional lives of the Campion children, in addition to the effects of the
emotional deprivation suffered by each of the parents: the extramarital
adventures of their father, which, judging by statements made by Anna
Campion, may have been the manifestation of a sexual addiction. In
Anna's words, Richard Campion was "a bit of a Ted Hughes figure"[20]—
not only in his artistic inclinations, but in his proclivity for relationships
with other women. The existence of a half sister from one of these affairs,
unknown to Jane until relatively late in her career, was a family secret
that would have a profound effect on the filmmaker.[21] The impact of
this revelation is registered by the accusatory reference to a love child
that Ruth hurls at her father in *Holy Smoke* and by the inclusion of a half
sister, Pauline, in *In the Cut*, for which no hint exists in the source novel
by Susanna Moore upon which the film was based.

Without Nola Millar, the viability of the New Zealand Players was
weakened. Several years later, in 1957, Richard Campion resigned from
the Players, and he joined the staff of Wellington College in 1958.[22] After
this, the romantic fantasy that had united Edith and Richard Campion
began to unwind. Their first daughter, Anna, whose "unpreferred birth
name" (according to the Turnbull Library's catalog) is "Dianna Margaret," had been born in 1952, while their second daughter, Jane, whose
"unpreferred birth name" is recorded as "Elizabeth Jane," was born on 30
April 1954. A son, Michael, would be born in 1961. Around this time, Jane
Campion recalls, "My mother gave up acting and after a while we kind of
[saw] that that wasn't a good decision. It didn't help her. My father only
did what he wanted to do, and of course, he enjoyed it."[23]

What Richard Campion occupied himself with—after having
mounted a number of productions with the boys at Wellington College,
including *Henry IV, Henry V,* and Anton Vogt's *Kiwi in Crete*—was the
establishment in the early 1960s of a stationary group of players, the New
Zealand Theatre Trust, located in Wellington.[24] Richard's new theater

company, of which he was artistic director, survived only two productions before it, too, collapsed.[25]

In 1962, Richard headed off to Sydney for a short time. After his
return to New Zealand, he worked with an all-Maori company that was
committed to presenting indigenous culture and produced an epic about
the settling of New Zealand: *Green Are the Islands*.[26] Richard also turned
to the world of opera, directing productions of Strauss's *Die Fledermaus*
in 1966 and Bizet's *Carmen* in 1969 (with the young Kiri Te Kanawa) for
the New Zealand Opera Company, and then a series of productions for
regional companies, including *La Traviata* in 1988 and *La Bohème* in 1990
for the Hawke's Bay Opera Trust, and Donizetti's bel canto opera, *Lucia
di Lammermoor*, in 1988 and Bizet's *The Pearl Fishers* in 1993 for the Wellington City Opera. In 1986, he wrote a docudrama, *Waitangi—"I Was
There,"* based on the missionary William Colenso's eyewitness account of
the signing of the historic Treaty of Waitangi between the Maori tribes
and the colonial British government in 1840, which was performed to
great acclaim at the first International Arts Festival in Wellington.

Meanwhile, Edith Campion, who had been awarded an MBE for
her services to New Zealand theater in 1961, turned to the writing of
imaginative literature. In 1977, she published *A Place to Pass Through*, a
collection of short stories, which was followed in 1979 by *The Chain*, a
novella published in tandem with another short novel, *En Route*, by the
doyen of New Zealand literature at that time, Frank Sargeson—who
would later be depicted in *An Angel at My Table* as the literary mentor
of Janet Frame. Throughout the 1970s and early 1980s, Edith published a
variety of poems and short stories in *Landfall* and *Islands*, the two main
outlets for literary artists in New Zealand.

Most of Edith's literary works express acute states of loneliness and
depression. Frank Sargeson summarizes her stories as being about "the
private agonies of the solitary individual made hopelessly lonely and
depressed by entanglement in the day-to-day trappings of contemporary
urbanised life."[27] In "Dialogue," for example, she evokes a world that is
like "a desert without oasis. No love in a world of sand without moisture."
"How do you take action against fear?" Edith's fictive persona wonders:
"Fear of water was easy. You wore a life-jacket. Fear of living. Fear of
dying. Fear that heaved up at sunrise and shadowed the coming day.

What action—what life-jacket?"[28] These despairing sentiments fore-shadow the statements that Edith would make in the short film (really, a docudrama) made in 1989 by Anna Campion, *The Audition,* which shows Jane Campion auditioning her mother for the role of Miss Lindsay that she would perform in *An Angel at My Table.* In this film, Edith reveals that, each day when she wakes up, she "feels frightened."[29] Clearly, the psychic perturbations suffered by Edith in her adult life were acute—a fact that was reflected in her recurrent hospitalizations for depression at Porirua Psychiatric Hospital near Wellington and at Ashburn Hall in Dunedin in 1980.

2 One of the clearest indications of Edith's state of mind during this time, and of the dynamics that operated within the Campion family, is to be found in *The Chain,* the short novel she published in 1979. For this reason, it is worthwhile examining this neglected work at some length.

The novel is based upon the gruesome real-life discovery in 1973 of the body of a man who had been chained to a tree in a Florida forest, where he had been left to die of starvation. Edith relocates this story to the New Zealand bush, turning it into a metaphor that symbolically evokes a state of psychological incapacity and entrapment, especially that of the main character in the novel, Murray Edward Scott, a husband and father whose ordeal prompts him to enter into a process of self-reflection, in the course of which he comes to realize his failings as a son, as a husband, and as a father. Although *The Chain* is far more than a simple roman à clef, the level of autobiographical significance is unmistakable and revealing.

There are plenty of indications of how personal this fiction was for Edith Campion, for she invests the narrative with a number of autobio-graphical references. Murray, for example, carries with him "the photo of his three children" (although their genders do not match those of the actual Campion children). He also has a photograph of his wife, Jean, who appears "dark-haired, vulnerable, timid"—which mirrors exactly the appearance of Edith in the photograph she chose for the dust jacket of the book.[30] Similarly, Murray is presented as having had an earlier lover, Sally, and he recalls that he had "played Brutus at Training College to Sally's Portia," which evokes not only the fact that Richard Campion was associated with the teachers training college in Wellington, but also the theatrical career of Richard and Edith Campion and especially their involvement with Shakespeare (28). Jean, we are told, went to an "exclusive school" that "hadn't managed to mould her to one of those easily recognisable private school girls," just as Edith was sent to Nga Tawa, where she similarly refused to conform to the norm (34). Furthermore, "marriage to Jean had taken him [Murray] from teaching to running a farm," which reflects the move of the Campions to a farm at Otaki, where Edith was living at the time of writing (20). The level of autobiographical allusion extends even to small details. As Murray grows more delirious from the effects of starvation, he notices, "High on a branch a small fawn cat regarded him with stern, wild, yellow eyes" (71), which recalls Edith's lifelong love of cats—an idiosyncrasy to which she alludes in the autobiographical blurb that appears on the dust jacket of the novel. Most tellingly, the novel itself is inscribed "for Dick,"[31] as if, in writing it, Edith was seeking to convey a plea to her real-life husband to try and understand the feelings and perceptions that she was representing in *The Chain* at a displaced remove—in order to arrest the disintegration of their marriage, which was by that time unraveling.

What message, then, does Edith try to convey? Her main purpose is to depict an interior process of discovery in the husband whereby he comes to realize the extent to which certain aspects of his own family circumstances have damaged him psychologically, and how that psychological damage negatively affects his wife and children on account of the angry and self-protective behaviors it induces in him. In Murray's treatment of his wife, for instance, "He often snapped, as if he were punishing her for something—as if she were in some way to blame for something of importance that he himself had lost. . . . the center of my sinful earth" (6).

Murray questions whether he has given her what she needed, or whether "like a miser, [he had] hung back—withheld—punishing her? Punishing her for not being someone else" (11). This idea is reiterated several times in the novel, as when he hears Jean's voice in his mind, saying, "Sometimes I feel you use me as if I'm a stand-in for someone else" (20).

As his reveries deepen, Murray comes to realize that the "someone else" he is always seeking is his mother. She is imaged as a tyrannical and domineering woman who left her son feeling that he could never give her what she was seeking from him:

> Beyond the immediate turn of leaf and fern the face of his mother superimposed. Face to face with dead eyes they looked at each other. She had always, always wanted something from him. She was the aging princess waiting to be kissed into being—her husband had failed and now she looked to the son. (29)

Here, then, is a classic instance of a mother who seeks to have her unmet needs supplied through an emotionally incestuous relationship with her son that, in this instance, takes the form of a negative attachment secured through the threat of emotional withholding. In the novel, this relationship is presented as one in which Murray is a helpless victim, with his mother being imaged phantasmagorically as a predatory spider:

> His mother came and wrapped him in a tight chrysalis of silk and held him between her eight legs and hugged him against her belly. He opened his mouth to protest but she filled it with candy floss. He was tumbling down the web—off the world. Down . . . down until he dangled from one delicate thread. . . .
>
> He dangled in space. Below was empty darkness. "Help! Please . . . help me." (64)[32]

Predictably, the son's reaction to this incestuous maternal invasion is deep resentment: "He had hated, resented the unspoken need to be loved, to be approved," and this had left him with a "Jehovah-like urge to punish" (29). His response had been to withdraw from his mother in a kind of emotional cut-off that had left him unsure even of how she died, his "sad, lost princess" (45). The problem, Murray now realizes, is that he had continued "the penny-pinching of emotional change" with his wife, Jean:

> He had allowed her to doubt her value. It was not always in things an outsider could see; they would have labelled him loving, considerate, a good father. But he knew, and Jean knew . . . tiny things. . . . So she believed that she had failed . . . fallen short . . . and he did not want her to read it in the mirrors of his soul. . . . he had no bloody soul, no heart—just a good calculator. He could have freed her, given her the chance to grow.

Perhaps he had been fearful of living with a whole woman, afraid she might find him out. (47)

The inhibited, withholding psychological condition that Edith Campion depicts in the husband figure in *The Chain* is remarkably similar to that in the heroes depicted by another New Zealand novelist of Edith

Campion's generation, Maurice Gee. Many of Gee's masculine characters suffer from what can be described as "inwardness":

> The term *inwardness* can be defined as a retreat into oneself, resulting in vari-
> ous degrees of a depersonalised mind state and a lifestyle characterised by
> diminution of feeling for oneself and others, reliance on painkilling habits and
> substances, and a defensive, self-nurturing posture toward life. . . . The inward
> posture represents a serious impairment of the ability to engage in emotional
> transactions and is especially damaging to the capacity for giving and receiving
> love.[33]

As I have argued elsewhere, Gee shows this condition of inwardness to
be a consequence of the repressive regime of subjectification enforced
by New Zealand puritanism during the twentieth century.[34] If Edith
Campion's Murray is indeed based on Richard Campion, as one suspects
it may be, the presence of this inwardness is not surprising, given the extreme religious repression enforced by the sect of the Exclusive Brethren
to which his family belonged. Moreover, as with Gee's male characters,
the adoption of a defended inward posture by Murray is induced by his
need to protect himself against the demands of his mother, which are
presented as simultaneously involving an invasive emotional intrusion
combined with a threatened withholding of affection that leaves her son
in a state of existential suspension.

Unsurprisingly, Murray, in Edith Campion's depiction, seeks to
avenge himself on his mother for what amounts to emotional abuse by
using other women as stand-ins for the evacuation of his anger. This is
shown most strikingly in the episode in which, in his fantasy, he violently rapes one of his imagined abductors, who is a woman, with a force
that leads him to actual orgasm, even though his victim is a phantasm
(56–57). Sex, for Murray, is shown to be a means of both surrendering
to the incestuous invitation and expressing a violent resentment at the
fact that it exists.[35]

The problem, Edith Campion shows, is that this pathological syndrome in Murray has a negative effect on the other members of his family—not merely on Jean, whom Murray confuses and conflates with his
mother in one imagined episode, but also on his daughter:

> The boys were all right, but he had made Mary too eager to please, unsure, want-
> ing love but feeling it withheld. Why? Why did he keep repeating this stutter
> of life, this damaging reluctance to give what was required, needed? He ran

his tongue round his teeth. His mind didn't know, or didn't want to answer the
question. (64)

The extent to which these words anticipate comments that Jane and
Anna Campion would later make and episodes that Jane would depict
in her movies is uncanny, suggesting that the family dynamics centering
on the father in Edith Campion's *The Chain* may have provided some of
the most important materials that motivated Jane Campion's creativity.
It is clear that Edith Campion's novel furnishes indispensable evidence
of the forces within the family to which each of its members responds
through their respective arts.

Sadly, the tensions between Richard and Edith Campion depicted
imaginatively in *The Chain* were not to be resolved, and the couple divorced in 1984. Following this, Edith, in the words of her obituary, "sad
and often depressed, withdrew to her beautiful garden in Otaki," where
she died on 13 September 2007.[36] Richard Campion continued to be
involved in Jane's career, assisting her, for example, on the set of *Holy
Smoke* (1999) and advising her on the script for *Bright Star* (2009).

3 Such powerful disturbances in the psychic terrain of the parents
were bound to exert a lasting influence on the children—for reasons that Freud explains in his exposition of what he terms the "family romance." According to Freud, "The freeing of an individual, as he
grows up, from the authority of his parents is one of the most necessary
though one of the most painful results brought about by the course of
his development." The achievement of this liberation, Freud asserts, is
what constitutes "a normal state." Conversely, a failure to achieve this
liberation results in a condition of neurosis.

There are various factors involved in the process that leads to the
separation which is a precondition for the full individuation of an adult
personality. In the early years of a child's life, his or her "most intense
and most momentous wish . . . is to be like his parents (that is, the parent
of his own sex) and to be big like his father and mother." As intellectual
growth increases, however, the child discovers that his or her parents are
neither unique nor incomparable (in the way that he or she had believed
them to be). This discovery is an essential prerequisite for the growth in
independence that allows a new generation to supplant the former one.

Freud recognizes that many factors can interfere with the successful achievement of this necessary liberation. In his words:

> There are only too many occasions on which a child is slighted, or at least feels he has been slighted, on which he feels he is not receiving the whole of his parents' love, and, most of all, on which he feels regrets at having to share it with his brothers and sisters. His sense that his own affection is not being fully reciprocated then finds a vent in the idea, which is often consciously recollected from early childhood, of being a step-child or an adopted child.

"The latter stage in the development of the neurotic's estrangement from his parents, begun in this manner," Freud continues, "might be described as 'the neurotic's family romance.'"[37]

In Freud's view, the creative imagination has a particularly important role to play in the attempt to achieve psychic liberation through this family romance:

> It [the family romance] is seldom remembered consciously but can almost always be revealed by psycho-analysis. For a quite specific form of imaginative activity is one of the essential characteristics of neurotics and also of all comparatively highly gifted people. This activity emerges first in children's play, and then, starting roughly from the period before puberty, takes over the topic of family relations. A characteristic example of this particular kind of fantasy is to be seen in the familiar day-dreams which persist far beyond puberty.[38]

The purpose of these "day-dreams," Freud avers, is, through the play of the imagination, to free the child "from the parents of whom he now has such a low opinion and [to] replac[e] them by others." These works of fiction, "which seem so full of hostility, are none of them really so badly intended," given that "they still preserve, under a slight disguise, the child's original affection for his parents."

> Indeed the whole effort at replacing the real father by a superior one is only an expression of the child's longing for the happy, vanished days when his father seemed to him the noblest and strongest of men and mother the dearest and loveliest of women. He is turning away from the father whom he knows to-day to the father in whom he believed in the earlier years of his childhood; and his phantasy is no more than the expression of a regret that those happy days have gone.[39]

In my view, this account by Freud of the dynamics of what he terms the "family romance" describes almost precisely the processes that can be observed in Jane Campion's films. In all of them, she seeks to work through the issues that constitute the legacy of having been raised in a family in which the parents were so deeply affected by issues arising from the unresolved traumas they had suffered in their childhoods. Moreover, the chronic depression of the mother, the inwardness and sexual proclivities of the father, and the mutual obsession of the parents with the theater meant that they were, in their separate ways, not emotionally available to their children. As contemporary psychoanalytic theory has recognized, when children are raised in such circumstances, they are likely to suffer from narcissistic deprivation, which in turn leads to various symptoms of disturbance within their psychic economy, leaving the children facing a need to confront the unresolved issues they have internalized from their parents, as well as their own unmet emotional needs.[40]

Both Campion daughters attest to the negative impact on them of their parents' predispositions. Anna Campion found her parents "distant" and "secretive"; her father was "uninterested in his daughters" and her mother "took everything personally," meaning that Anna "never felt safe." As a result, she retreated into her head, "into a fantasy haze where the real world didn't impinge."[41] Jane Campion, more circumspect, despite insisting on her closeness to both her parents, nevertheless conveys a sense to her audiences of the distress she suffered as a result of her family circumstances. In her interviews and director's commentaries, she repeatedly invites viewers to make connections between her life and her art in a way that almost suggests a psychological compulsion to make known her own personal suffering—however obliquely—as part of a process whereby she is seeking liberation from them. For example, commenting on the "irrational eroticism" she had shown in *In the Cut* (2003)—"this savage energy that takes hold, which is impossible to control"—Campion reveals that her interest in the dynamics of this kind of sexual compulsion springs from her consternation at how it can be that "a sudden eruption of mad passion can destroy the life of a couple who enjoy a wonderful marriage."[42] It is not too difficult to discern here an allusion to the marriage of Edith and Richard Campion—"marvellously" in love, but torn apart by infidelity. Similarly, attempting to explain why she included the skating sequences in *In the Cut*, Campion adds to the suggestion of Laurie Parker, one of the producers, that "we're the ones who didn't have as much love as we wanted from our fathers" the further information that "the problem is that the fathers themselves never got enough [i.e., love]"—a clear allusion to her real-life father.[43] On another occasion, when discussing the "tragic underbelly" of the family depicted in Sweetie, Campion admits the existence of a parallel between the film and her own family, particularly in terms of a shadowy comparison between herself-as-Kay and Edith Campion: "[in] my late 20s . . . I realized how similar I was getting to Mum."[44] What becomes clear from such revelations, is that Jane Campion uses movie-making as an instrument to deal with the issues deriving from family dysfunction that she "carries round" with her. For her, the act of fictive invention and representation functions as a form of psychotherapy.

She is not entirely aware of the process by which she does so. "I'm not conscious of my choices," she admits.[45] Her images often arise from her unconscious and serve a metonymic purpose,[46] as in the case of the New Zealand bush setting in The Piano, which for her "carried secrets and hidden things" relating to sexuality.[47] Campion, trying to explain her relationship with filmmaking, comments on the intuitiveness of the process:

> it's the same as going to see a psychic—part of me already knows something's doomed, but I can only read it in signs. . . . all the good ideas just arrive, you don't figure them out, they just arrive. You don't know how they come. A lot of the time you're trying to block that instinct because it's more than you want to know about.[48]

We are presented, then, with a filmmaker who uses films to access what, because it resides at the unconscious level, has been described as the "unthought known."[49] The invention of images and actions in Campion's films is a way of accessing her unconscious as a means of working through personal issues—which, as we have seen, mostly concern aspects of her experience within a troubled, though brilliant, family. Filmmaking, as Campion says, serves the same function as visiting a psychic—a practice in which she confesses that she has engaged (like Kay in Sweetie)—which is "to find out what you think yourself that you can't know you think because you're blocking it."[50] For this reason, her films provide an unusual depth of insight into the psychic life of the filmmaker, as well as exemplifying the process whereby a troubled subject seeks to grow into self-understanding and a fully liberated personality. Because of the high degree of symbolic condensation and displacement involved, these films contain episodes and images that often strike the viewer as overdetermined—that is, they appear to have a latent content that is greater than the manifest content, even though the meaning of that latent content, as in a dream, is not made clear. The presence of this personal dimension helps to explain, too, the function of the expressive cinematic style that has been noted by Dana Polan as conveying, through the evocation of forms of affect, a sense of personally felt emotional trauma, or, as Kathleen McHugh puts it in describing Campion's use of surrealism, the "unseeable, unspeakable" that "makes itself felt in the 'return of the repressed' in the diegetic field, a field whose status as objective or subjective reality is put into question for its spectator."[51] The presence of this depth of unspecified signification, brought into being by cinematic techniques that are selected in order to bring it into being, makes for an unusually rich and complex filmic textuality, which probably accounts, at least in part, for why Jane Campion's films are so highly valued by those who favor them.

4 What, then, are the issues that are revealed implicitly and explicitly in the fictive worlds of Campion's films, and how do they relate to the effects of her having grown up in this troubled family?

Both Anna and Jane Campion emphasize how absorbed their parents were in their "unreal world" of the theater during the time when the two girls were in the formative stages of their early childhood. As Jane puts it, "our parents were above all absorbed in their own story—they were very much in love, and the children came second."[52] This self-absorption of the parents, which suggests a fantasy of fusion arising out of codependency, had two effects on the children. First, it left an impression in Jane of a strongly romantic ideal, in which her mother and father played the role of ideal lovers—a romanticism that was doomed to suffer disillusionment when it came into collision with the harsh realities of real life, which did indeed happen with the financial collapse of the New Zealand Players and the distressing fact of Richard Campion's sexual adventures. Second, and more negatively, it left the children with an acute hunger for their parents' attention and a feeling of neglect.

Such feelings of neglect can leave a child suffering from an acute feeling of emotional deprivation that she will attempt to counter by adopting certain behaviors. As Joyce McDougall notes, people who must struggle to maintain their "narcissistic homeostasis" tend to attempt this in two ways: either by keeping a distance from others or, at the opposite extreme, by grasping others, "displaying an unquenchable need of the person chosen to reflect the image that is missing in the inner psychic world."[53] The Campion sisters, according to Jane, in their childhoods manifested this syndrome. Confronted with their parents' self-absorption, they tended to act out or to play the fool (*jouer les branques*): "It was the only way of attracting the attention of our parents, who were too absorbed in their career[s] as actors in the theatre."[54] In fact, both of the responses to narcissistic deprivation described by McDougall find representation in Campion's films. The tendency to keep a distance from others is shown in extreme form in Janet Frame in *An Angel at My Table,* who mirrors the shyness that Jane Campion confesses made the experience of being a student a lonely one for her: "At first, when I went to university, I was unhappy, very alone. I didn't manage to insert myself in any group, in fact I'm a bit quirky [*tordue*], and that meant that it took me a while before I could find others who were prepared to share my sense of humour."[55] Similarly, the "unquenchable need" of another person to reflect what is missing in the inner object world is all too apparent in what Campion describes as the "sad and inevitable quest for talent . . . and attention" displayed by Dawn in *Sweetie.*[56]

Predictably, the other legacy of the Campions' self-absorption was the development of an intense rivalry between the siblings, generated by the need to compete for their parents' attention. Anna was born five years after the death of the Campions' first child, a son, and, according to Anna, she was greeted as a miracle baby: "Mum was so thrilled to see me, a strong tantrummy little girl." This special place that the firstborn sister held in her mother's affection, Anna continues, meant that "Jane always wanted my father's attention" out of a need to define herself through difference.[57] This competition between the two sisters for their parents' love generated a lot of conflict between them. In Jane's words, "We hated each other growing up. I hated everything about her [Anna], her competitiveness, I hated her." Jane's resentment of and antipathy toward her sister was so intense, Jane says, that it caused her to leave New Zealand altogether: "Because I'd had enough. I was so sick of the fighting, the competition. I just wanted her to let me be."[58] For her part, Anna concedes that "[i]t's taken us a while to connect. . . . There's a

Darwinian aspect to it. Another child comes along, and how does each get enough nurturing?"[59]

It is not too difficult to detect in this rivalry the origins of Campion's interest in siblings—sisters, specifically—that Kathleen McHugh has identified,[60] as in the relationship between Pam and her sister in *A Girl's Own Story*; between Kay and her sister, Dawn, in *Sweetie*; and, in a more complex variation, between Frannie and her half sister, Pauline, in *In the Cut*. Significantly, even though Anna and Jane had a younger brother, there is virtually no reference to him in their public comments; it is as if he has been erased. One can only speculate as to the cause, but one reason may reside in the fact that, according to Ellen Cheshire, Richard Campion "only became an active father with the arrival of his son, Michael, which coincided with the decline in fortunes of the theatre company leading to its final collapse."[61] Anna Campion has confirmed this, recalling, "When their brother, Michael, was born, seven years after Jane, the father said to the mother, 'You take the girls, I'll look after the boy.'"[62] One can well imagine that if, as we have surmised, Richard Campion was himself narcissistically deprived, his emotional investment in his son as a potentially unimpaired reflection of himself may well have accorded to the latter a degree of attention that the two sisters may have had cause to resent. It is significant that Michael is the one Campion sibling who did not follow his parents into a theatrical or cinematic career—today, he is a successful business manager.[63] For whatever reason, he has chosen another pathway that places him outside the realm of occupations pursued by the rest of his family.

Another powerful influence on Jane Campion's psychic economy was her awareness of her father's infidelities and the effect that these had on her mother. In film after film, she shows husbands and fathers who have affairs, for example, the father in *A Girl's Own Story* and Ruth's father in *Holy Smoke*. These men are depicted as being cowardly and weak, and they are presented as objects of contempt. Campion's feelings about paternal sexuality appear to be deeply ambivalent, however, for she also portrays the masculine sexuality of father figures as being irresistibly seductive and as exciting curiosity, even to the extent of an incestuous desire—as when Dawn reaches between the legs of her naked father in the bathroom scene of *Sweetie*, or when Ruth, in the novelized version of *Holy Smoke*, casts PJ (who, like Baines in *The Piano*, is an older man) in the role of her father and says to him, "Come on Daddy. Daddy FUCK ME!!!"[64] One can infer that this complex mixture of love and hate for father stand-ins is largely what motivates the preoccupation with transgressive eroticism in Campion's films,[65] reflected not only in the actions of heroines like Ada, Ruth, and Frannie, but also in the impulse of a woman such as Isabel in *The Portrait of a Lady*—whom Campion has likened to herself—to be irresistibly attracted to a "bad boy" like Osmond. There is far more to the eroticism of Campion's heroines than the simple valorization of personal desire or an affirmation of a woman's self-determination, as alleged by Polan and various feminist scholars.[66] Eroticism as transgression not only offers hope in the face of a world that is felt to have failed one, but also, in the case of Campion's imaginary scenarios, gives access to an understanding of the force in her father that had the power to divert his attention from the children and to destroy a marriage that seemed, on the face of it, to be a closely bonded one.

It is readily apparent that an equally powerful influence was the combination of romanticism and depression in Edith Campion. Both predispositions appear to have been deeply internalized by her daughter, and they find expression in the speechless rage against men of the mute Ada in *The Piano* and in the uncontrollable fear of the world displayed by Janet in *An Angel at My Table*. Jane Campion's compassionate understanding of her mother is beautifully caught at the end of Anna Campion's short film, *The Audition*, when a tear appears in Jane's eye as she listens to her mother recite some lines from *Juno and the Paycock*—lines that symbolically capture the pathos and tragedy of Edith's ill treatment by life. The correlative emotion induced in Jane by her mother's plight— bitter resentment at her father's treatment of Edith—is graphically and violently represented in the skating scenes of *In the Cut*, in which the husband-father, depicted as a handsome matinee idol, severs the limbs of his fiancée and is heading toward slicing off her head when the sequence abruptly ends. As with her father, Campion's sentiments toward her mother appear to be complex. In making *An Angel at My Table*, she sought to both identify with and separate from her; in *The Piano*, the primal closeness between mother and daughter is symbolically figured in the bond between Ada and Flora.

The presence of a powerful impulse toward transgression in Jane Campion's movies is striking. The son in *Peel* defiantly continues to throw orange peels out the window of the car even after his father orders him to stop; the brother and sister in *A Girl's Own Story* engage in incestuous sex; Janet in *An Angel at My Table* steals money from her father's pocket; Ada in *The Piano* is drawn into adultery; Isabel in *The Portrait of a Lady* embarks upon "a young girl's voyage towards darkness and underground regions" by rejecting all her socially acceptable suitors in order to marry the sinister, yet sexually irresistible Osmond.[67] The origins of this dramatized impulse toward transgression, one can infer, can be traced back to the family circumstances of the Campions. When children are subjected to narcissistic deprivation as a result of their developmental needs not being met, as occurs when parents neglect their children or when the parents manifest the pathological symptoms of unresolved personal issues, the children often seek escape through transgression. Transgression appears to offer hope, because it presents the possibility of acting according to values and expectations that provide an alternative to those of the world that has failed the child.[68] This impulse, I believe, is what one recurrently finds in the films of Campion. It is manifest both in the rebellious eccentricity of her cinematic style and in the content of her films, and it is largely responsible for the "quirky-ness" that many critics have identified.[69] In Campion's own words, her impulse as a young filmmaker was to deal with "what was nasty, what isn't spoken about in life."[70]

Along with the representations of dysfunction and transgression, there also occurs a sustained attempt on Campion's part to articulate a corrective ideal. This can be found in her efforts to show a redeemed masculinity, as in the cases of Baines in *The Piano* and PJ in *Holy Smoke*, who let go of their attempt to assert an oppressive patriarchal power and are led to mitigate the brutal aspects of their masculinity by giving expression to their feminine side. It is seen equally in Campion's depiction of the search of her heroines to find an escape from puritanical repression. This can take the form of sexual liberation through eroticism, as in the cases of Ada and Frannie, or of self-realization through the discovery of oneself as a creative artist, as in the case of Janet Frame. In all instances, Campion appears to be seeking to find corrective alternatives to the forces in her parents' lives that caused misery both to the parents and to their children.

Finally, it is evident that, when these lines of connection between Campion's art and the circumstances of her early life are traced, it is impossible to understand either her or her work fully unless the formative influence of her New Zealand background is acknowledged. Scholars have debated whether Campion should be regarded as an Australian rather than a New Zealand filmmaker, given that she has lived in Australia for much of her adult life. Campion is ambivalent on this point, at times presenting herself emphatically as Australian, as when she comments on *Holy Smoke:* "Ruth has a strength that is very Australian, and I feel that I am fundamentally Australian—these are my landscapes, my life."[71] It is clear, too, that both she and her sister fled New Zealand partly because they found it oppressive. As Anna observes, "I couldn't reinvent myself in New Zealand. . . . It's not a place where individuation is encouraged."[72] Jane also repeatedly voices her distaste for the repression that marks New Zealand society, together with the inclination of New Zealanders to cut down anyone who is perceived to be a tall poppy.[73] Nevertheless, at other times, Campion is fulsome in acknowledging the debt she owes to New Zealand because of "the specialness" of her New Zealand childhood and the way that New Zealand "fashioned her way of seeing."[74] Jane Campion's attitude toward her birthplace is exactly comparable to the attitude she displays toward her parents; it is one of love-hate, deep attachment but also a desperate need to escape from the oppressive psychic effects of it and attain the self-repair and fulfillment that her films show her to be seeking. It is out of this deep and ambivalent complexity, fueled by the psychological tensions generated by an intense family romance, that the richness of her art arises.

What this account of Jane Campion's familial background has shown is how the existence of a problematic that derives from personal circumstances can exert a determining influence on the nature and purpose of a filmmaker's authorial motivations and preoccupations. In the chapters that follow, I will excavate the process of imaginative creativity whereby she has transformed the tensions inherent in this problematic into works of art, in order to demonstrate how this process constitutes the prime authoring influence in each of Campion's films.

2 The "Tragic Underbelly" of the Family: Fantasies of Transgression in the Early Films

1 Although Jane Campion attests to having grown up in a loving family, she, like her sister, Anna, nevertheless made haste to distance herself both from its dysfunctions and from the repressiveness of New Zealand society generally. At the earliest opportunity, around the age of twenty—having studied anthropology and psychology at Victoria University of Wellington in 1975—Jane Campion traveled to Europe, where she studied art in Venice, learned Italian in Perugia, and worked as an assistant for an advertising company in London, feeling fairly lonely and miserable in all of these places. Following this OE (the "overseas experience" characteristically undertaken by many young New Zealanders), she then relocated to Australia, while Anna, who had moved to London shortly after Jane left New Zealand, remained in England. In Sydney, Jane first studied painting at the Sydney College of the Arts from 1979 to 1981, and then enrolled in the Australian Film, Television, and Radio School between 1981 and 1984. Campion completed several acclaimed shorts while still a student: *Mishaps: Seduction and Conquest* (1981), *Peel* (1982), *Passionless Moments* (1983), and *A Girl's Own Story* (1984). *Peel*, in particular, drew attention to Jane Campion's unusual talent, when it was selected by the important French producer Pierre Rissient to be shown at Cannes in the section "Un certain regard," where it won the Palme d'Or for the best short film at the 1986 Cannes Festival.

Even though she and her sister had left New Zealand in an attempt to escape from their family, Jane Campion found that in actuality they continued to be very much with her. As she later confessed: "Everybody has a family and there's a legacy you carry from that.... Suddenly you realize that you haven't left your family at all, that you've been carrying them with you, and you've been living under the illusion that you haven't."[1]

By the time Jane Campion returned to the Antipodes, she had come to realize that she was beginning to replicate aspects of her mother's experience and that all families have "a tragic underbelly."[2] The short films she made between 1980 and 1984, together with two she made after completing film school—*After Hours* (1984), made for the government-funded Women's Film Unit, and *Two Friends* (1986), a feature produced for television—represent her first attempts to explore the forbidden subjects that were hidden in the shadows, to grapple with "what was nasty, what isn't spoken about in life," in an effort to understand the family legacy that she had come to recognize she was carrying around with her.

Campion's efforts to grapple with those forbidden subjects, the nature of which is apparent in the deeply personal symbolic images that recur in these early films, are essential to an understanding of her authorship. As Campion has admitted on several occasions, acknowledging the singularity of the way she works, she cannot let herself know things directly but, as she revealed in a conversation with Kathleen McHugh, "trusts her unconscious and does not interrogate the images it produces."[3] She discovered this need to rely on images that arise from the unconscious when, at the age of twenty-five, she encountered writer's block after drafting three pages of the script for her first film. To overcome this block, she "handed the matter over to her subconscious." She warns, however, that such a process can only work if one believes in the possibility of a response from the subconscious.[4] On another occasion, speaking to Michel Ciment, she explained: "I think that people understand the world in terms of symbols. Things are rarely what they seem. They are metaphors of what is or what could be. And that also goes for our interior torments."[5] That Jane Campion was able to develop such a purposeful and deliberate way of accessing her unconscious owes a lot, one assumes, to her deep interest in psychoanalysis, which probably originated in her awareness of her mother's battle with depression and the psychotherapy that this entailed. At one point, she reveals, she even thought of training as a psychoanalyst,[6] and her sister actually became one—a fact reflected in Anna Campion's full-length feature, *Loaded*, by the presence of a psychoanalyst as a character. Jane Campion's impulse to harness symbolic images from the unconscious was also greatly strengthened by her exposure to structural anthropology during her B.A. studies at Victoria University of Wellington and by her deep interest in the ideas of Jung, especially concerning archetypes.[7]

To gain a sense of the full richness of meaning in Campion's films, therefore, one needs to be sensitive to the symbolic images through which she explores the meanings of the stories and events she depicts, while recognizing that the main purpose of the radical displacement involved, as Campion has explained, is to gain knowledge about the inner perturbations of the psyche that she needs to know about, but is fearful of knowing. In the rest of this chapter, I will identify how this process of accessing the subconscious works, and to what effect.

2 The symbolic images and the themes in Campion's early films reveal a number of interlocking preoccupations, all of which involve disturbed relationships within a dysfunctional family. Many of them refer to sexual matters, or to transgression, and often to both—most often in relation to men (fathers, in particular) who are regarded both with longing and resentment.

For her first film, *Tissues,* made on Super 8 in 1980 prior to her entry into the Australian Film, Television, and Radio School, we are dependent on Campion's own testimony, as the work is not available for general viewing. Campion has dismissed this film as a "European-influenced nonsense piece," but her description suggests that it was far from being such. *Tissues* is an account of a man arrested for child molestation, with the title deriving from the use of a tissue in every scene. Hence, this first experiment in filmmaking announces the preoccupation with the sexual abuse of children that resurfaces in *A Girl's Own Story* and, in a modified form, in *After Hours.* Indeed, Campion has said that it "announces" *A Girl's Own Story.*[8] *Tissues* also relates in general terms to the theme of incest, or of incestuous fantasies, between daughters and fathers, or their stand-ins, that reappears in *Sweetie* and *Holy Smoke.*

Jane Campion's intense interest in eroticism and perverse sexuality is equally apparent in her next short film, *Mishaps: Seduction and Conquest,* shot on video in 1981. This film interleaves scenes from the real-life attempt of George Mallory to scale Mount Everest in 1924 with scenes showing a fictional brother, Geoffrey, back in England, trying to seduce a woman called Emma, who is not very interested in him. It thus juxtaposes two apparently contrasting styles of conquest, in order to show the similarity that unites them—the nature of a compulsive desire that resides in the pursuit of the desired object, and not in the object itself. As Campion explains it: "I was very moved by the way the men on the expedition talked about the mountain as though it had the qualities of a temptress: the closer you got to it the less you wanted it. It just seemed so much like the nature of desire."[9] The idea of desire finds an imagistic correlative in the striking use of the color red, suggesting passion, in this otherwise black-and-white film.

A question arises as to whose desire is at issue here. At one level, Campion's statement could be taken as referring to desire generally, but the reference to the mountain as a "temptress" that needs to be overcome and the doubling of the nonsexual conquest with an attempted sexual one—reinforced by the phonic link between the names "George" and "Geoffrey"—suggest an awareness of the force that could lead a husband-father to betray his marriage in the pursuit of affairs. This seems probable when one views these early films in the sequence in which they were made, which reveals a recurring symbolic displacement that becomes progressively overt until it finds an almost literalized transcription in *A Girl's Own Story*. The suggestion of a biographical allusion to the relationship between Richard and Edith Campion is also strengthened by the outcome of Geoffrey's attempt to seduce Emma. As Kathleen McHugh has astutely observed, "though the majority of this film [*Mishaps*] is about two brothers . . . their relative styles of seduction and conquest, it ends with a dramatic shift, suddenly about a woman writer's loss of focus and inability to write after she has been seduced and politely abandoned."[10]

If one recalls that Richard and Edith Campion were to divorce in 1984, and that *Mishaps: Seduction and Conquest* was shot in 1981, it seems likely that the seduction and abandonment of Emma is, at one level, a displaced allusion to Richard's abandonment of Edith—a writer who was on the verge of achieving national prominence in New Zealand after the publication of her collection of short stories in 1977 and of her novel, *The Chain*, in 1979. Like Emma in the film, Edith seems to have lost heart as a writer after the breakup of her marriage, publishing virtually nothing after 1980.[11] It is also possible that, at another level, there may be an allusion to Jane Campion's own experience—which so often seems to reproduce that of her mother—given that she repeats the situation of Emma in that of Ada in *The Piano*. Again, McHugh is percipient on this point: "In each case, the woman, engaged in her own art, her own endeavours, becomes infected by the failed desire of the other, and then loses herself to that position."[12] Jane Campion has confessed that, when she was young, she was prone to do "a con-job" on herself when pursuing romantic relationships, "occasionally with very unsuitable people."[13] It is conceivable that the onset of creative paralysis induced by "the failed desire of the other" shown in *Mishaps: Seduction and Conquest* symbolically depicts not merely the experience of the mother, but also the experience that the daughter herself, on occasion, has had—in an ironic reenactment of the experience of her mother, just as various of her fictive heroines become, in McHugh's words, "doubles for their mothers."[14]

Peel—An Exercise in Discipline, the short film made in 1982 for which Campion won a Palme d'Or at Cannes, continues to explore the central issue intimated in *Mishaps: Seduction and Conquest,* but through an even more extreme form of symbolic displacement. In terms of its thematic focus on the idea of discipline, this film has been excellently analyzed by Dana Polan, who notes that it is about discipline in three ways: characters striving for self-discipline; characters striving to impose discipline on others; and the discipline involved in making a film.[15] Other critics have commented on its representation of the dynamics of power relations within a family. There exists as well another level of signification in *Peel* which is apparent only through a decoding of its symbolic imagery, and this layer of meaning has received virtually no attention.

At the center of the symbolic structure of *Peel* is the orange. In terms of color, its visual impact is reinforced by the orange dots on the father's shirt, the red hair of the three protagonists, and the pile of oranges shown at one point during the film's progression, which multiplies the visual reference to the first orange which the son bounces against the windscreen of the car out of boredom and then peels—the scraps of which he throws out the window onto the road, to his father's great annoyance. The film thus emphasizes four interrelated ideas: fruit/the act of peeling/forbid-

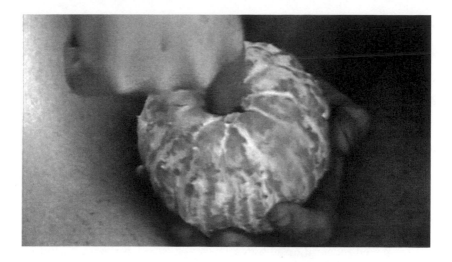

An image of displaced awareness of sexual secrets in *Peel*.

denness/rebelliousness. The associations inhering in this imagery are compounded when the son, having peeled the orange, thrusts his finger into the hole at the center of its segments, with the camera emphasizing this action through a cut to a close-up shot. This is a striking cinematic moment, as Polan observes, because of its "visceral" representation of "intense tactility or palpability."[16] It is also strikingly suggestive as a phallic image, evoking sexual intercourse. In this respect, it links up associatively with the condom the boy inflates when he finds it lying by the side of the road, which he holds in a way which visually evokes a giant penis. Both images serve to intimate the existence of sexual activity that is not being overtly acknowledged, but is omnipresent beneath the surface.

It seems to me that, at a deeply displaced and condensed symbolic remove, *Peel* is dealing with the same issue that is to be found in Campion's other short films: illicit sexuality, associated with the father, residing as a dark secret within the family, which cannot be acknowledged overtly and which produces simultaneously a fascination and an aversion in the perspective offered by the filmmaker. Although Campion has drawn attention to the connection of *Peel* to a real couple, the Pyes, who play Brother/Father and Sister/Aunt in the film, she has also revealed that the film is based on a real episode that occurred in her own family when her father decided to impose discipline.[17] Viewed in this context, the peeling of the orange takes on another connotation: at a symbolic level, it represents the peeling away of the surface layers of the family's history, revealing the sexual desire and compulsiveness underneath that generates the perturbations Campion depicts in one film after another. In this sense, the orange depicted in the film is symbolically, as well as literally, a "forbidden fruit," a biblical "fruit of knowledge" that the filmmaker is drawn toward, but fears ingesting.

It is significant that, when the boy, in response to his father's coercive injunctions, attempts to put the peel back together again—that is, at a symbolic level, to maintain the surface fiction that conceals the truth underneath—he becomes complicit with the father in attempting to assert a rigid discipline over his older sister. To me, this suggests an unspoken recognition of how the excessive concern with discipline displayed by the father functions as the masking opposite to the transgressive, illicit sexuality intimated through the symbolic structure of the film. In a stroke of brilliant psychological insight, Campion then shows the sister's awareness of this hypocrisy, reinforced by an attempt at patriarchal dominance on the part of the father and the son (who are now in league), as provoking her own defiant rebelliousness, when she begins to peel an orange and discard its skin on the road. In short, the film draws a lot of its power from its dramatization of the deep source of rage experienced by a woman who feels the injustice of being subjected to a masculine power that is grounded in self-deception and pretense of a grotesquely culpable order. The sister's angry defiance at the end of *Peel* can be viewed as preparing the way for Ada's muteness in *The Piano*.

Stylistically, the systematic "deforming [of] norms" that Polan detects in *Peel*, as in Campion's other early shorts—manifest in such techniques as shooting high angles downward, the eccentric placing of characters in the frame, exaggerated contrasts of scale, and the use of extreme contrasts of color and lighting[18]—does far more than simply generate quirkiness for its own sake. It serves as the register of an emotional perturbation that is having difficulty in finding expression except through the nature of the images that are assembled to narrate what is ostensibly a very simple event, and the way in which those images communicate a complex mixture of resentment and anger through the unease that is generated by the style in which they are presented. This perfect marriage of form and context, when the motivation of this short film is properly understood, turns *Peel* into an astonishing achievement that well merits the admiration and acclaim that it has enjoyed.

Jane Campion's next film, *Passionless Moments* (1983), is the one production that stands outside the general thematic preoccupations that I have been outlining. The reason is not hard to discern. At this stage in her life, Campion was in a relationship and living with Gerard Lee, her co-director. Although they thought up most of the scenes and directed the film together, Gerard Lee wrote the narration, which is delivered as a voice-over. The relative absence in this work of the high degree of symbolization and displacement observable in Campion's other films is instructive: it demonstrates just how personal her cinematic fictions are in the movies over which she exerts authorial control. *Passionless Moments* is a less deeply layered work. As Campion describes it, "Gerard and I wanted to show sweet, ordinary people that you rarely see on screen" with the banal episodes from their daily lives "told with a certain ironic distance."[19] For the purposes of this book, therefore, this film is less significant than her others. It does, however, in its difference from Campion's other films, highlight the necessity of a personal element that connects to the director's own experience of life as the origins of genuine authorship. As far as authorship is concerned, one senses that the greater part of this film (but not all of it) is more Gerard Lee's than Jane Campion's, despite the impact of Campion's cinematography.

A Girl's Own Story, made in 1984, is an altogether different matter. Indeed, it is the most overtly autobiographical of all Jane Campion's early films, despite her occasional protestations to the contrary. Campion is aware of her own inconsistencies in this regard, admitting that she is "ashamed of her own propensity for contradicting herself."[20] In an interview in the *Sydney Daily Telegraph* in 1990, she confessed that she had used a dress belonging to her mother in the production: "'Mum never noticed', she commented, 'until my sister said, "Don't you see. We're all in that film."'"[21]

Indeed they are, as becomes plain when one matches up the episodes and motifs depicted in *A Girl's Own Story* with what is known about the real-life circumstances of the Campion family. The film abounds in personal allusions. One of the opening shots shows Pam and a friend tracing with a finger the erect penis of a naked man in a line drawing, which displays the caption "This sight may shock young girls." Not only does it recall the image of the inflated condom in *Peel,* but the inclusion of this drawing also foreshadows Jane Campion's admission that, when she went to art school in Sydney, "I started doing these crude porno-graphic paintings . . . but nobody told me off."[22] Later, in *In the Cut,* she will again include an aggressively phallic drawing—the red lighthouse on the blackboard of the classroom where Frannie gives her lesson on Virginia Woolf's *To the Lighthouse*—which Campion, somewhat to her embarrassment, admits she drew herself.[23] In a very particular sense, then, *A Girl's Own Story* is the director's own story.[24] This idea is further reinforced when the film shows us Pam and her friends in their school uniforms—the same kind of uniforms that can be seen in the photos that survive of Jane Campion in her schoolgirl years and that will reappear in the school uniform that she has Janet wear in *An Angel at My Table,* thus reinforcing the autobiographical association in that film also.

A similar correspondence is established when we are introduced to Pam's mother. She is shown sitting motionless in a shot from behind that helps to establish her unhappiness and depression, and she is wearing a fur-rimmed dress with a price tag on it. As noted above, Campion later revealed that she borrowed a dress belonging to her own mother, Edith, for the film, and it is possible that this is the dress in question, given that it is the garment that Pam's mother wears in most of her scenes. The film establishes a parallel between the mother in the story and Edith Campion—an identification that is further reinforced by the hairdo that Pam's mother wears, which exactly replicates Edith Campion's in the portrait that appears on the dust jacket of her novel, *The Chain.* More-over, the numerous cats that appear as a recurrent motif in the movie recall Edith's own recurrently proclaimed passion for cats—one of the enthusiasms she lists, for example, in the biographical blurbs on the dust jackets of both her published books. The allusion to cats, while carrying its own range of symbolic connotations, reinforces the suggestion that *A Girl's Own Story* has the story of Edith Campion and her troubled marriage at its center. Edith wrote a powerful poem, published in the New Zealand literary journal *Landfall,* describing the deep personal comfort she gained from the companionship of her cats and, especially,

The depressed mother in a dress with a price tag in *A Girl's Own Story*.

the soothing effects of stroking their fur. At the conclusion of this moving piece, she writes that, even if she were to go to hell, her cat would be loyally waiting for her.[25]

The sisters in the film, too, recall the Campion sisters, especially in the fighting that takes place between them. Both Jane and Anna Campion have attested to their mutual hostility as siblings during their youth, with Jane admitting that the fighting she shows between Dawn and Kay in *Sweetie* reflects "the sort of fighting my sister and I used to do—pulling the hair, like furies."[26] For her part, Anna has confessed, "It's taken us a while to connect. . . . There's a Darwinian aspect to it. Another child comes along, and how does each get enough nurturing?"[27] In *A Girl's Own Story,* this dynamic is played out between Prue and Pam, with Prue representing Anna, and Pam representing Jane.

Not surprisingly in the context of this family allegory, the father in *A Girl's Own Story* replicates the marital infidelity of Richard Campion. In the film, Jane Campion fictively recreates this as an affair with a younger woman, whose existence Pam's father attempts to mask by professing to love his wife, whom he is able to dominate by manipulating the seductive power his erotic attractiveness holds for her.

Once the correspondences between the characters in *A Girl's Own Story* and the members of Campion's own family are recognized, it becomes possible to see how she constructs the film as a representation that allows her to explore the "interior torments" that are, in her view, most readily accessible through symbols. *A Girl's Own Story* can be viewed as a more extended and overt symbolic presentation of the issues hinted at implicitly in *Peel* and *Mishaps*. At the heart of the film is the distress caused by the father's infidelity and its consequences, not only for his wife, who plunges into depression, but also for the psychic life of his daughters. In the case of the mother, the price tag attached to the dress she is wearing (Edith Campion's real-life dress) suggests the cost of a passionately romantic attachment to her husband and, thus, metaphorically speaking, of her marriage. (We should remember that Edith literally lost a fortune, as well as being cheated on.) For the daughters, Pam especially, the effect is equally damaging. The film, as many commentators have observed, deals with the rites of passage of adolescent girls—in particular, through their discovery of sexuality. While that is true, the film is more preoccupied with the disturbed impulses concerning sexuality that are experienced by its central character, Pam, as a result of her father's conduct and its impact on the rest of the family.

What disturbs Pam is her simultaneous experience of contradictory impulses concerning sex, both of which arise from her awareness of her father's illicit sexual activity. On one hand, she is drawn toward the idea of sex because of its power of visceral and emotional attraction—something that her father is manifestly unable to resist—and because of the excitement implicit in the sense of transgression involved. This transgressive dimension, manifesting as an incestuous sexual curiosity, is doubled and dramatized in the subplot involving Gloria and her brother, Graeme, in which the two have sexual intercourse under the pretense of being cats (an episode which subsumes the several other occasions in the film in which the image of a cat is associated with the use of sex for self-soothing, or as a substitute for that satisfaction). At another level, Pam also experiences a deep recoiling at the idea of sexuality as a result of her awareness of its power to destroy—exemplified in the sad case of her betrayed mother.

The complexity and confusion Pam comes to feel about the motives and objectives of sexuality are manifested in various ways. Her
ambivalence is apparent in a fantasy of incest she entertains toward her
father, expressed in her longing to be the object of his attention and
admiration. She dresses up provocatively in a miniskirt, with her hair
untypically curled, to accompany her father to a restaurant, where they
intend to celebrate her birthday. When the father drops in on "an old
pal"—his current mistress, Deirdre—to invite her to join them, the
distressed Pam, whose earlier happiness at the prospect of being alone
with her father had been expressed in a brief tap dance, protests that
she had wanted it "to be just the two of us," as if they had been going on
a date.

The complexity of Pam's attitude is also shown to be linked to the
possibility that, as a young child, she suffered sexual abuse—imaged in a
scene in which the little Pam is lured into a stranger's car by the prospect
of stroking a kitten. Whether or not this scene attests to a literal molestation, it certainly confirms the presence in Pam's imaginary of the blend
of excitement and fear regarding sexuality that is manifested in the film
in other ways.

The most clear statement of this conflict-ridden syndrome is the
final, surrealistic scene in *A Girl's Own Story* that shows Pam and her
friends singing "I feel the cold / I fear it's here to stay / There is no end
to this lake of ice / I want to melt away," while shots of ice skating are
superimposed on the scene taking place in the present. The content of
this sequence is then contrasted with a shot of four girls sitting in front of
heaters—another recurrent motif in the film that suggests, symbolically,
a desire to find a way of thawing out a frigidity of response generated
by fear, not only of the cruelty of the world, but of masculine sexuality
itself, because of its power to cause harm. By depicting this overwhelming sense of a world in which terrible things can happen, *A Girl's Own
Story* prefigures the frigidity of Kay in *Sweetie* and anticipates the sexual
repression of Ada in *The Piano*, while suggesting the psychodynamic
influences that can produce such sorts of dysfunction.

Of all Jane Campion's films, *A Girl's Own Story*, as its title invites us
to surmise, is the one that approximates most closely her own real-life
story—which is undoubtedly one of the reasons that it is invested with
an uncanny and disturbing power. It announces all the main themes that

Campion will systematically elaborate, with various permutations, in the course of all her subsequent movies.

3 *After Hours* (1984), Jane Campion's next film, was made at the request of a feminist action group, the Women's Film Unit, with the intention of raising awareness about sexual harassment. This topic provided Campion, as writer and director, with an opportunity to pick up the theme of sexual molestation and abuse that she had already depicted in two of her movies, in *A Girl's Own Story* in particular.

Campion has been remarkably cagey about this movie, even to the point of virtually disowning it—on the grounds that the need to make it "openly feminist" had resulted in a conflict between the project and her artistic conscience: "I wasn't comfortable because I don't like films that say how one should or shouldn't behave. I think that the world is more complicated than that.... I would have preferred to have put this film in a closet but it toured the world!"[28] These words are revealing, because they indicate the presence of an ambivalence in the filmmaker's vision that is comparable to the contradictory impulses that *A Girl's Own Story* depicts in Pam. Although Campion has explained her discomfort with the film in terms of its need to conform to a feminist agenda, this explanation is far from convincing, especially when one considers the extent to which the purported feminist agenda is subverted from within the film itself.

The film is implicitly critical of most of the women it depicts, as Dana Polan has meticulously detailed.[29] The wife of the molester, Mr. Phillips, is shown to be an empty-headed woman whose main concern is with the frivolities of life, such as landscape decoration and interior design, and who is hence oblivious to the furtive sexual adventures her husband is conducting under her nose. Phillips's elderly secretary is equally obtuse, displaying an uncritical hero worship that helps to sabotage the investigation into the alleged abuse. So, too, the investigator herself, who seems very willing to abandon the investigation as soon as it becomes obvious that it will be difficult to prove that the abuse occurred. Even Lorraine's mother, from whom she should be able to expect understanding, implicitly blames Lorraine for having worn a miniskirt to work—a reproach that is mirrored in the recrimination of her boyfriend. The victim of the abuse is thus deserted by the very women who should be the guardians

The daughter taking her father's pulse in *After Hours*.

of her safety and sympathetic to her cause. This seems far from the articulation of a feminist agenda.

Just as disturbingly, there is an equal degree of ambivalence in the depiction of the molester himself. Phillips is a father and, perhaps, in the eyes of Lorraine, a father figure (Lorraine's natural father is not present in the movie). In his role as a father, Phillips is seen as the object of his own daughter's devoted attention. In one scene, his daughter, dressed in the uniform of a nurse, is solicitously trying to hear her father's pulse through a toy stethoscope, protesting that "it doesn't work." At a symbolic level, this action is resonant with possible connotations, suggesting on one hand the concern of a loving daughter to help her father get well from a malaise that is afflicting him, but without the means of doing so, and, on the other, her consternation at finding that, metaphorically speaking, he does not "have a pulse"—in other words, he is either heartless, or something vital to healthy functioning is lacking in him.

Similarly, in the scene in which the molestation actually occurs, Lorraine does appear to encourage the abuse. When Phillips turns off

the lights in the office, a switch in the film to low lighting with dark attached shadows as the result of strong side lighting, combined with a
series of close-up shots that alternately show the faces of Lorraine and
Phillips, generates a subjective sense that, to some degree, Lorraine finds
this moment exciting, however dangerous she might also feel it to be. In
this respect, the scene anticipates the moment in *The Portrait of a Lady*
when Osmond emerges from the shadows of the catacombs to begin
his seduction of Isabel, with the whole scene playing on the contrast
between light and darkness to suggest the mixture of fear and attraction
that the heroine is experiencing at that moment. After initially fondling
Lorraine's shoulder under the pretense of scaring her in the dark, Phillips
switches the lights back on and returns to work. At this point, Lorraine
could leave to return home, but chooses not to. Instead, she remains
with Phillips in his office and tells him she is not feeling well. When he
touches her on the side of her throat to ask whether that is where the pain
is, she encourages him to touch her on the stomach by saying that that is
the site of her malaise. The image of Phillips doing this, once again presented in a close-up shot to draw attention to it, anticipates Isabel's view
of Osmond's arm encircling the waist of Pansy, his daughter—which
is one of the things that draws her to him—a parallel that indicates the
presence of an unconscious desire for a bonded relationship with a father
(figure) that trembles on the verge of crossing boundaries. Thus, to a
certain extent, Lorraine—like Pam in *A Girl's Own Story*—seems to be
living out a fantasy of incest with a father figure at the same time that she
feels abhorrence and anger at the outcome of it. Like Pam, metaphorically speaking, she is left "feeling the cold," which is revealed when she
later recoils from the touch of her swimming coach, suggesting that she
has developed a fear of men in general.

For Lorraine, the experience of these conflicted feelings, especially
in the absence of any help from those who should be supporting her, not
only results in isolation, but leaves her prone to suicidal ideation. We
see this in a scene late in the film when she first touches the surface of
the water in a swimming pool, making concentric circles on it, and then
allows herself to fall into the pool's depths, causing the viewer initially
to wonder whether she intends to drown herself. There is a strong resemblance between this episode and the equivalent scene in *The Piano* where
Ada, having entertained a suicidal fantasy, places her foot in the coils of

a rope tied to her piano, which has been thrown overboard, and thus allows herself to be drawn underwater into the depths of the sea. Likewise, the opening and closing scenes of *After Hours* show the windows of the offices in the building where Lorraine works illuminated from within by a blue fluorescent light. This makes the interior of the offices look like an aquarium, filled with water—an effect that anticipates the bush scenes in *The Piano*, which are filmed in a blue autochrome that makes them seem as if they are taking place underwater. Not only does this visual effect in *After Hours* create an associative link between the office scenes and the swimming pool scenes in the movie, but it also suggests an imaginative continuity between the preoccupations of *After Hours* and those to be found in *The Piano*.

This depth of associative resonance makes it all the more unlikely that Jane Campion's discomfort with the film arose simply from a feeling that she had been required to make it conform to a feminist agenda—which, in any case, it does not. Campion was compromised by the nature of her personal concerns, and she knew it. The deep ambivalence about fathers and father figures that Campion had already depicted in Pam in *A Girl's Own Story*, and would again depict in Ruth in *Holy Smoke*, made it unlikely that she could bring herself unequivocally to condemn a man like Phillips, however much she might resent what he did. That is why she thought that the world is more complicated than anything that the Women's Film Unit could want her to show.

A coda may be added to this account of *After Hours*. One of the other films Jane Campion considered making around this time was to have been called *Ebb:*

> It was an imaginary story about a country where one day the sea leaves to never return, and the way in which the people have to find a spiritual solution to this problem. The natural world had become artificial and unpredictable and the film spoke about faith and doubt. The inhabitants of this country had developed a certain form of spirituality, hearing voices, having visions. At the end, the father of a family central to the story, the man who was the least inclined towards a spiritual adventure, had the most extraordinary experiences. It's for him that the sea returned and his tongue/language began to have a salty taste! He became a sacrificial victim.[30]

It would appear that this film, through the use of mythological symbolism, was to have presented a remedy for the psychic perturbations of the kind of world depicted in *A Girl's Own Story* and *After Hours* in the form of a spiritual solution. What links this mythological fable with *After Hours,* specifically, is the centrality in *Ebb* of a father "who was the least inclined towards a spiritual adventure" and who had to undergo conversion before the sea could return—metaphorically speaking, before the world could be put right again. This idea recalls the episode in *After Hours* where the little girl, dressed as a nurse, is seeking to find her father's pulse. In Campion's imaginary, the curing of the father (figure) is the essential prerequisite for the restoration of a happy condition of existence—which is presumably what *Ebb* would have shown. Campion will elect in her subsequent films to convey this idea through different means.

4   Jane Campion's next assay was *Two Friends* (1986), a seventy-six-minute-long feature made for television to a script by the Australian novelist Helen Garner. The screenplay had been inspired by the actual experiences of Garner's daughter and one of her friends, investing it with a "freshness of observation and the truth of the situations," in Campion's eyes. When approached by the producer, Jan Chapman, Campion chose the script because she felt she could "get something out of it."[31] For the purposes of this book, *Two Friends* is illuminating, because it shows how film authorship does not depend upon a literal authoring of the screenplay by the director. Even when the screenplay is written by someone else, as in this instance, the director can still "get something out of it" through the way in which he or she contrives and executes the mise-en-scène. That is precisely what Campion did with Helen Garner's novel and screenplay, converting the work, in the process, into a film that unmistakably bears the stamp of her own authorship because of the way in which it is converted into a vehicle for her own personal issues. As such, it foreshadows the authoring strategy that Campion would use again in converting Henry James's novel *The Portrait of a Lady* and Susanna Moore's novel *In the Cut* into films that are fully transformed into her personal cinema.

It is not hard to see why Campion would have been attracted to Garner's novel. The story of *Two Friends* contains many elements that she had already depicted in *A Girl's Own Story*—especially in its depiction of dysfunctional families and the psychodynamics they produce. Both girls alluded to in the title, Louise and Kelly, are yearning for the attention of and an attachment with fathers who are estranged from their wives. In this respect, the two girls are doubled in a way that Campion will repeat with Kay and Dawn in *Sweetie* and with Frannie and Pauline in *In the Cut*, with Kay and Frannie representing a more repressed version of their respective sisters, and their sisters acting out the aspects of themselves that Kay and Frannie have repressed. With Louise and Kelly, there are strong suggestions of a fantasy of incest that is characteristic of individuals caught up in a disturbed family romance in which boundaries are not clear, or else transgressed.

Louise's father is shown to be complicit in this fantasy. When Louise introduces Matthew, a friend, to her father, the latter says, "Looks like we're visiting the same girl," as if they are rival lovers. Later, when Louise is alone with her father in a restaurant (in a version of the situation that would have ensued had the presence of Deirdre not interfered with the similar event in *A Girl's Own Story*), she says to him, "Dad, do you think anyone would mistake us for boyfriend and girlfriend?" to which he replies, "I dunno—what d'you think?"

Kelly's yearning for a "romance" with her father is equally intense. Distressed by the hostility of her stepfather, Malcolm, she longs to move out and live with her father in his apartment. During the evening when she goes to stay with him, however, he receives a call from his lover and immediately abandons her to join his mistress, which leaves Kelly alone in the apartment with his friend. In terms of the mechanisms of neglect and disappointed expectation involved, this episode replicates those in the sequence in *A Girl's Own Story* when Pam's father similarly lets her down.

The consequences for Kelly are dire. Driven by a desire to find some substitute for the paternal affection of which she has been deprived, she goes to the bedroom of her father's friend, who is staying the night in the apartment, and lies down next to him. In response, this man begins to make love to her, which prompts the alarmed Kelly to jump up and flee. Again, the psychic mechanism at the heart of this episode is very close to Campion's concerns: narcissistic deprivation, as a result of paternal neglect, is recurrently shown to motivate an attempt to find compensation for what is missing in the woman's internal world through engagement in physical intimacy with a man who is a stand-in for a longed-for, but missing, father. This impulse in the girl or woman is then perceived to be persecutory, because it activates a prohibition against incest—triggered by the fact that the man evokes the idea and presence of the neglectful father. We see this again in *Sweetie* in the reversal of desire in Kay, and in *Holy Smoke* in the way that Ruth's seduction and conquest of PJ Waters is followed by an overwhelming desire to flee from him.

The extent to which Campion was able to identify her personal concerns with the characters and situations in Helen Garner's screenplay is further demonstrated by the presence of numerous symbolic images that link the events of the film with aspects of *A Girl's Own Story*. When we first see Louise, for example, on the occasion when she meets her friend Matthew in her mother's house, she carries an electric heater across the room, recalling the innumerable heaters that appeared as a recurrent motif in the earlier film. Likewise, there is a great emphasis on school uniforms in *Two Friends,* visually recalling the uniforms of Pam and her friends in the earlier film—even to the extent of replicating the scene in which the schoolgirls display their legs, dressed with white socks and shoes, in parallel. Through these images, Campion associates the situation of the girls within the story not only with her own experience— she went to a girls' school—but also with the experience of her mother, who was similarly sent to a girls' school. The image of a school uniform serves as a powerful symbol in Jane Campion's imaginary because of its association with a myth in the family that Edith Campion was so poor in her youth that her school uniform was the only respectable item of clothing she possessed.[32] Even if there is a degree of fancifulness in this statement (it is hard to believe that Edith Campion could have been *that* poor, given that she was the heiress of a very large fortune), it does attest to another associative connotation that inhered in the image of a school uniform for Jane Campion—which is repeated not only in *A Girl's Own Story* and *Two Friends,* but also in *An Angel at My Table* in her presentation of the young Janet Frame. For Campion, the image is associated with the miseries of girlhood in general, and with narcissistic deprivation in particular.

The final aspect of Helen Garner's screenplay that engaged Campion's attention was the connection that the script establishes between emotional deprivation and delinquency, as represented in the sad decline of Kelly into sexual promiscuity, drug taking, vagrancy, and, it is implied, the probability of a premature death—signaled in the death of another girl at the beginning of the movie. The decline begins when her stepfather refuses to let her accompany Louise after the two girls have succeeded in gaining entry to an elitist girls' school. Deprived of motivation and the supportive connection with her best friend, Kelly seeks solace in the company of boys, and when her real father shows no interest in her and she realizes, from the attempt of his friend to convert her need for affection into an opportunity for sex, that sex is all she has to offer, she loses all sense of self-worth and takes to the streets. Her attempt to regain contact with her family merely leaves her with a deepened sense of hopelessness, expressed when she smashes the ceramic vase she has bought for her mother to celebrate the latter's birthday. As in *After Hours,* the mother has no will to support Kelly against the injustice that is perpetrated against her by an insensitive and self-interested man—in this case, her stepfather. By the end of the movie, one feels the inevitability of the self-destructive trajectory which is the only path left for Kelly to follow. In terms of the psychodynamics involved, Garner and Campion, between them, have put the spectator in the presence not only of the sources of delinquency, but, behind that, of the wellsprings of depression itself, including, one senses, the depression that affected Edith Campion and, by her own admission, her filmmaking daughter (on occasion). Despite the verdict of many critics who say that *Two Friends* is anomalous in the oeuvre of Jane Campion in seeming not to be a "Campion film," to the contrary, it seems to me to manifest her personal cinema as much as any of her other early films.

5 I will briefly speculate on what these early films reveal about the function of filmmaking for this enigmatic auteur. It seems to me that the visual nature of cinematic representation makes it possible for Jane Campion to construct images that are able to serve the function of "objects" as understood in contemporary psychoanalytic theory. Because the visual images Campion constructs relate at a symbolic level to her perception of her own family background (whether literally, or in a metaphorically transliterated form), the images themselves are able to release the subjectivities of the objectifying self. More than that, they hold out the possibility to the spectator of sharing in the experience of these subjectivities, mostly at an intuitive level, given that the registration of the states of thought and feeling depicted does not depend upon any awareness of their origins in Campion's life story.

I would go further. In one of her French interviews, Jane Campion confessed that, for her, "the cinema is, above all, a way of gaining the attention of people" ("Pour moi, le cinéma, c'est d'abord un moyen de retenir l'attention des gens").[33] This statement is capable of being interpreted in at least two ways: in one sense, it means that cinema has the power to keep people interested, but in a deeper sense, it means that cinema is a way of attracting people's attention. While the first sense is obviously important to Campion, it is the second sense that provides, in my estimation, the most profound motivation. Campion *wants* her audience to share in the experience of these elaborating subjectivities of the objectifying self; she wants them to see what she is trying to get at. That is why she so insistently invites viewers in her interviews and commentaries to make the connections and links with her personal life, and the desire to have this involvement on the part of the audience is largely what informs the construction of the public persona she projects through the media.[34] The negative self-feelings that derive from such familial histories can be evacuated, or at least allayed, through the participation of viewers who are invited to share, imaginatively, the experience itself. As Campion has revealed, she makes films because she wants to "be loved"[35]—a desire that is motivated, one suspects, by a personal experience of acute narcissistic deprivation as a result of paternal neglect, reinforced by whatever negative feelings she may have internalized from her depressed mother. I speculate, therefore, that one of the motives for a director to make personal cinema is precisely the need to gain from audiences, through their vicarious engagement with the fiction, some validation, through empathic understanding, of those factors in the filmmaker's life that have led to the creation of the film in the first place.

The primal situations and psychological problematics articulated in Jane Campion's early films resurface in all of her subsequent feature-length movies. Indeed, as we examine the later films in the order of their production, it will become clear that their main purpose is to elaborate, in greater depth, aspects of these issues to which the early films, because of their brevity, had not been able to do justice. In the chapters that follow, I will trace the stages by which Campion achieved this further elaboration.

3 Living in the Shadow of the Family Tree: *Sweetie*

1 Having established in her early films what her main thematic preoccupations would be, and now confident in her ability to tackle a full-length movie as a result of her two features made for television, Jane Campion was ready to extend her exploration of the issues that she now recognized as inherent in her personal problematic. By 1989, the year that *Sweetie* was released, she had also experienced the failure of several relationships—most notably with Gerard Lee, with whom she had lived for a number of years while attending film school. It was to be expected, then, that her new feature-length film would have a dual focus. On one hand, it would, in Campion's own words, "push in all the directions I'd taken earlier because we knew we hadn't gone as far as we could"—that is, it would deal with the consequences of growing up in a dysfunctional family.[1] On the other hand, it would be preoccupied with relationships, particularly relationships that "don't work."[2] Jane Campion's genius would show, in a profoundly imaginative way, the connections that she intuited lay between the two.

The connections between a disturbed family romance and relationship dysfunction, however, is not made entirely explicit in *Sweetie*, even though they are apparent at all stages in the film. Being a highly intuitive filmmaker whose method is to represent images arising from her unconscious, Jane Campion ends up showing far more in *Sweetie* than either its narrator, Kay, or the filmmaker herself are able to put into verbal expression. Within the film, Kay tells a story that "she herself does not fully know." Indeed, as Kathleen McHugh has suggested, Kay is "afraid of the back story, of her family tree."[3] In this, she truly does reflect her creator. When an interviewer asked Campion what *Sweetie* was about, she could offer little more by way of explanation than her fictional surrogate could: "It's really hard to say what it's about because it sort of begs that question." The best she could come up with was to suggest that the film presents "a look at the underbelly" and that "it's about love, too, and about family"—but beyond these vague generalizations, she could not, or would not, venture any opinions.[4] As she later admitted to Michel Ciment, *Sweetie* was "a film that I controlled the least, which brought me where I didn't really know I was going, and in this sense it was a great adventure."[5]

Apart from this lack of conscious control on the part of the director, the cryptic nature of Campion's mode of symbolic representation also adds to the interpretive burden that is thrust on the viewer, and in the case of *Sweetie,* interpretation presents a considerable challenge. As McHugh has observed, the film's narrative is presented less as a "hermeneutic chain of cause and effect culminating in coherent resolution and closure than a puzzle from which some of the pieces have been permanently lost,"[6] which puts one in mind of Campion's belief that "[y]ou don't discover the truth just by developing a plot," but rather "by exploring many levels," especially through the symbols and metaphors by which people gain access to a sense of their "interior torments."[7]

Campion's statement alerts us to the need, when seeking to interpret this film, to look for the kinds of metaphoric and metonymical displacements that are at work, and the ways that these are used to conduct an exploration that is operating at different levels of meaning. Such displacements, I suggest, constitute one of the most basic strategies of authorship. The reference to "interior torments" should also prompt us to realize that there is a connection between the nature of the symbolic displacements and the inner psychic world of the creator, for whom the fictive representation serves a function similar to that of a dream, or an imaginative fantasy. In the rest of this chapter, I will demonstrate how and why, in the case of *Sweetie,* this is so.

2 As with *A Girl's Own Story,* the raw material for many of the elements of *Sweetie* is drawn directly out of Jane Campion's real-life experience.

> It started off being about a couple—myself and the co-writer on "Sweetie,"
> Gerard Lee—and the problems of feeling like we were in love but not having the
> relationship work. And how mysterious it felt, and frustrating, and unhappy-
> making, and how our families kept intersecting. You couldn't seem to solve a
> problem without something else happening. It just had a mystical quality to it.[8]

The first third of *Sweetie* is preoccupied first with the formation of this relationship and then with its breakdown—mirrored in the relationship between Kay (Karen Colston) and Louis (Tom Lycos, an actor chosen for his remarkable physical resemblance to Gerard Lee). The most striking aspects of the filmic relationship are the superstition that motivates Kay to enter into it and the onset of a sexual dysfunction that makes the relationship feel like one between brother and sister, in which sex is prohibited as if it were a form of incest. Just how closely this relationship reflects Campion's real-life one is suggested by the origins of the sapling that Louis plants, which Kay subsequently pulls out and hides:

> In film school, I was obsessed with making films and wasn't paying much atten-
> tion to Gerard. We had this tree growing in the backyard, and I remember him
> saying to me, "You don't look after anything. Two trees have died now, and if this
> last one does it's because you don't care about things. And that's how I feel; I feel
> like that tree." So I just kept looking at this tree, worrying whether it was going
> to die or not.[9]

Of itself, the baby tree provides an object that registers Kay's superstition, yet in the context of the movie as a whole, it takes on a much larger symbolic dimension, serving to register the more general existential anxiety that is generated in her by the psychodynamics deriving from her familial legacy.

Indeed, even though the movie begins with a depiction of Campion's troubled relationship with Lee, its focus quickly expands to encompass other players who are caught up in a drama extending across several generations. Again, the raw material for this expanded focus was drawn from real life—in particular, from those aspects of familial life in which the experiences of the Campion and Lee families "intersected." The major point at which they did intersect was in the parallel breakdowns in the relationship of the parents. Gerard Lee's mother had split from his father for a time and gone to live in the country for a trial separation, while Jane Campion's parents had divorced in 1984.[10] By basing the relationship between Flo and Gordon in *Sweetie* on that between Gerard Lee's own

parents, Campion was able to use it also as a vehicle for exploring vicariously the forces that led to the separation of Richard and Edith Campion.
Campion's strategy was to "mix and match" elements from her and Lee's
real-life experience for the sake of constructing an archetypal story that
would suit her thematic purpose—which is, as one French newspaper
accurately observed when the film appeared, to present "la thérapie fil-
mée d'une névrose familiale" (the filmed therapy of a family neurosis).[11]

This mixing and matching takes the characters far from their original sources, as can be seen from the presentation of Sweetie (Dawn)
herself. Campion has revealed that the character of Dawn was actually
inspired by one of Gerard Lee's male relatives, with the gender of the
character being changed "for family reasons," out of respect for the feelings of Lee.[12] Certain other aspects of Dawn were drawn from Jane Campion's real-life relationship with her own sister, Anna. Even though Jane
is at pains to insist that Dawn is not to be equated with Anna, she nevertheless concedes that "there is a kind of wildness to my sister Anna, and
she did actually have a horse collection."[13] Moreover, the fighting that
takes place between Kay and Dawn recalls "the sort of fighting my sister
and I used to do—pulling the hair, like furies."[14] Indeed, one senses that
Dawn, despite Campion's protestations, derives from the latter's desire to
exact some kind of fantasy revenge on her sister in the film, to evacuate
the "hatred" Jane confesses she felt for Anna when they were growing
up together in Wellington. Certainly, Anna felt sufficiently uncomfort-
able that she expressed some concern about Jane's dedication of Sweetie
"to my sister":

> "It would have been better to say, 'to Anna', for *obvious reasons*." She pauses.
> "At Cannes, she [Jane] decided it was a convenient diversion for the press, and
> would try to encourage me to be Sweetie-ish. I'd say, 'Actually, I don't really ap-
> preciate you stealing hunks of my personality and mixing it up with this nutcase.
> And not exactly expressing to the press that it's nothing to do with me.'"[15]

Even though by the time Sweetie was made the two Campion sisters
had become the best of friends—as a result of Anna's initiative—it is
clear that in the film Jane was still engaged in exorcising the traumatic
sense of disadvantage in the competition for their parents' love that she
had felt when she and Anna were growing up. This is why—even though
by Jane's account there was never anyone quite like Dawn in the Campion family—she combined "hunks" of Anna's personality with other

The collection of toy horses in *Sweetie*.

elements relating to a person in Gerard Lee's family to make a new composite character, with the difference that "it's mixed and matched, and exaggerated." As Campion puts it, "we're all muddled up," as when she gives Kay, rather than Dawn, the horse collection that had belonged to Anna Campion in real life.[16]

As I have suggested, this deliberate mingling of elements points to a creative reshaping in which details drawn from real life are recombined in order to make them conform to a larger purpose—one that may not be entirely formulated in the filmmaker's conscious awareness, but which nevertheless reflects a concern to understand certain things that, in her words, are "more than you want to know about" but are necessary to be known, all the same.[17] This kind of reshaping—achieved through a process of metaphoric condensation and metonymic displacement—I would maintain, constitutes an essential dimension of authorship. It remains now to show how such an imaginative reworking can, through the activation of a process that is set in motion at a displaced remove, bring to light, through a dramatized exemplification, the things that are "more than you want to know" but which the filmmaker feels a need to know nonetheless.

3 The deeper preoccupations that make *Sweetie* such a fascinating exploration of the psychodynamic influences that can operate within a

troubled family are suggested by the thematic patterns that result from a reorganization of the elements drawn from Campion's own experiences.

A context for this patterning is provided by a leitmotif that recurs throughout the film: trees, including their power to affect people's lives. The symbolic connotations inherent in this metaphor are evident in Kay's voice-over as the film begins:

> KAY   We had a tree in our yard with a palace in the branches. It was built for my sister and it had fairy lights that went on and off. . . . She was the princess. It was her tree. She wouldn't let me in.
>   At night the darkness frightens me. Someone could be watching from behind it. Someone who wishes you harm. I used to imagine the roots of that tree crawling, crawling right under the house, right under my bed. Maybe that's why trees scare me. It's like they have hidden powers.

In this brief passage, Campion, with a remarkable economy achieved through symbolic condensation, sets in motion the major thematic associations that will inform the rest of the film. The tree, metaphorically speaking, suggests a family tree. The palace in its branches, built for Kay's sister and from which she is excluded, signifies a privileged place, invested with romantic fantasy, in which a daughter can be the object of her adoring father's admiration. In its sinister aspect, however, the tree has a hidden power to cause harm through the invasiveness of its spreading roots. These roots can crack concrete, crawl under a house, and creep right under one's bed. At a symbolic level, the tree represents the family legacy that Campion believes you carry around with you. The fact that its roots are capable of crawling right under one's bed metaphorically foreshadows a link between the legacy of the family and the sexual dysfunction that Kay will soon experience in her relationship with Louis.

The image of the tree is reiterated throughout the movie. When Louis plants a sapling in the backyard, we are informed that it is an elder tree, with the pun on "elder" indicating the influence of the family's legacy, which was earlier associated with the tree's roots. The foliage of the tree is present as a shadow on the walls of the bedroom that Kay and Louis share. In the inset sequence of black-and-white time-lapse photography that shows a seed germinating, the sight of the "erection" of the seedling, as Nicolas Ripoche has recognized, invests the idea of the tree with sexual connotations.[18] A later shot records the root system of a large

A symbolic image of subterranean forces at work in *Sweetie*.

old tree cracking through pavement, after which the camera tracks fast along the ground to an extreme close-up of a thick tree trunk—again, with phallic overtones. When Sweetie arrives to stay with Kay, the latter attempts, symbolically, to sweep the leaves of the tree she has deracinated under the bed, indicating an association between the boundaryless libidinousness that Sweetie incarnates and the closing down of her own sexuality, and the connection of both to the sapling, the existence of which she has tried to disavow by attempting to destroy it. Eventually, Sweetie is killed in the wreckage of her fantasy palace when her own desperate actions cause it to collapse out of the tree in her parents' backyard. Finally, in the scene of Sweetie's burial, there is this statement in Kay's voice-over: "Trees never seem to leave us alone. We couldn't even get the coffin down for some tree root sticking out the side." The persistence of these references makes it clear that Campion intends the viewer to register the idea of trees as an omnipresent metaphor with a range of suggestive connotations, all of them connected to the idea of a lingering family legacy and the effects it can have on the younger generation.

Within the context of this encompassing metaphoric mindscape, Jane Campion builds a structure of symbolic contrasts that enables her to explore how narcissistic deprivation, on one hand, and an emotionally incestuous cross-generational investment between father and daughter, on the other, can affect the psychic well-being of a child as she grows into adulthood. This, rather than the relationship between Kay and Louis that provided the film's original pretext, turns out to be the primary preoccupation of *Sweetie,* and, one can infer, it relates back to the same set of family circumstances in Jane Campion's life that, as we have seen, informs each of her earlier films. The large degree of symbolic displacement and condensation that is at work, however, makes the preoccupation in this film into an enigmatic presence, rather than an insight that has been brought fully into conscious thought.

4 The key to an understanding of the film's symbolic subtext resides in the central relationship between the two sisters, Kay and Dawn. As a number of critics have recognized, Kay and Dawn exist as dialectical opposites. They are, in fact, doubles for each other, constructed as if they are the two halves of a single personality.[19] It may be useful at this point to invoke Carl Jung's theory of the "shadow," given that we know Jane Campion was interested in Jungian psychology during the period in which she was a student of structural anthropology.[20]

According to Jung, every human being has a persona, or mask, through which "we codify ourselves in a form which we hope will prove acceptable to others."[21] The achievement of this acceptability involves the repression of unacceptable traits that tend to be relegated to the unconscious, where they coalesce to form a disowned part of the self that Jung called the shadow: "Everyone carries a shadow, and the less it is embodied in the individual's conscious life, the blacker and denser it is."[22] Even though we may seek to disavow this unwanted part of our personality, it tends to resurface in dreams and visions, often as a feared, threatening, or despised figure of the same sex as the dreamer. As Anthony Stevens puts it, "Inevitably, the shadow comes to possess qualities opposite to those of the persona, the shadow compensating, as it were, for the superficial pretensions of the persona, the persona balancing the antisocial characteristics of the shadow."[23] In order to protect ourselves against the threat of these unwanted aspects of the self, we unconsciously adopt a variety of ego-defense mechanisms: "Not only do we repress the shadow in personal unconsciousness, but we deny its existence in ourselves, and project it out on to others."[24] The purpose of such projection, then, is to deny our own badness by attributing it to others, who can then be used as scapegoats.

This, it seems to me, is precisely what Jane Campion has done in contriving the symbolic structure found in *Sweetie*. Campion has revealed that "an alter ego part of me is Kay—a very extreme version of a part of me."[25] It seems just as likely that Dawn is also a "very extreme version of a part" of her—the disavowed shadow who, because of the need to repress it, is experienced as persecutory and threatening. As Campion puts it, Dawn "has this access to her animal self, if you will—the stuff that Kay is too frightened to contact."[26] The close link between Dawn and Jane Campion is also evident from other statements Campion has made, her filmic preoccupations, and even her practices as a filmmaker. In a number of interviews, for example, she has revealed her impulse to rebel. As a young filmmaker, she tells us, she was "particularly committed to what was nasty, what isn't spoken about in life,"[27] and at art school, she started doing "crude, pornographic paintings."[28] Her curiosity, she confesses, "has always been on those margins of what's acceptable . . . what we as wild creatures really are, as distinct from what society wants us to buy into."[29] Consequently, all of her movies depict transgression, the crossing of boundaries, and the flouting of convention of one sort or another, whether it be incest (in *A Girl's Own Story*), or adulterous eroticism (in *The Piano*), or even murder (in *In the Cut*). Generally, Campion displays a powerful impulse to rebel against any forms of repression that seek to impose limits or to constrain the spontaneous expression of emotion and desire. We see this in the camera work of *Sweetie*, which, with its off-center framing, bizarre angles, discontinuous editing, and refusal to satisfy viewers' expectations, betrays an intention (admitted by Jane Campion and her cinematographer, Sally Bongers) to break the rules of conventional filmmaking.

We see the same thing again in one of her more recent films, *The Lady Bug*, which was released at Cannes in 2007 as one segment in a compilation of short films titled *Chacun son cinéma; ou, Ce petit coup au coeur quand la lumière s'éteint et que le film commence*. In this bizarre *court métrage*, a woman dressed as an insect—the Ladybug—is spied lurking within one of the speakers in a cinema theater. When a gruff old janitor goes to kill it with a broom handle, the Ladybug comes out onto the stage of the cinema hall and does a song-and-dance routine until she is half-squashed when the janitor stomps on her. Apart from being a metaphor for the suppression of women in the film world, such as Campion herself,[30] the short piece could be viewed as an updated replay of Dawn's behavior in *Sweetie*—a possibility that is enhanced by the fact that Genevieve Lemon, who played Sweetie, also articulates the voice-over through which the Ladybug speaks. What Sweetie and the Ladybug share, apart from their aspiration to be allowed to "perform" on the stage, is the ability to "bug" people through outrageous and bizarre "acting out" in a world where they fear being oppressed by men. From this parallel between Sweetie and the Ladybug, it is apparent that Dawn in the earlier film is merely an extreme incarnation of the tendencies that Jane Campion has exhibited as a filmmaker throughout her whole career.

It seems likely, therefore, that Kay and Sweetie represent a splitting out of two extreme parts of Campion's own personality, which are then embodied and personified in two antithetical characters so that the impulses residing in them can be investigated. Additionally, their relationship as sisters mirrors the real-life relationship of Anna and Jane Campion as sisters, but without exactly replicating it. The purpose of these strategies, as I have suggested, is to enable an exploration of the range of reactions that a certain kind of pathological formation in parents can generate in their children. We find that the reactions exhibited by both Kay and Sweetie emanate, paradoxically, from the same cause; indeed, they represent the contradictory impulses experienced by the filmmaker in response to the circumstances of her own family background.

5 What, then, are Kay and Dawn responding to, and what are the consequences of their response? In the course of the movie, it becomes clear that both Kay and Dawn are suffering from the effects of emotional deprivation as they try to satisfy the exigencies of forbidden libidinal longings and impossible narcissistic desires. In the ordinary course of human development, infantile fantasies, first, of fusion with the mother and, then, of possession of the parents of both sexes are inevitably disrupted by the necessity of oedipal separation, which in turn leads to a discovery of one's individual identity: "The realization that one will never be both sexes or possess either parent sexually is rewarded with the gift of sexual desire and the promise of fulfillment in the future."[31]

If parents are suffering from unconscious problems, their unresolved psychic issues can interfere with a child's ability to come to terms with the forbidden and the impossible:

> If parents' internal dramas drive them to use their children—either their bodies or their minds—to settle scores with the past and repair their own narcissistic images or damaged libidinal relationships, the small megalomaniac is not likely to receive the help required to find solutions to the inevitable traumas of human life. For it is parents who give their children a sense of self, enjoyment in their individuality, masculinity and femininity, and the right to enjoy as fully as possible all aspects of adult life.[32]

When parents are unable to provide their child with a secure and confident self-sense, the child, in order to maintain psychic survival in the face of feelings of guilt, shame, and inadequacy, will tend to adopt neurotic or perverse solutions as a protection against psychic pain.

In *Sweetie,* there is every sign that such a failure of the parental function has indeed occurred. It is reflected, on one hand, in Kay's deep existential anxiety, which causes her to withdraw into herself, and, on the other hand, in Dawn's propensity to act out. Both responses are shown to arise from a need felt by the sisters to receive a kind of love and attention from their parents—their father in particular—that has not been given, leading them to adopt defensive postures which, although diametrically opposed, serve the same purpose, which is to protect them against a fear of the forbidden, in Kay's case, and a desire to perpetuate the impossible, in Dawn's case.

In Campion's depiction, it is the father who is chiefly to blame—which is ironic, given his fixation with Sweetie and the excessive emotional investment he places on her supposed talent. His culpability resides in the fact that, by constructing Sweetie as a "princess" and as a performer who will achieve great success on the stage, he is failing to see her or treat her as she really is. Instead, he uses Sweetie as a stand-in for someone else in his own fantasies, to supply something that is missing in his inner psychic world. This leaves Dawn feeling just as neglected as Kay does, despite the enormous amount of attention that Gordon, her father, lavishes on her.

It is possible that Jane Campion may be reflecting a real-life struggle she may have had with her father to maintain a sense of her individual identity. The evidence for this is provided by Richard Campion. A decade after *Sweetie* was made, Richard recalled how the young Jane had defied him at the age of five: "I was doing the parental thing about what she might want to do later on. She looked up at me with those big blue eyes and her golden hair and said, 'Dad, I am my own self!'"[33] This revelation helps to explain why Campion in later life felt a need to reject the theatrical world of her parents: like Sweetie, it is likely that she felt pressure to realize the unfulfilled ambitions of her parents, her father in particular. This is also suggested by the fact that Richard Campion in 1993 declared himself to be engaged in writing a book called "I'm My Own Self," which was to recount his battle to establish a New Zealand theater.[34] Interestingly, Anna Campion remained active in the world of New Zealand theater until at least 1973, taking part in productions directed by Nola Millar, her parents' erstwhile colleague.[35] It is possible, therefore, that Jane Campion's depiction of Sweetie reflects her sense of an implicit acquiescence on the part of her elder sister to a paternal pressure to fulfill his unrealized aspirations that she, Jane, had managed to resist—or, at least, to transplant into the different, but closely related, domain of cinema.

The pressure her father exerts on Dawn to achieve success in a theatrical career prompts her to seek rescue by transgressing the boundaries of the world that offers her no reassuring sense of an identity she can realistically assume, in an attempt, like that of the young Jane Campion, to secure some sense of an independent, determinate self. In addition, she frequently takes refuge in a regression to a childlike or nonhuman state—as when she barks like a dog or joins the young boy Clayton in his infantile pranks—as a means of avoiding a fear that she might not exist as a person. As her mother, Flo, affirms when Kay suggests that Sweetie is "evil," "she's not evil . . . she's just frightened." This perception echoes Jane Campion's view that Dawn is by no means "mad": "In my opinion she is normal, or at least was normal. Since her childhood, she has been pushed by her environment little by little and ends up by losing her equilibrium and her sense of responsibility. In other circumstances she could have been different."[36]

Dawn is the victim of an excess of the wrong kind of love—one that takes no account of who she actually is. This absence leaves her—as the song at the end of the movie, which pathetically captures the longing of the young Sweetie, suggests—hungering after genuine love and affection, just as much as if she had been entirely neglected.

If, in Jane Campion's words, Sweetie was loved "too much" by her father, Kay "is not being loved enough."[37] The effect on Kay's psychic economy is very much the same as on Dawn's, even though it results in behaviors that appear at first sight to be diametrically the opposite. As Campion points out, Kay is cripplingly fearful and anxious in the face of the world, taking refuge in superstition as a way of trying to control her anxiety.[38] In this respect, she is modeled closely on her creator, who admits that superstition has been "part of my whole life," and that she too has visited psychics.[39] Kay is equally as needy of her father's affection as Dawn is, with the difference that whereas Dawn literally enacts an incestuous fantasy, Kay represses her fantasy of incest so completely that it causes her to shut down her sexuality altogether. This is revealed in the scene where Kay sees Sweetie bathing her father, in which the sight of Dawn reaching between his legs causes Kay, in the scene that immediately follows, to draw the sheets of her bed tightly up to her neck—signifying a need to protect herself against the attractiveness of this incestuous fantasy in her own imagination by emptying herself of sexual desire altogether. This is what induces her to cease sleeping with Louis and to experience their relationship as one between brother and sister, rather than between lovers.

On another level, Kay feels an acute jealousy of Sweetie, reflecting the real-life competition of the Campion sisters to attract the attention of their parents, who, by Jane's account, were completely absorbed in their theatrical careers. This prompts in Kay a desire to "really hurt" her sister, so she kicks Dawn while the latter is crawling to Louis. Dawn reciprocates this jealousy, as is evident in the fighting that occurs between the two and in the way Dawn chews up Kay's collection of porcelain toy horses. Although it is not made explicit, this sibling rivalry possibly masks a repressed homicidal impulse on Kay's part, which makes her feel all the more guilty when Sweetie is killed at the end of the film, achieving, in effect, what Kay had wished for.

Dawn thus stands simultaneously for two different things within the metonymic rhetoric of the movie. At one level, in Kay's imaginary, she stands for the resented rival who is a competitor for their father's admiring and approving attention and who therefore must be "killed off" in order to make the forbidden (that is, the maintenance of an incestuous fantasy bond with the father) possible. At another level, Dawn is Kay's own feared shadow, a compendium of all the impulses and reactions in which Kay could potentially indulge, should her concern to repress them in order to make herself seem acceptable fail. Here, then, is another reason that Sweetie needs to be killed off: to make Kay feel safe within the defended form of self-construction she has fashioned for herself.

It is peculiar that the father should occupy such prominence as a cause of dysfunction within the family when the mother's potential responsibility is virtually occluded. To find an explanation for why this should be so, one must delve deeper into the psychic motives that are imputed to Gordon in the film. One of the most astute commentators on *Sweetie,* Kathleen McHugh, has pointed to the existence of a strange "mother-daughter replacement and exchange" that has taken place. Flo, Gordon's estranged wife, turns out to be the one who is really talented at singing and dancing, rather than Sweetie. Gordon, nevertheless, fails to recognize this and persists in investing his hopes and fantasies in his daughter, rather than his wife. This substitution, I believe, indicates the presence of a shortsightedness in the father that helps to explain why Campion places such a heavy emphasis on his role.

Gordon uncannily resembles Murray, the male protagonist in Edith Campion's novel, *The Chain,* in the way that he invests a real-life relationship with the imputed qualities of an imaginary one, thus leaving the person concerned feeling inadequate about the status of her own being. In Murray's case, he uses his wife, Jean, as a stand-in for a missing ideal that is associated with his mother, whose love he could never obtain. Gordon, on the other hand, chooses his daughter Dawn to be the equivalent stand-in. In both instances, the fantasy ideal to which each man clings is imaged as a "princess." For Murray in *The Chain,* this "sad, lost princess" is a fantasy version of his actual mother. She is imaged as a Sleeping Beauty whom Murray could never kiss into being because, being asked by his mother to supply unmet needs that her husband had been unable to satisfy, he, as a son, could never give her what she sought from him. When Murray in turn uses his wife as a stand-in for his mother in his attempt to secure what is missing from his inner psychic world— that is, a loving, approving mother whose imago he could internalize for the sake of self-parenting—Jean's realization that she is simply being used as a surrogate for this missing fantasy ideal fills her with resentment and despair.

In *Sweetie,* Jane Campion shows something similar at work in Gordon's relationship with Dawn, even though the connection between Gordon's fantasy ideal and the possibility of a disturbed mother-son relationship in the past is less explicitly represented than in Edith Campion's novel. The existence of a similar psychic economy can be inferred from the way that Gordon seeks to use Dawn as a means of repairing a sense of his own inadequacy. He does this by requiring her to succeed as a brilliant performer on the stage. In the event that she could accomplish this, it would serve two purposes: first, it would enable her to embody the image of an idealized femininity—the "princess" of his imagination—and, second, it would, through a process of vicarious substitution, enable him to succeed in the eyes of his disappointed internalized mother and thus satisfy her expectations. As with Murray in Edith Campion's novel, Gordon is seeking, through the unconscionable pressure he exerts on his daughter to deliver what she is unable to provide, to repair a deep lack in his own imaginary, a lack that should have been supplied by the imago of a loving, affirming internalized mother.

In both *The Chain* and *Sweetie,* then, the female family member who is chosen to be the stand-in for the fantasy princess figure of their respective male characters ends up with a deep sense of failure because of her inability to actualize the fantasy entertained by the damaged husband-father. It is this strong awareness of the existence of disturbance in the father's psychic space—perhaps inherited by Jane Campion from the understanding of the syndrome expressed by her mother in *The Chain*—that helps to explain why the father, and not the mother, occupies such a central place in this depiction of family dysfunction.

6   Even though she is exempted from being a cause of the family's dysfunction, the mother is nevertheless accorded an important role as an agent of the family's potential rehabilitation. Significantly, Flo diverges from the other members of the family in her attitude toward trees; when Louis mentions that someone has stolen the sapling he planted, she says, "I can't imagine living without my trees . . . they give me hope." This ability to nurture hope makes it possible for Flo to initiate a movement

toward potential redemption, which begins when she forces Gordon, whom she realizes has put Sweetie on a pedestal, to choose between Sweetie and herself. By forcing him to make this choice, she is insisting that he relinquish the unhealthy cross-generational bond he has with his daughter in order to recover an emotionally healthy relationship by affirming his choice of herself, his wife, as the object of his libidinous attachment. To achieve this, she proposes a trial separation, leaves Gordon, and goes to live as a housekeeper with a gang of jackaroos (farmhands) in the Australian outback. This movement from the town into the country is archetypal, in much the way that the movement from the city into the green world of nature in Shakespearean comedy is archetypal. According to Campion, "a theme for me is the redemptive power of nature," and this is precisely what she shows in the world of the jackaroos: "The jackaroos are mythical Aussie men to me—gentle beings because they have been modified by their relationship with nature. . . . [They are] relaxed, and hopefully can teach Kay how to relax."[40]

Everyone who enters into this world experiences some form of healing. For Flo, this is expressed in her ability to sing—which astonishes the other members of her family—and in the words of the song she sings, which affirm the possibility of discovering a true, restorative form of love:

> FLO [sings] There's a love that waits for you
> And there's a love that waits for me,
> It's a love so good and true . . .
> And I know will always be.
> Let me hold you in my arms
> And you won't be sorry dear,
> For I know that you're the one
> You're the love that waits for me.
>
> So forget about the heartache . . .
> And the troubles you've been through . . .
> Somewhere there is someone,
> For someone . . . just like you.

At first, the troubled men in the family, Gordon and Louis, refuse to open themselves to this possibility. Gordon refuses to remain in the camp, and Louis refuses to participate in the life of the camp. Flo, however, persists in her belief that "we can begin again" and encourages Kay and Louis to join her in a symbolic baptism by swimming in the river on whose bank they have a picnic. Eventually, Gordon returns to the camp, where he cuts in to join Flo in the dance—which is a sign of the restoration of the bond with his wife.

The depiction of these scenes in the jackaroos' camp takes on a surrealistic quality, as if a wish-fulfillment fantasy is being enacted. Images of a redeemed masculinity abound: one jackaroo dances with a dwarf, indicating an acceptance of difference that is conspicuously absent in the rest of the film; two other jackaroos dance in unison to a complicated shuffle involving a physical proximity so close as to suggest a homoerotic bonding; Gordon is shown in a frilly "pinny," engaged in homely kitchen chores, suggesting a discovery of a hitherto repressed feminine side; and so on. All of this suggests a vision in which masculinity itself has been purged of those attributes that have the capacity to cause harm or fear to a mother like Flo or a daughter like Kay, having been emptied of the predispositions and behaviors that reflect disturbances in the psychic economy of men. To this extent, these episodes appear to suggest what Campion believes would be necessary were the dysfunction she depicts earlier in the film to be avoided or healed.

7 Campion is too much of a realist, however, to allow the film to end there, for she makes it apparent that the idyll depicted in the camp of the jackaroos can only last so long as the existence of Sweetie and what she represents—both literally and in the world of symbolic signification—is ignored. Inevitably, the characters need to return to the real world, at which point Campion's sense of the likely outcome reasserts itself.

Unsurprisingly, the redemptive vision begins to dissipate. Gordon begins to backslide when he contemplates the actual emotional cost of sending Sweetie away to a specialized institution; Louis realizes the depth of Kay's phobic pathology when he discovers the dead tree she had uprooted and, denouncing her as "abnormal," leaves her; any notion that Dawn could be reintegrated into the family flies out the window when she and Kay engage in vicious physical fighting; and Dawn attempts to ward off the threat of reality—that is, of being sent to an institution—by retreating into a psychotic reversal of the place she is meant to occupy in her father's fantasy when she takes refuge within her "palace" in the (family) tree. Instead of displaying the attributes of a princess, however,

Sweetie provocatively confronts her family with the opposite: she strips naked, paints her body black, utters obscenities, farts at her family, and generally regresses to the state of a frightened (and therefore aggressive) child. All this amounts to an extreme form of defiance and rebellion.

The denouement is highly ambivalent. Throughout the movie, Kay has appeared to wish Dawn, insofar as she represents the feared shadow part of herself, "dead" (in fantasy). At a metaphorical level, this would make it seem that, in order to be psychologically healthy, Kay has to kill off the dark, anarchic side of her own impulses (embodied in Sweetie) so that she can be released from the fear of them that causes the repression from which she suffers. When Dawn actually dies, however, Kay is reluctant to let her go, attempting desperately to breathe life back into her by giving her mouth-to-mouth resuscitation. There is some indication that the sexual dysfunction caused by Kay's repression might be in the process of being ameliorated. This is suggested by the scene at the end of the movie that shows Kay and Louis lying opposite each other. Her feet gently caress those of Louis, and she asks him if he knows that his toes curl up when he is making love. The implication is that he has returned to her and that they are once more enjoying a healthy sexual relationship—but Campion at this point obtrudes another significant symbolic image that suggests that such an outcome is uncertain.

I am referring to the collection of toy porcelain horses that Kay regards as extremely precious, which Sweetie destroys. An earlier scene in the movie associates "riding horses" with sex, when Clayton—to whom Kay has shown her collection of toy horses—asks Bob, Sweetie's lover-manager, to pretend to be a horse: "You be 'Thunder' Bob." This occurs shortly before the scene in which Sweetie and Bob, who has taken on the attributes of "Thunder," have loud sex in the room next door, prompting Kay to disrupt their lovemaking under the pretext of wanting to go to the toilet. Moreover, immediately following the scene in which Kay witnesses the incest between Dawn and her father, the camera pans from the shot of Kay pulling up the covers to her chin across to the broken porcelain horses. Through a process of metonymic transfer, therefore, the toy horses become associated with sexuality, with Kay's simultaneous attraction toward it, motivated by a repressed incestuous fantasy, accompanied by a fear of her own latent impulses. This makes it significant that, once Sweetie is dead, we are shown another shot of Kay's toy horses, which

Kay has tried to reassemble. The horses, however, are only partially re-stored; they remain cracked, with limbs missing, suggesting that the restoration of healthy libidinous impulses in Kay is far from complete. Finally, the fact that a tree root interferes with the lowering of Dawn's coffin into her grave suggests that Sweetie, and what she represents, are far from buried and gone even though Dawn has died. As Kay says in her voice-over, "Trees never seem to leave us alone," which implies that the troubling legacy of this dysfunctional family might continue to disturb the mental well-being of its members.

There was at least one compelling reason for the ambivalence and skepticism that mark the ending of *Sweetie*. Even though Jane Campion had attempted to show the possibility of a redemptive remedy for dys-functional relating between parents—in the reunion of Flo and Gor-don—in real life, her own parents had failed to achieve such a reconcili-ation: Edith and Richard Campion had finalized their divorce in 1984, an event that so greatly distressed Edith that she attempted suicide during the final weeks when *Sweetie* was being shot.[41] In view of these circum-stances, it is not surprising that the ending of *Sweetie* should contain elements that undermine confidence in the happy resolution that the filmmaker, at one level, would like to believe is possible.

At the conclusion of *Sweetie,* we are left with the impression that behind all the metaphoric displacements and multilayered symbolic sig-nification that constitute the film there remain the shadowy lineaments of an unresolved, long-term family romance. In making this film, Jane Campion had indeed "pushed further" in the directions she had initi-ated in her earlier movies, by penetrating deeper into the intricacies of the psychological reactions to which she recognized she was prone, but she must have realized that there was much, much more that remained to be explored and brought to light before her own inner torments were likely to be alleviated. In particular, there was much more to be brought into consciousness concerning her relationship with her mother and her understanding of her mother's condition. As I will show, her need to comprehend these things motivated Campion to make her next three movies, *An Angel at My Table, The Piano,* and *The Portrait of a Lady.*

4 "How painful it is to have a family member with a problem like that": Authorship as Creative Adaptation in *An Angel at My Table*

1 Even though Jane Campion's films up to and including *Sweetie* laid out the dynamics of a family problematic in a fairly comprehensive manner, there was one major factor that she had not yet explored in depth: the influence on her of her mother's lifelong battle with depression. Indeed, there is a curious downplaying of the mother's role, and even presence, in many of Campion's films. The mother is absent altogether from the family group depicted in *Peel*; although there is a father and a son, the mother's place is taken by an elder sister, which foreshadows Gordon's substitution of Dawn for Flo as his *femme* in *Sweetie*.[1] In *A Girl's Own Story*, the mother is present but is virtually mute (foreshadowing Ada in *The Piano*), and she is presented as a passive victim who is easily dominated by her husband when the latter exploits sex as a weapon to play upon her needy hunger for personal affirmation. In both *The Piano* and *The Portrait of a Lady*, neither of the heroine's parents is present: Ada's mother is dead, and Isabel Archer is an orphan. In *Holy Smoke*, Ruth's mother makes brief, intermittent appearances, much like Flo in *Sweetie*, and Ruth does end up with her at the end of the movie, but her role is far less significant than that of the father stand-in, PJ Waters, who assumes a more prominent place in the film than Ruth's biological father. Finally, in *In the Cut*, the parents of Frannie and Pauline are presented only in fantasy, and while we learn that the father is still alive and intending to marry his fifth wife, we get the impression that the mother is dead. At any rate, in Frannie's fantasy recollection, her mother has been killed off by Frannie's father.

Despite these absences of significant maternal figures, Jane Campion's own mother had exerted a profound influence on her daughter's formation. In particular, Jane had found the experience of her mother's depression deeply traumatic. When Jane was a teenager, she recalls, Edith Campion had been affected so badly by depression that Jane had offered to help her mother die: "It really scared me to feel close to her complete lack of hope." On that occasion, her mother turned her down, but the experience left "a deep and lasting impact" on Campion. As she puts it, "I had to get away, I couldn't breathe, I couldn't see for myself my own optimism any more." To Jane, Edith's way of looking at the world "seemed almost contagious."[2]

At the same time, Jane was deeply attached to her mother, and the empathic bond between them was exceedingly strong. Some sense of the paradoxical nature of the relationship between them, in which affection, compassion, and resentment on both sides played off against the other, can be glimpsed in Anna Campion's short film, *The Audition*, made in 1989, the year before Jane Campion's *An Angel at My Table* was released. As Harriet Margolis has argued, *The Audition* could almost be viewed as an early exercise in reality TV, on account of the literal way it focuses on the manifestations of Edith's state of mind and the reactions they provoke in her daughter.[3] The opening sequences, which show Jane driving her mother's car to Otaki after her mother has picked her up from the Wellington airport, reveal an apparently peremptory bossiness in Edith as she orders her daughter to watch her speed, change gears, and not stray into the oncoming lane. This simple sequence allows one to infer an impulse to control springing from Edith's need to master her anxiety. As the film proceeds, she links the fear she feels each morning to the breakdown of her marriage, which draws attention to the absence of the husband and father: "I suppose I cared about my marriage too much." Jane, as she listens, is shown to take a breath from an inhaler—itself suggestive of a nervous psychosomatic reaction—which serves as preparation for the revelation that Edith also suffered from asthma as a child. This, as Margolis has proposed, implies a psychological connection between mother and daughter grounded in their vulnerability: "In a sense, *The Audition* is a film about the extent to which mother and daughter are alike rather than having separate personalities."[4] Despite the impatience Jane displays toward her mother—as when she berates her for "that fat negativity of yours," which she accuses her of "always giving . . . something to eat"—the ending of the film reveals a great degree of empathic identification between mother and daughter. When Edith gives a rendition of a scene from Sean O'Casey's *Juno and the Paycock,* one of the triumphs of her theatrical career, the camera shows a tear welling up in Jane's eye. Margolis aptly sums up the final impression that is left by the film: "From a psychological point of view, Anna's film already suggests perhaps some difficulty in separation, or some form of narcissism, between both the mother and the daughter, on the one hand, and at least *one* of the sisters with the other."[5]

These insights into the complexity of Campion's relationship with her mother help to explain why mothers are not more prominent in her films; it has been simply too painful for Campion to deal directly with such a topic when her relationship with her own mother was so problematic. On the other hand, she needed to come to terms with what that relationship implied for her, especially given her awareness of how similar she was becoming to her mother as she advanced through her thirties.

Adaptation gave Campion the means to address this topic in a manner that was psychologically safe. All fictive invention provides for vicarious substitution, but an adaptation has the added advantage of allowing a particularly painful subject to be addressed at an even greater displaced remove, under the guise of another person's invention. Such a strategy enables the person making the adaptation to explore feelings that she might otherwise have been tempted to block. Campion has admitted that she often finds it difficult to let herself know things in a direct way, which is why she has "always understood and known more than . . . [she can] know directly through metaphor."[6] Adaptation, for Campion, serves the same function as metaphor, except that the even more radical displacement involved offers an even stronger degree of self-protection.

When adaptation is used in this way, the strategies used by the adapter to convert the source work to his or her purpose require a kind of creativity that constitutes a form of authorship in its own right. In the case of Campion's *An Angel at My Table*, an adaptation of the autobiography of the renowned New Zealand writer Janet Frame, this creative element is manifest both in Campion's selection of the episodes she chooses to show or suppress and in the nature of the mise-en-scène. Both serve to introduce a new set of referents which, for the filmmaker, coexist alongside the original ones, which has the effect of turning the work into a highly personal object, into a new work that manifests Campion's personal cinema.

In the rest of this chapter, I will retrace how Janet Frame came to be associated with Edith Campion in Jane Campion's imaginary and the cinematic consequences of that imaginative association.

2 From the time she first read Janet Frame's novel *Owls Do Cry* at the age of fourteen, Jane Campion strongly identified Frame with both her mother and herself. As a young teenager, Jane recalls, whenever the Campions would drive on weekends past "the notorious loony bin" at Porirua on their way to the family's beach house in Plimmerton, she used to ask whether Janet Frame was in Porirua Hospital.[7] Given the helplessness and desperation Campion admits she felt because of Edith's depression, one can surmise that this was the reason for Jane's early interest in Janet Frame. *Owls Do Cry*, with its story of a young woman institutionalized on account of the extreme anxiety she experienced in the face of the world, would have provided the young Jane with a fictionalized correlative for the distressing situation she recognized within her own family.

The potential parallel between Janet Frame and Edith Campion was made explicit when Edith was hospitalized in Porirua Hospital, just as Frame had been admitted first to Seacliff Hospital in Dunedin and then to mental hospitals in Christchurch and Auckland. As Jane Campion records:

> Fifteen years later I was to become sadly familiar with Porirua Hospital, Ward K2, as my mother tried repeatedly to find some relief from the overwhelming terror and bleakness of her late-life depression. I visited Janet Frame territory, stepping over Max's false leg left lying in the corridor, and trying to fend off an elderly man who shuffled with alarming purpose up to my mother in the day room, put his hands on her armrests and asked, "Edith what will it cost me to sleep in your bedroom?"[8]

In her commentary on *An Angel at My Table,* Campion admits that she found her helplessness in the face of her mother's illness harrowing and traumatic:

> The issue of mental illness . . . even now is still incredibly difficult in our society, and anybody who has a family member or anyone they're close to who suffers any mental problems—depression, schizophrenia—knows just how painful it is to have a family member with a problem like that, or, in fact, to be the person with the problem, because it's just so badly understood, and really there's very little you can do to help people.[9]

It is not surprising, therefore, that when Campion felt moved to explore the nature of her experience of her mother and its consequences in her own makeup, she chose as her vehicle the story of a prominent figure who, in her mind, strikingly resembled Edith in certain respects.

There are further signs that this associative link was uppermost in Campion's mind when she decided to make *An Angel at My Table.* The immediate trigger, she tells us, occurred in 1982, when Edith sent Jane the first volume of Frame's autobiography, *To the Is-Land,* which had just been published.[10] This occurred soon after Edith had entered Ashburn Hall—the famous psychiatric clinic in Janet Frame's hometown of Dunedin—to undergo treatment for her depression, a period during which she compiled a number of writings, papers, and scrapbooks on unipolar depression that are now deposited at the Alexander Turnbull Library.[11] Yet another sign of the association between Janet Frame and Edith Campion occurs in Jane Campion's recollection that, when she finally met with Frame on 24 December 1982, she "drove in [her] mother's car to Levin, to ask her for the rights to her autobiography."[12] The use of Edith's car for this purpose might seem a small detail, but the fact that Campion remembered it more than twenty-five years later attests to the lingering power the association held for her. The detail suggests how Jane's awareness of Edith was metonymically transferred to Edith's car, while the journey was associated with a quest for understanding that Campion imagined an adaptation of Frame's *Autobiography* might provide.

Campion records that the first volume of *Autobiography* had an enormous effect on her: "As I read, I sobbed and sobbed. She had struck a blow right to my heart. But it was not only about Janet's life, I was also experiencing my own childhood."[13] The intensity of this reaction is also suggestive, for it indicates a dual identification in which Campion identifies Janet Frame not only with her mother, but also with herself—especially in terms of growing up feeling frightened, lonely, and emotionally isolated. As has been well described in the psychoanalytic literature, such a reaction is characteristic of a child who "gets caught up in the maternal world by identifying with her internal representations, then enacting these differing selves in her presence." Such children, according to Christopher Bollas, "have managed to cultivate a type of empathic skill in which they get inside the other and act the other out" at an unconscious level, "driven by anxiety about being left out in the cold" unless they can find the self in the other through "a form of mirroring in which the child reflects the mother's internal objects."[14] The weeping that was triggered in Jane as a response to *To the Is-Land* shows Jane identifying with Janet as if she (both Janet and Jane) were Jane's mother, Edith—which suggests a mirroring in Jane's own life of her mother's unhappiness, which she is moved to act out as a result of intense empathic identification.

This peculiarly complex nexus of identifications that informs Campion's reaction to *To the Is-Land* precisely reflects the identifications one can detect in her filmic adaptation of Frame's *Autobiography*. Furthermore, as I will show, these identifications exerted a determining influence on the character of the adaptation itself because of the cinematic strategies they promote.

3 Campion has revealed that her life and her cinema reflect one another, even though her life is much less intense than her films: "I live through my films, and it is only later that I find out how much of myself I have invested in them."[15] Of *An Angel at My Table,* she has said that she could "really see [her]self" in the story that Janet Frame tells in her autobiography and that, when she read it, she "would just kind of invest [her] own childhood memories along with it."[16] The result, Campion avers, is that "there is certainly more of me in the final result than I was conscious of when I started."[17]

Even had the filmmaker been less forthright than she has been in identifying them, the nature of her personal investments in *An Angel at*

My Table could be inferred from her selection of which material from Frame's *Autobiography* to include or omit. The screenplay itself was written by Laura Jones, but Campion makes it clear that she had formative input into the shaping of the final script. According to Campion, "she and Jones worked closely in the making of the screenplay, with Frame's books working as 'a mediator' between them."[18] Even then, she did not follow Jones's screenplay rigidly, subjecting it to a further process of selection that greatly reduced the material from the autobiography originally retained by Jones.[19]

The principle governing Campion's further reshaping of the screenplay seems to derive from a desire to focus primarily on scenes that serve as correlatives either for Edith's story or for her own. For example, she omits the scene of "Dad, in his kilt and old suit-coat . . . striding up and down in the snow outside the shed, playing his bagpipes" that Jones had proposed.[20] Similarly, she omits the reference to the dropping of the atomic bomb on Japan, together with most of the other material relating to World War II, and she deletes the scene of the dance held in the Dunedin Town Hall, where no one asks Janet to dance. All of the scenes in Andorra involving El Vici, who had wanted to marry Janet, are omitted, which limits Janet's romantic and sexual experience to one man (Bernhard), with whom, like Edith, she believes she has a lasting attachment but who ends up betraying her.

Most significantly, as Lawrence Jones has pointed out, Campion greatly reduces the role of Lottie Frame, Janet's mother, in a move that reflects the tendency I have noted in her other movies. "The 'virtual disappearance' of Frame's mother began with Laura Jones's screenplay, which omitted references to Lottie's own dedication to writing poetry. Jones had, however, included scenes showing Lottie's formative influence on Janet, and Janet's love and concern for her, that Campion cut."[21] My surmise is that this otherwise unaccountable suppression of Frame's mother occurred because in Campion's imagination it was to be Janet Frame herself, and not her mother, who was to serve as the surrogate for her own mother, Edith. Indeed, this reduction in the role of Lottie Frame semi-orphaned Janet in a way that strengthened the parallel with Jane's mother, who had been orphaned at an early age.

Predictably, the scenes from *Autobiography* that Campion did choose to dramatize were retained because of their relevance to Edith's story. Like Edith, who attempted suicide on several occasions,[22] Janet attempts to kill herself—in this instance, by swallowing a bottle of aspirins. Also like Edith, she undergoes electric shock treatment, and she turns to writing as a source of respite from her unhappiness. The exactness of the parallel is reinforced by scenes depicting Frank Sargeson as Janet's literary mentor, which mirrors Sargeson's role as a mentor for Edith when the latter turned to creative writing—to the extent that he allowed one of his own novellas, *En Route,* to be published in the same volume as Edith's *The Chain.* Finally, Campion extends the implicit parallel between Edith and Janet by showing the latter losing her baby in London, just as Edith had lost a baby soon after his birth in London in 1949. In Frame's *Autobiography* this event takes place in Andorra; the fact that Campion shifts the location from Andorra to London in the film serves not only to tighten the narrative, but also to invest the episode with a specific level of personal relevance for Edith.

As Anna Campion had done in *The Audition,* Jane also uses her mother as an actress in the movie, having her appear in a memorable scene where, as Miss Lindsay, she recites a passage from Tennyson's *Idylls of the King* to the enthrallment of the children in the class; later, she encounters Janet in the cemetery, grieving for the death of her sister, Myrtle. At this time, Edith Campion was approaching seventy, which means that, in terms of her visual appearance, she is far older than is consistent with the depiction of a high school teacher. Jane Campion's reason for casting her, however, was not motivated by a concern for verisimilitude, but by her overriding personal association of Edith with Janet Frame. Moreover, there was a further parallel between the inspiration Miss Lindsay had provided for the young Janet Frame through her love of poetry and the inspiration for the young Jane Campion that Edith had provided through her comparable love of poetry, especially passages from Shakespeare, which she was constantly reciting. The casting of Edith Campion for this role in the movie was not casual; it was intrinsic to the process whereby Jane Campion was converting the story to accord with her personal frame of reference.

To strengthen the associative parallels between Janet and Edith still further, Campion imported into her film scenes from Frame's earlier novel *Faces in the Water* that depict in harrowing detail the kind of scenes Campion witnessed when she visited her mother in Porirua Hospital. In *Autobiography*, Janet Frame touched only lightly on her experiences in various mental institutions, and she was unhappy about the inclusion of the scenes from *Faces in the Water* in the screenplay for *An Angel at My Table*—to the extent that she expressed concern through her agent.[23] Campion's persistence in retaining these scenes despite Frame's wishes suggests that she may have associated them less with Janet Frame than with Edith Campion, who similarly underwent electric shock treatment and participated in dances with the other patients like that shown in *An Angel at My Table*.

The close association between Janet Frame and Edith Campion extends throughout the mise-en-scène. Fairly early in the movie, for example, Campion shows Janet in a school uniform. Commenting on why she included this scene, Campion notes that, like Janet, her mother as a child was "very poor." Edith's school uniform was the only clothes that she possessed—to the extent that when she was invited to the birthday parties of other children, she had to go in her uniform, "while all the other girls wore pretty dresses." "It is for that reason," Campion adds, "that I included this scene in the film."[24]

The same thing happens when Campion explains why she showed Janet wearing gumboots. Having described how everyone wears gumboots in the countryside because of the mud, she is moved to recall her own childhood experience in the country: "I grew up in the city, but my parents moved to the country when I was 13 years old. My mother did a lot of horse-riding, and for that reason, so did I and my sister. That is how I came to own a mare."[25]

The way that one image here triggers a chain of related associations shows the depth of connotative significance that inheres in Campion's images, with several levels of signification operating at the same time. At the simplest level, there is the literal application of the image to Janet; at a secondary level, there is the association of the image with Jane's own experience, relived vicariously through Janet; and at another level beyond that, there is the application of the image to Edith, involving Jane

Campion's awareness of her similarity to her mother and the empathic identification between them.

There are many other images in the film that similarly evoke Edith Campion. When Jane reflects on the scenes showing Janet at school, she observes that "school was a real trial for me. . . . I could not behave myself. I could not be good."[26] One detects here a recollection of the experience of the mother—Edith had been a delinquent at school and eventually ran away—as relived in the behavior of the daughter, with the recollection being triggered by the connotations that Campion has invested in the depiction of Janet in the movie.

Finally, Campion incorporated into the film a motif that she recurrently uses to activate an associative link between what is unfolding in the action and her issues relating to her mother: the image of a cat, recalling Edith Campion's enthusiasm for cats and the metaphoric transfer of this enthusiasm to her passion for romance. Significantly, Campion shows Janet surrounded by cats when, in part 3 of *An Angel at My Table*, she brings Bernhard his breakfast as their relationship is developing—just before the lovemaking scene when he interrupts their foreplay to read Janet a poem he has written that morning, which indicates the extreme egotism that obscures his sense of her as a person in her own right.

4 Apart from establishing a parallel between Janet Frame and Edith Campion, Jane Campion's creative maneuvers also establish a parallel between Janet and herself. As she has admitted, she could identify with Frame's autobiographical account, which led her to "just kind of invest [her] own childhood memories along with it."[27]

It is in this respect that one sees the peculiar conflation of identifications that I mentioned earlier, in which Jane seems to identify with Janet as if she (Janet) were Jane's mother, Edith, and then acts from inside this identification as if she (Jane) is actually her mother, so that three levels of parallel identification coexist simultaneously. The effect is to turn the representation into something that resembles, metaphorically speaking, a hologram: look at it from one perspective, and one will see Edith in Janet; slightly change the angle from which it is viewed, and one will see Jane in Janet. What we are getting through the various substitutions in the adaptation is a displaced representation of the complex relationship between the Campion mother and daughter, showing the deep mutual identifications and dependency needs that cause one to be mirrored in the other.

As a result, the representation focuses on the depiction in Janet of a narcissistic fragility that is actually shared by the two Campion women, which is shown to be a consequence of a fearful dependency on a mother who is experienced as also providing some kind of threat. This complex feeling is conveyed in the opening shot of Janet's mother, who is seen from baby Janet's perspective as a huge black silhouette reaching down to seize her. The image is not a comforting one; rather, it suggests a threatening maternal imago who is featureless and shadowy, literally blocking Janet's sight of the sky and hence eliciting fear, even though the mother's words are affectionate and solicitous. Janet's existential loneliness is next indicated in the famous shot of her as a little girl walking toward the viewer down a long gravel road. As she nears the camera, she pauses, strokes the velvet of her dress as if to seek some private comfort, then turns and runs away, shielding her face with her arm, as if to escape from the invasive gaze of the onlooker.

The syndrome that is being depicted here is consistent with that found in a child who has suffered emotional deprivation because of some disturbance in the process of primordial psychic structuring that should take place through the infant-mother relationship. Campion appears to have constructed Janet as an embodiment, or emblem, of this condition of narcissistic fragility, and in her director's commentary on *An Angel at My Table,* she identifies herself strongly with it: "We all feel vulnerable and unchosen, unlovable, uncared about in one way or another."[28] Campion also refers to Janet's "desperate need for attention," a comment that reminds one not only of Sweetie's "sad and inevitable quest for talent and attention,"[29] but also of the frantic competition of the Campion children to gain the attention of their distracted parents. There is nothing in Frame's *Autobiography* to suggest that Janet's parents neglected her or left her feeling unloved, nor that she felt a "desperate need for attention." These states of mind appear to be imputed as a result of Jane Campion's projections.

In part 1 of the movie, "To the Is-Land," the scenes Jane Campion chooses to depict are either ones that show Janet suffering damage to her

In the shadow of the mother in *An Angel at My Table.*

sense of herself, or else ones that portray her attempts to repair this damaged self-sense. A good example is when the young Janet steals money
from her father's pocket in order to buy chewing gum, which she then
offers to the other children in her class at school in order to be liked by
them. In this act, one senses Janet's yearning to secure compensation for
a sense of self-affirmation that is otherwise lacking in her inner space.
When her teacher, Miss Botting, ritually humiliates and punishes her
in front of the whole class, her sense of self-esteem, far from being reinforced, is damaged still further, and this erosion of Janet's self-sense
becomes progressively more extreme as the movie proceeds. Similarly,
when Janet is shamed by her father's angry reaction at the dinner table
to her revelation that Myrtle and Ted "did it" in the "plannies" that af-
ternoon—which reminds us of the father's comparable shaming of the
son in *Peel*—we are shown Janet suffering from the onset of intense
narcissistic mortification; she feels both culpable and worthless, without
fully knowing why.

Janet's need for affirmation to compensate for this recurrent experience of narcissistic mortification is highlighted by the effect on her of the
rare instances when people do offer affirmation. We see this in part 1 of
the film when Janet is praised for a poem she has written and receives a
prize at a school ceremony, and in part 2 when her first collection of short

stories wins a national award. Again, Jane Campion identifies closely
with the restorative effect of such affirming events: "I had the same experience myself," she confesses, admitting that things turned around for
her when her short film *Peel* won the Palme d'Or at Cannes.[30]

It is easy to see why Campion felt that she could "see herself" in Janet
Frame's story. As she puts it, when she first read Frame's novel *Owls Do
Cry,* "what I really found happening was that I was discovering my own
childhood again . . . feeling the specialness of that New Zealand childhood"[31]—even though that childhood has been shown to have been a
fairly unhappy one. Campion's identification with Frame extends far
beyond this childhood period. As an adolescent, she reveals that, like
Janet, she was "incredibly embarrassed" when she got her first period.
She made her father go into a drugstore to buy pads, because she found
it too shameful to think of the pharmacist knowing she had her period.[32]
In Janet's case, however, it is her mother who helps her deal with her first
period. The fact that Jane Campion had her father assist her, rather than
her mother, implies the same kind of investment in the father, at the
apparent cost of the mother, that one witnesses in the adaptation as a
whole.

Campion's experience of going to university, she says, was also comparable to that of Janet at the Dunedin Teachers' College, which was
another miserable time for Frame: "Too shy to mix. Too shy to go into
the Union, my only romance was in poetry and literature." Campion's
experience when she went to Victoria University of Wellington was similar: "At first, when I went to university, I was rather unhappy and very
lonely. I didn't succeed in inserting myself into a group; indeed, I am
rather quirky, and that meant that it took me a long time to find anyone
who wanted to share my sense of humour. I had also been to a school
for girls."[33]

As an adult, Campion had been miserably lonely in London, just as
Janet had been, and the scene in which she shows Janet in Ibiza wrapped
up in a blanket while writing was based on Jane Campion's experience
of writing in a Tibetan monastery in the Lake District of England.[34] Finally, Campion identified deeply with Janet's aspirations to be an artist.
Like Janet, at the time she was making *An Angel at My Table,* she "really
believed" in her own "projections": "I believed my interior world was

reality."[35] Her sense of the reality of this interior world was so intense that, like Janet, she had a sense of her muse as a personified presence:

> I very much identified with Janet when she speaks of her inspiration and about her relationship with her muse. I myself personalized this muse in the form of a man, from the time I was a child. I had a very strong feeling that this person was by my side to assist me, and to give me ideas. All of that has finished now, however.[36]

Janet and Jane are comparable, therefore, in the degree to which they use their art—writing in the case of Frame and filmmaking in the case of Campion—to construct a world of imaginative projections capable of serving as a self-object to protect them against the possibility of narcissistic hemorrhaging.

5 Having established the grounds for an identification of Janet Frame with both her mother and herself, Campion switches to focus on the way that all three of them—Janet explicitly in the film, and Edith and Jane implicitly through the parallels that are intimated—seek to find protection against psychic pain through a romantic relationship, and through the invention of an imaginative world through art when that possibility fails.

As Campion reveals in her director's commentary, she "really identified" with Janet's loneliness in London and with her aspirations to be an artist. She also identified with Janet's "longing for a man of her own, a boyfriend, or a partner."[37] This, one surmises, is why Campion places much more emphasis in the film on Janet's romantic and sexual encounter with Bernhard, a visiting American history professor, than Frame does in the book. The more extended treatment reflects Campion's own interest in "love and delusions" and sexuality, to which she confessed around this time,[38] just as it reflects the disillusionment with romance of Edith Campion, whose marriage had disintegrated several years prior to the making of this movie.

One sign of Campion's personal investment in Janet's disillusionment at the collapse of her romantic fantasy is the inclusion of one of her recurrent motifs, a heater, in the scene in which the fetus Janet is carrying is aborted. As in *A Girl's Own Story,* in which heaters are invested with an important symbolic signification, the presence of this heater in the scene of Janet's abortion, at a symbolic level, suggests the reactivation of a retreat into the self as a result of an awareness of masculine perfidy—especially that which arises out of the discovery that men are able to engage in sexual relationships that are devoid of any romantic commitment.

It is in the context of an encounter with a reality that is felt to be threatening or disillusioning that Janet, and through her Jane Campion, and prior even to that, Edith Campion, engage in imaginative creation, whether by writing fiction or by making films. It is worth speculating on the respective psychological motivations of the three women, as inferred from their works, in engaging in this artistic activity.

For each of them, artistic creation provides a means of allaying, as Milton would say, "the perturbations of the mind" arising from the encounter with reality. For Frame, the imagination has the power to translate what might otherwise seem abject in life—the "apparent rubbish" of which she speaks at the end of *Autobiography*—into something precious that furnishes a compensatory space one can inhabit in the mind. She likens the process of imaginative recreation to that of a child who takes mundane objects that are worthless in the real world and places them in a playhouse, where they come alive. As Frame puts it:

> In trying to secure and bring home to their place the treasures of my recent past I find that, like . . . [her niece] with her playhouse of fantasy, carpeting her floor with old treasures, pouring her teas out of cups and saucers removed from their home but transformed in their new setting, I prefer to take my treasures to my home, my playhouse, Mirror City.[39]

The motivations of the Campions, both mother and daughter, should be distinguished from Frame's practice, which amounts to an attempt to bolster the defenses of a psychic retreat. Edith Campion in her fiction and Jane Campion in her films seek to invest fictive representation with the function of a dream in which, through symbolic condensation and displacement, they can work out the meaning of the things in their experience which are giving rise to perturbation or dysfunction. This is why, I believe, Jane Campion in *An Angel at My Table* alters the relative proportions in the depictions of Janet's parents that Frame gives in *Autobiography*. For Frame, her mother, Lottie, had been the one who showed her how to discover the magical in the mundane: "She had only to say of any commonplace object, 'Look, kiddies, a stone' to fill that stone with a wonder as if it were a holy object."[40] Hence, Lottie furnished her daughter with a means of escaping her crippling anxiety. In contrast, Edith Campion, being chronically depressed, could only convey a sense of her own anxiety and her conviction of life's "meaninglessness" (as Anna Campion shows in *The Audition*). It is for this reason, one suspects, that Jane Campion places so much emphasis on the father as a character in her movies. The father is felt to be the one who should be able to offer help (implicitly in the context of the mother's inability to provide the psychic nurturing that should ordinarily occur). The fact that the father, or father figure, in Campion's movies is almost invariably shown to be unreliable (on account of his own narcissistic insufficiency or sexual impulses) greatly compounds the sense of a deep-seated perturbation, with the existence of which the film attempts to grapple.

In *An Angel at My Table*, Janet's father, Curly, provides the exception, and it is he, rather than Lottie Frame, whom Campion places most prominently in the viewer's attention. He is the one who gives Janet an exercise book in which to write her poems; he is the one who, out of his love and concern for her, does not want Janet to leave home again after she has been institutionalized for schizophrenia; and it is he who appears at Frank Sargeson's hut to assist Janet on her journey to Europe, thus enacting a role as her biological father that is parallel to the one Frank Sargeson plays as her literary father.[41] It would appear as if Janet's father represents in the filmmaker's imagination an idealized paternal imago of the sort she could have wished for herself.

Once the importance of the father in Jane Campion's imaginary is recognized, the function of artistic creation for her and her avatars becomes clear. It is represented symbolically in the images of the final scene, which show Janet stepping into her father's shoes. This scene is not present at all in Frame's *Autobiography*. In Laura Jones's screenplay, it appears in an embryonic form, with Janet putting her feet into "Dad's slippers."[42] In the movie, Campion completes the realization of the symbol that must have been shaping in her subconscious by converting the slippers into boots. What this image signifies is the degree to which Janet has grown—through the experience she has gained and, especially, through the exercise of her art—to the point where she can occupy, in her imagination, the place that her father occupied in her earlier life. In

Janet steps into her father's boots in *An Angel at My Table*.

terms of the larger symbolic rhetoric of the film as a whole, this image also stands as a representation of the filmmaker's own desire to secure this imaginary assurance, associated with an idealized paternal function, for herself.

Some sense of the complexity of the connotations inhering in the images in the final sequence of the movie can be gauged from Campion's remarks. Commenting on the shots that show Janet composing one of her novels in a caravan (trailer), Campion draws attention to an association with her father:

> I love caravans. My father won a caravan in a raffle and I wrote quite a number
> of scripts in that caravan, which he still owns. He's now 80, and he's had the
> caravan for about 20, 30 years, and it sits outside his house in New Zealand now.
> . . . [I] had so many happy and important times in that caravan exploring my own
> storytelling, film-writing. . . . I'm still crazy about caravans, and I dream about
> outfitting one absolutely particularly to me.[43]

Here, then, in real life is an expression of the same desire that Campion, in the movie, attributes to Janet: a desire to occupy a space, associated metaphorically with the father, in which the individual, through art, can construct an imaginary world capable of providing a palliation of her psychic unease. In this sense, art becomes an "object" (in psychoanalytic terms) that offers the possibility of rescue from the narcissistic deprivation into which the "fat negativity" of the mother's depression could potentially plunge her. It does not matter that in other places Campion shows fathers in an equally negative light. The essential thing is that, whether in reality or idealized in fantasy, the father represents a protective capacity that is longed for, as well as a source of affirmation that can compensate for the emotional absence of the mother (who is largely missing as a character in her own right).

6 Campion's decision to make a cinematic adaptation of *An Angel at My Table*, therefore, attests to her readiness to commence an exploration of what was involved in her mother's disturbed psychic condition and how this might be affecting her. It also attests to a deeply compassionate identification with her mother—so deep that it appears to have led her to repeat Edith's experiences in many aspects of her own life. Like her mother, she was a keen equestrian, joining her in horse riding at the family's farm in Otaki. Like her mother, she acted in plays, and in her twenties she retraced the journey to London that her mother had made in 1948. When she entered adulthood, Jane Campion realized "how similar . . . [she] was getting to Mum," and as her career proceeded, this similarity became even more marked, despite her attempts to get away and define herself differently.[44] Like her mother, she published several works of literary fiction, including a short story,[45] and became an avid reader of the kind of romantic fiction for which her mother had been "a very strong advocate."[46] Tragically, the parallels between Edith's life and Jane's would be replicated in an unthinkable way, with the death of Jane's son, Jasper, soon after birth, mirroring the death of Edith's firstborn son in London. And the pattern has continued with the failure of Jane Campion's marriage to Colin Englert, which parallels the breakdown of her parents' marriage.[47] It is no wonder, then, that Jane Campion, whether consciously or unconsciously, has felt a need to tackle the issues pertaining to her relationship with her mother.

By the time she completed *An Angel at My Table,* Campion had made an impressive start at sounding the heart of the mystery surrounding her mother's depression, and, through her personal investment in Janet Frame's story, she had come to understand the nature of the narcissistic mortification that a person suffering from that kind of psychic fragility is liable to experience. Her comments suggest that, in the course of doing this, she was able to discover why she had been becoming so "similar to Mum." Nevertheless, there remained a great deal to be uncovered—particularly concerning the secondary effects of the influence of emotionally troubled parents on matters such as adult sexuality and the ability to attain a secure equilibrium as an independent, fully individuated self. That would be the topic of Campion's next movie, *The Piano*, to which I will now turn.

5 Traumas of Separation and the Encounter with the Phallic Other: *The Piano*

1 Whereas the making of *An Angel at My Table* allowed Jane Campion to acknowledge through her art the existence of a profound empathic bond with her mother which, in her earlier films, had appeared to be disavowed, it also showed that there were other consequences of that relationship in her own life still waiting, and needing, to be explored. She had deepened her understanding of her mother's depressive illness through her adaptation of the story of Janet Frame and could also see how, in the course of growing up, she had internalized certain of her mother's predispositions and tendencies; she had not only begun to grow "similar to Mum," but had also relived aspects of her mother's experience. What Campion had not yet come to terms with, however, were the ways in which her mother's psychic condition had influenced the formation of her own adult personality, particularly with respect to her ability to form successful relationships with men. For that larger understanding to be achieved, she needed to integrate her new sense of how her mother had influenced her with the awareness revealed in her student films and *Two Friends* of how her relationship with her father had affected her. By doing this, she would be able to see how these two influences had worked together to produce the feelings and personality predispositions that she recognized in herself. In short, she needed to attain a fuller, more rounded, more coherent understanding of the influence of her family background in its totality, rather than just parts of it, and it is this aim, I will argue, that prompted and informed the making of *The Piano*. The rest of this chapter will be devoted to a demonstration of how and why Campion drew upon her own experiences in creating this remarkable

film, so as to turn it into a vehicle for advancing the understanding of her personal issues and how they might be resolved.

2 The screenplay for *The Piano* took over six years to develop, and the process is illuminating. According to Campion, she was only just out of the Australian Film, Television, and Radio School (from which she graduated in 1984) when she first thought of the idea for the film. We can infer, although Campion has never directly said so, that this occurred when the producers John Maynard and Bridget Ikin—for whom Campion would soon make *An Angel at My Table*—approached her to direct a film adaptation of a novel by an earlier New Zealand woman novelist, Jane Mander, *The Story of a New Zealand River*. Maynard and Ikin, who had bought the film rights to this novel, wanted to cast Sam Neill in the film they planned to make with financial backing from the New Zealand Film Commission, which was to have been called *The River*.[1]

The plot of Mander's novel strikingly foreshadows a number of the plot elements that resurface in *The Piano*. Its heroine, Alice, is a severely repressed unwed mother from Scotland, who arrives in colonial New Zealand, accompanied by her vivacious nine-year-old daughter, and marries a man she does not love for reasons of social propriety. Like Ada in the film, Alice brings with her a piano, to which she is deeply attached because it provides her with a means of emotional expression she does not otherwise have, and, like Ada, she is attracted to a bushman, David Bruce, who lives in a shanty near by and who is more sensitive to music than is her husband.[2]

Campion was interested in this project, and it is easy to see why. She has professed her love of novels in general: "As a whole, they satisfy me much more than most films, since they illuminate things much more patiently and deeply."[3] In particular, she admits to a special liking for romantic novels of the sort written by Charlotte and Emily Brontë, and *Wuthering Heights* is specifically mentioned as an influence: "She [Emily Brontë] . . . writes about the bareness of these marshy areas. I . . . [could] well imagine that feeling in the New Zealand landscapes."[4] Furthermore, her mother, Edith, had long been "a very strong advocate" for this type of story: "She always held up to my sister and myself the role of martyr. She believes in love and its redemptive power. She is extremely romantic, which is something that both of us recoiled against, but her flame is still there."[5] In addition, Campion had become interested in her ancestors and "how they were, how it must have been for them, a very puritanical society, going to a place like New Zealand, which was so astonishingly different, not only physically from England, but also culturally in the sense of what the Maori culture was like."[6] Jane Mander's story of an emotionally starved woman trapped in a loveless marriage in the wilds of colonial New Zealand, who seeks liberation from the "awful disease" of puritanism by engaging in a passionately intense, but forbidden relationship with a sensitive man, provided a basic plot structure that allowed all of these interests to be brought together.[7]

Campion's initial openness to the idea of directing the planned film was sufficiently strong for her to begin a story outline for the adaptation, even though the other Maynard-Ikin project in which she was involved— the filming of Janet Frame's *Autobiography* for television—would interrupt her progress on this early draft. As she informed Maynard and Ikin in a letter written in 1985: "The first thing I ended up working on was The Piano Lesson, my inspiration from Jane Mander's melodrama and you will see there is precious little of the original, but the inspiration was still there."[8] The story outline itself begins, "New Zealand's first piano was left abandoned on a beach. Alice's husband could not see the use for it. However, Alice's attachment to her piano was unique, for she was mute."[9] After beginning a first draft, however, Campion put it away and turned to the making of *Sweetie*, realizing that her self-understanding was not yet mature enough to tackle the material she was trying to shape in *The Piano Lesson*. As she puts it: "I didn't have enough experience as a director and I wasn't in a position to really understand all the themes that I wanted to focus on, this archetypal story, the relationships between primitivism and civilization, a whole construction based upon oppositions. I thus decided to let the project rest."[10]

In 1990, after completing *Sweetie*, she returned to the embryonic screenplay and wrote the second draft in two and a half months, making changes and adding new material, before filming *An Angel at My Table*.[11] The final version of *The Piano Lesson* was written in six weeks, once the filming of *An Angel at My Table* had finished.[12]

By the time Jane Campion had finally completed her screenplay for *The Piano Lesson*, it must have been clear to everyone that it could no longer be viewed simply as an adaptation of Mander's novel. On the basis of the changes Campion had made—including her decision to make the heroine mute—one can infer that she had recognized that to remain bound by the constraints of Mander's conceptualization of the characters would not allow her to do what she wanted to do with the story. In particular, it would not allow her to explore issues relating to eroticism and desire with the degree of freedom she needed. As she confessed to a French interviewer in 1993, she had become "obsessed with understanding the nature of desire" when she was in her twenties and thirties, and this obsession furnished a strong motive for making the film:

> For me, *The Piano Lesson* [the original title, by which *The Piano* remains known in Europe, where copyright reasons do not preclude it] was an opportunity to study this force in the way a researcher studies an organism. You could say that I put the embryo of desire, curiosity, and eroticism under my microscope, and then observed these three elements transform themselves into love.[13]

Mander's novel could not provide the scope for an exploration of desire and eroticism to be pursued in this way, because Alice—despite her frustration and the intensity of her feelings for David Bruce, the bushman—remains sexually faithful to her husband, Tom Roland, until the latter is killed in an accident near the end of the novel. Campion needed to shift the focus so that the heroine's sexual liberation, rather than the suffering that results from her repression, became the main focus of the film. In order to put this process "under the microscope," Campion had to invent the notion of several bartering arrangements concerning Ada's piano—the symbol of her repressed passion. The first of these bartering arrangements is struck between Ada's husband, Alasdair Stewart, and the bushman, Baines (the David Bruce figure in the film), when Baines proposes that Stewart give him the piano in exchange for some of the land Baines owns. The second arrangement is between Baines and Ada: he will trade the keys of her piano in exchange for letting him "do things" while she plays her piano, until she has earned all of them back, at which time he will return the instrument to her. Apart from the obvious symbolism involved (which suggests the different attitude each man has toward Ada and her sexuality), these bartering arrangements serve as a device for imparting "the lesson" that each of the three protagonists needs to learn through their relationship to the piano: Stewart has to learn that patriarchal authority cannot compel love; Baines has to learn that seduction lies not in turning the woman he desires into a "whore," but in discovering the feminine side of himself, so that she can make her own choice freely, without fear of his masculine power; and Ada has to discover that she wants to transfer her erotic impulse into sexual lovemaking with Baines, rather than displacing it into the playing of her piano. (The coexistence of these three different levels of symbolic connotation invests the original title of the film, *The Piano Lesson,* with more resonance than its eventual one, and it is a pity that it needed to be changed for copyright reasons.)

There was an even more important reason that Campion needed to free herself from the constraints imposed by an adaptation of *The Story of a New Zealand River.* She wanted to convert the story into an archetypal, mythic fable capable of accommodating the personal concerns of her earlier movies. The archetypal quality of *The Piano* and its exploration of desire have received a lot of attention from critics. Dana Polan has characterized the film as being "in large part about a woman who gains new forms of self-expression by taking control of the erotic dimension of her life." To represent such a liberation, Polan argues, Campion drew upon two established cinematic genres: the "romantic film" that delivers "a narrative of longing and desire, of desire for objects but also for qualities beyond inanimate worldly things," and the "woman's gothic" film, in which

> a simple woman, often from a modest class background, finds the cyclical regularity of her limited lifestyle transformed when a stranger comes brusquely into her life, marries her and spirits her [a]way to a wild abode away from civilisation where she is trapped and where she begins to suspect that he hates her or even has murderous designs on her.[14]

In a similar vein, Kathleen McHugh points to the extreme romanticism of the cinematic mode Campion adopts, noting the "surreal visual flourishes" that accompany a "wildly romantic plot," in which the heroine "embodies a complex transnational and transhistorical feminine imaginary." Ada, McHugh believes, is a "composite" of the attributes of the women artists who inspired Campion, combining "Emily Brontë's silence, Emily Dickinson's secrecy, and Frida Kahlo's fierce gaze."[15]

Campion's exploitation of the generic elements identified by Polan and McHugh to create a feminine imaginary helps to explain why *The*

Piano was received so rapturously by female audiences around the world: its focus on self-realization achieved through a liberated eroticism answered to the zeitgeist, which, as Hilary Radner has shown, from the late 1980s onward has produced a distinct line of films informed by the values of "neo-feminism," a doctrine of self-fulfillment advocated by, among others, Helen Gurley Brown, the former editor of *Cosmopolitan*.[16] Female viewers were able to read in Ada's experience a paradigm of their own aspirations.

While an identification of stylistic and generic elements can illuminate the nature of *The Piano*'s construction and reception, it still does not explain what prompted Campion to make the movie in the first place. Moreover, there are so many particularities in the film that exceed, diverge from, or overturn the expectations generated by its mode that one is prompted to look for a broader explanation. In the rest of this discussion, I will explore the reasons for the overdetermination that one can detect in *The Piano* and show how it maps the filmmaker's personal preoccupations in real life, in order to illuminate her creative process.

The degree of Campion's personal investment in the reconceived fable she developed from hints in Mander (and others) is apparent in the clear links between *The Piano* and the films that preceded it. Ada's muteness, for instance, bears an obvious relationship to the muteness of the mother in *A Girl's Own Story,* who has not spoken to her husband for two years, while Ada's sexual frigidity and repression bear a resemblance to that of Kay in *Sweetie*. At another level, the mother-daughter relationship depicted in *The Piano* actualizes, in a dramatic embodiment, the (con)fusion of imaginative identifications found in *An Angel at My Table,* in which Campion identified herself with Janet Frame at some moments, and at other times identified her mother, Edith, with Janet Frame, and at still other times identified herself with her mother.[17] In *The Piano*, these fused identifications are explicitly embodied in the visual doubling that defines the characters of Ada and Flora, with the emotional fusion between them being suggested literally as well as figuratively by the similarity of their appearance and actions. Finally, the version of the father figure who appears in the earlier movies as an object of fear, on account of his attempt to impose patriarchal authority (as in *Peel*) reappears in the form of Stewart in *The Piano,* while the version of the father, or father figure, who appears as the object of forbidden desire (as with the fathers in *A Girl's Own Story* and *Two Friends,* and with Gordon in *Sweetie*) reappears in the form of Baines (who is represented as a man much older than Ada) and in the shadowy figure of Bluebeard in the theatrical performance put on by the settlers. These parallels indicate the high degree of symbolic displacement and condensation that is taking place in Campion's reconception of the fable.

Given the magnitude of these changes that Jane Campion wanted to make—especially in the light of the profound personal relevance they had for her—it was inevitable that she would end up making a film of her own, rather than persisting with the original project to make an adaptation.[18] It would have been impossible for Campion to have continued with that enterprise, because the whole mode and focus of the fiction had become utterly transformed in the screenplay she wrote,[19] especially given that the story had been redesigned to function like a dream, rather than as a narrative operating exclusively at the level of literal realism, as Mander's novel had done.[20]

Campion's intent in this regard is expressed explicitly in some comments she entered into her workbook for *The Piano,* in which she noted as "Considerations" for "the feeling of the story":

1. Clarity in storyline
2. Complex psychological/subconscious mechanisms
3. The forces below that drive
4. The hiddenness, secretiveness[21]

This preoccupation with subconscious mechanisms and the driving forces that exist below the surface not only attests to a major shift in mode and emphasis, but also points to a need to look for the presence of these elements when interpreting the story. In the rest of this chapter, I will identify these subconscious mechanisms and forces, extrapolating the associations they carried in the filmmaker's imagination.

3 What is it, then, that invests *The Piano* with its archetypal, mythic, and oneiric qualities? Richard O'Neill-Dean has proposed that the film can be read as the dream of a dreamer who is having trouble separating from the mother-child dyad—the symbiotic relationship that exists in the early months of life when the infant cannot distinguish itself from

its mother. In psychoanalytic theory, the process of individuation that should take place as the child develops depends upon a dissolution of this dyadic relationship in order for the child to register his or her own separateness. For this to happen, the mother must assist the child by being emotionally available out of a concern for his or her well-being, but without developing a narcissistic over-investment in the child as an extension of herself. If the mother's interactions with the child during this stage are "good enough," the child will gradually internalize the caretaking capacity arising out of the relationship with the mother and will thus develop an ability to function confidently as an independent being.

In the case of Ada, O'Neill-Dean observes, this process became arrested when the young Ada was six years old, leaving her "stuck" at an arrested stage of psychological development that is represented in the symbiotic mother-daughter relationship between Ada and her daughter, Flora, with its extraordinary mirroring. O'Neill-Dean also proposes that the piano itself stands for the duality of mother and child in the dyadic world, and that the cut that separates Ada from her exclusive investment in the piano symbolically represents the collapse of narcissism that is necessary for her to resume progress toward healthy psychological development. In my view, this thesis is worthy of serious consideration and is, I believe, supported by the evidence in many respects (even though my own interpretation of Ada's mutilation, as will become apparent, is somewhat different).

A full understanding of the way *The Piano* functions as a dream depends upon being able to discern the latent content that lies under the manifest content—the "hiddenness" associated with the "subconscious mechanisms" that Jane Campion mentions in her workbook. This latent content, I will argue, derives from Campion's sense of the dynamics that were operant in her family.

Campion has given us a preliminary glimpse into the associative complexity of the process that is involved, for her, in the conversion of latent content into manifest content in this film. When she was deliberating on how she would depict Ada and Flora on the deserted beach, she tells us, she drew a little picture of "two glossy, brown-haired schoolgirls walking along, in Darlington, in their brown school uniforms—Ada and

Jane Campion displays the drawing in her workbook that expressed
the germ of the idea for Ada and Flora in *The Piano*.

Flora; they stop to pat two cats."[22] At first sight, this sketch might appear
to have nothing to do with the way that Ada and Flora were eventually
represented in these scenes, but if one unravels the chain of associations inhering for Jane Campion in these images, its relevance becomes
apparent.

To take the image of the girls in their school uniforms first. This image appeared in Campion's earlier movies, as we have already discussed:
the sisters in *A Girl's Own Story* are shown in their school uniforms, as
are the two girls in *Two Friends* and the young Janet in *An Angel at My
Table*. Not only is this image associated with Jane Campion's experience of being a pupil at a girls' school, but it also is associated with Edith
Campion.[23] There is an associative elision inherent in the image that
merges Jane Campion's identification of the image with herself, with
her identification of the image with her mother. In this way, the image
points toward the fusion that is signaled visually through the mirrored
appearances and actions of Ada and Flora.

The reference to cats is also significant, as I have already shown.[24] By
having the two schoolgirls stop to pat two cats, Jane Campion was allowing her imagination to reinforce the association between Ada and Flora

and herself and her mother—particularly with regard to the comfort that is shown to be imparted through the close bond between mother and daughter, which is, the image implies, comparable to the comfort that Edith gained from her cats in real life.

A further level of personal reference inheres in the fact that the two schoolgirls Campion drew in her workbook appear to be identical. This conjures up the idea of sisters, or friends, thus subsuming the personal preoccupations with issues relating to siblings that Campion had already explored in *A Girl's Own Story* and *Sweetie,* as well as those relating to friends in her television feature, *Two Friends.* Finally, the location of the two girls in Darlington, an inner-city suburb of Sydney, the city in which Jane Campion lives, firmly associates the image with the film-maker, leaving us in no doubt as to the deeply personal nature of its latent signification.

Most of the images in *The Piano* have a similar depth of associative meaning, the origins of which can be traced to the circumstances of Jane Campion's family background. Richard Campion, for example, is present in the figure of Bluebeard who appears in the Christmas play put on in the mission hall by the Reverend Campbell. Once again, the layers of allusion that inhere in this episode are complex and multifaceted. The play, as a phenomenon in its own right, recalls the theatrical careers of Jane Campion's parents and their efforts to establish a professional national theater. The content of the play, which shows Bluebeard killing his youngest wife because she has learned his "secret," metaphorically suggests Campion's sense of the effect on her mother of her husband's infidelities and his eventual desertion. The fact that the play—with its gruesome, bloody presentation of the severed heads of Bluebeard's previous wives—is produced by a "reverend," evokes the extremely repressive religious sect of the Exclusive Brethren in which Richard Campion was raised, suggesting a link between the repression of that background and the destructive effects on women that are produced by it.

Another powerful image in the film emerges directly out of the experience of Jane Campion and her mother: Stewart's mutilation of Ada when he chops off her finger. In her director's commentary on *An Angel at My Table,* Campion reveals that this incident originated in an event she witnessed when her mother was receiving treatment for depression:

The phantasmal legacy of an autobiographical incident, imaged as a shadow in *The Piano*.

> I went to one of these dances at a mental hospital. They had it in a gym. I can still remember this woman was there, and she'd chopped her hand off, her left hand off, because her husband was having an affair with someone, and she was trying to pull off her wedding ring, but it wouldn't come off, and in the heat of her desperation she went into the garage, got the axe, and hacked her hand off, and my mother was explaining this to me at the same time as we were watching her and her husband dancing at the dance in the gym. [This is] part of where I got the inspiration for the idea in *The Piano*, when Stewart chops Holly Hunter's [Ada's] finger off.[25]

Apart from registering the filmmaker's sense of trauma and horror, reflected in the marked parataxis of this passage, the statement indicates, once again, the chain of displaced associations that are latent in the image of the mutilation as it was eventually presented in the film. The real-life episode in the mental hospital, in which a wife ends up mutilated because of her desperation that her husband was having an affair, lent itself to being interpreted metonymically by the filmmaker as a displaced manifestation of the effects on her mother of her father's infidelity. It explains why, when Campion presented the Bluebeard play within the movie, she decided not only to present the instrument of marital murder as an ax, but also to replicate the real-life incident in the rehearsal of the shadow play, when the reverend appears to chop off Nessie's hand, and then to convert it into the later mutilation of Ada by her husband.

The New Zealand bush, too, has deeply symbolic overtones for Campion. She observes:

> [I]n the bush it is very dark, hardly any light penetrates. That is why the settlers burned down all the woods, so as not to become claustrophobic. It's claustro-phobic, impenetrable, it's like swimming under water. It's a mysterious, beautiful and fairy-like world but it can just as well be unsettling and nightmarish. For me, this landscape is very fascinating.[26]

For the settlers, she says, "the bush carried secrets and hidden things."[27] One can sense here the emergence, in Campion's imagination, of the bush as a symbol for what lies concealed, which is simultaneously fright-ening and exciting. In carrying "secrets and hidden things," it is also as-sociated with the existence of secrets within the family, as well as those aspects of oneself, as Campion says, that one is scared to know about, and, as such, the bush functions like the orange peel in *Peel*—as some-thing that masks from outward sight a viscerally moist and sensuously exciting interior beneath the seemingly hard carapace that contains it.

Campion makes it clear that one of the secrets signified by the bush are the forces involved in sexuality itself. The bush provides the cover under which Ada can pursue an extramarital affair. It is a place of sexual initiation, as when Flora and the Maori children simulate lovemaking by embracing the tree trunks. Significantly, Campion also associated the bush with her father, having gone on long tramps with him in it ("I loved that"),[28] just as, at the beginning and end of the movie, she appears to associate the sea with her mother.

4   It is in the context of these symbolic reference points, redolent with personal associations for the filmmaker, that the action of *The Piano* unfolds, and the action itself becomes the symbolic enactment of the psychological movement that takes place in the heroine, Ada. There are three distinct stages in this movement, which I will now trace.

When we first see Ada, she is looking out at the world through the gaps in her fingers, suggesting, as in the case of Janet Frame, a defensive retreat into a narcissistic autarky, or emotional enclosure within the self. Her "mind's voice" tells us that she has not spoken since she was six years old and that no one knows why, not even her. Within the precincts of this psychic fortress, she lives in the company of her treasured relation-ships—in particular, her relationship with her piano and her relationship with her nine-year-old daughter, Flora.

Once Ada and Flora have arrived in New Zealand and are left on a deserted beach, they are shown to have a relationship so closely bonded as to suggest some kind of mirroring narcissistic interdependency. Visually, they are versions of one another, being dressed similarly, with identical bonnets; they present and defend each other's interests; they release deep inner feelings through art—Ada in her piano playing, and Flora in her dancing and shell pictures—and they interpret each other's desires without words. The primitive nature of this preverbal, symbiotic fusion is symbolically figured in the tent erected from Ada's hooped petticoat, which encloses a warm (and warmly lit), womb-like space in which the intersubjective interchange between the mother and daughter can take place without impediment and without intrusion from the outer world.

This is a world from which men are excluded. Given the chance to rejoin the sailors and be taken on to Nelson, she signs, through Flora, that "she'd rather be boiled alive by natives than get back on your stinking tub," thus delivering a stinging rebuff to what had been a generous and considerate suggestion. Most conspicuously, there is no father present. Ada's father has sent her to the colonies to marry a man she has never met, and Flora's father is present only in the young girl's imagination, having "stopped listening" to Ada, as we learn later. The two females, mother and daughter, compensate for this absence—or rather, fortify themselves against it—by taking refuge in their relationship with one another. Inside the petticoat tent, Flora expresses her determination not to accord Ada's future husband any recognition of his paternal role or even of his masculine identity: "I'm not going to call him Papa, I'm not going to call HIM anything. I'm not even going to look at HIM."[29] In this refusal to give symbolic significance to the phallic other, she is mirroring the repressed self-containment into which her mother has withdrawn.

This rejection of the masculine was not always the case, however. In the novelized elaboration of *The Piano*'s screenplay that Jane Campion published in 1994 with the assistance of Kate Pullinger, a detailed backstory to explain Ada's muteness is supplied in the two chapters that Campion wrote. In this account, Ada's muteness was triggered by a traumatic incident involving her father that she endured when she was six.

Prior to this, we learn, she had always been "his favored pet." But when, during a visit of two neighboring aunts, the young Ada emptied some sugar granules onto the dinner table in order to pretend to be drawing in the snow, her father breached their intimate bond by chastising her with a force she had never known him to use. Bellowing at her with "a great spray of spit," Wyston McGrath ordered her to go to her room and not speak for the rest of the day. The effect on the young Ada was unbearable mortification: "The child's face burned a fantastic red and a sweat that prickled needles burst across her upper lip." Even McGrath was surprised by the force of his temper, ascribing it to the aggravating presence of the aunts and the need for children to be "obedient." Ada's shame, we learn, was "complete," causing her to hold her hands up across her face "so that none could look upon it" (this gesture is picked up in the opening shot of the film, which places the viewer in the perspective of Ada looking out through the fingers she has placed over her face).[30]

Campion's elaboration of this episode in the novelization helps to explain the psychic economy that is implicit in the representation of Ada in the film. When the little girl reaches "the safety of her bedroom" and, "taking a bite-sized piece of pillow into her mouth to muffle her cries," prepares to sob, "[t]o her surprise no sobs came."[31] From this, we can infer that Ada's involuntary muteness is the manifestation of an unconscious strategy to protect herself from the pain of intense narcissistic mortification. When the condition persists, her father comes to realize that her silence is a device to punish him for his betrayal of their intimacy:

> "Ada," he said, "I have punished you and now this last week you have punished me." He looked at her and she looked back at him with a forgiving unmoving quiet. "In my calculation, we are even," and he added, "don't you think?" He bent forward so his big-featured face was on her level. "Are we even?"
>   Ada heard her father's kind voice and looked into the face she loved so dearly, the face she had called "Beast," and despite her enormous love for him, and his utter devotion to her, she could not contradict the edict of her own small iron will. She, as firm as a window grille, would not speak.[32]

The effect of little Ada's unconsciously motivated muteness is to bind her father into an even closer bond with her: "soon daughter and father became even tighter, he in his mocking, admiring tolerance, she in her tiny child firmness," with her father recognizing that her muteness "is a dark talent."[33]

What we see represented in this backstory is a highly condensed and symbolically displaced expression of the psychic forces at work in a repressed incestuous fantasy, in which both father and daughter are complicit. On one hand, the father is despised as a "beast" because of his imposition of a paternal authority that does violence to the daughter's fantasy of being the object of his devotion, and, on the other hand, he is adored as the forbidden object of her primitive desire that cannot be attained. As a result of these conflicting impulses, the girl is left trapped in an arrested state—which we see perpetuated in the adult Ada before she encounters Baines—that leaves her incapable of accepting the oedipal conflict. This means that she cannot accept the necessity of transferring her fantasy desires from her father to another man, and she is left in a state of psychic dependency on her mother, which is replicated in the dependency of her own daughter on her, and hers on her daughter. The psychic economy depicted here renders more visible that which is implicit in all of Campion's other films that show a daughter entertaining an incestuous fantasy involving her father, or a father figure.

In Campion's novelized elaboration, the situation is made even more complex by the fact that Ada's mother, Cecilia, is dead—killed off in fantasy, if you like. Although she died three weeks after Ada was born, Ada maintains an attachment to her through her piano, which had been given to her mother by her father as an anniversary present. Cecilia, too, "had loved the instrument with a passion that could have been unseemly in other circumstances" and "played the piano every day for the last six months of her confinement."[34] These associations invest the piano with a complex significance for Ada. Insofar as the piano belonged to her mother, it provides a substitute for the mother in her absence: "little Ada would blush with pleasure as if the piano itself was her mother."[35] Insofar as the piano was a gift of her father to Cecilia on the anniversary of their marriage, by playing it, Ada is able, in her imagination, to take her mother's place as the object of his adoration. Implicitly, too, in giving Ada the piano, McGrath is unconsciously asking her to be a stand-in for his dead wife. This becomes clear in McGrath's response to Ada following her second trauma, when she is deserted by Delwar Haussler, her piano teacher, after he has made her pregnant: "Some of the staff maintained that there were times when . . . [McGrath] confused his daughter with his dead wife, slipping back through the years to when Cecilia had carried Ada. Others in the town insinuated with shameful whispers that perhaps it was Wyston himself who had fathered the child."[36]

Even though this later part of the novelization of *The Piano,* according to Kate Pullinger's account, was invented by Pullinger,[37] she and Campion worked in close collaboration, and one can assume that the material is consistent with the filmmaker's conception of the work.[38] Certainly, the thought in these passages, with its hint of incestuous possibilities (if only in fantasy) is consistent with similar suggestions in Campion's other films, as I have shown, and with the sense of Ada that the filmic representation imparts.

What all this material makes abundantly clear is that the psychodynamics motivating the repression that grips Ada owe more to complexities inherent in her family background than to the influence of Presbyterian puritanism alone. In particular, we are shown a daughter who is stuck because of the combined effects of an incestuous attachment that has to be disavowed, a resentment at the patriarchal authority that enforces the law of the father, and a fear of the phallus as a symbol of a sexuality that has the power to destroy, at the same time as it excites a fantasy of desire.

Perhaps the clearest manifestation of this nexus of contradictory and conflicting impulses is in the inset Bluebeard play. Seen as a shadow projected against a sheet, the figure of Bluebeard appears to have an enormous phallus, which turns him into a symbol of masculine sexuality.[39] The secret that his "youngest and sweetest wife" learns, for which she must die, is that he has killed all his earlier wives. Thus, while the image of the phallus provides a source of titillation with its intimation of erotic possibility, the image of the ax Bluebeard is about to wield is a symbol of the danger inherent in yielding to that sexual impulse.

Ada's fear of the destructive potential latent in phallic sexuality partly explains her frigidity toward her husband. It also explains why she rips off the faux wedding dress in which she is garbed for the photograph—inasmuch as it is a symbol of parental coupling.[40] Ada also imparts her fears to Flora, as when, from inside the security of the feminine petticoat-tent-refuge, she signs to her daughter the story of the wind:

And the wind said,
"Remember how we used to play?"
Then the wind took her hand and said,
"Come come with me."
But she refused.

In this little allegory, we detect an allusion to the forces at work in the backstory. The reference to an earlier time when a girl used to play with the wind recalls a primal time when a father would play with his daughter. The ensuing reference to the wind seeking to take the hand of the adult woman, with an invitation to join him, alludes to the courtship of a man who is seeking to make her his sexual partner. The woman's refusal signifies Ada's own recoiling from such a possibility, which suggests that the wind outside the tent, with its metaphoric ability to "impregnate"[41] and from which mother and daughter are protected in their refuge, signifies sexual coupling. Flora certainly interprets it this way, for her response is to assert vehemently that she is not going to call Stewart "Papa," which shows that she has assimilated Ada's psychic revulsion in that regard.

Understandably, Flora initially is just as reluctant to allow her mother to enter into an erotic relationship with a man as Ada is to enter it. Instead, she wants mother and daughter to remain enclosed within the confines of their narcissistic dyad. We see this in Flora's insistence that she "wants to be in the photograph"—that is, not to be left out of the coupled male-female partnership that the photograph is supposed to record. We see it again when she does not want to be left outside the hut on the occasions when Ada visits Baines, but wants to be allowed to "watch." Indeed, the idea of watching becomes a motif in the movie that suggests a primal trauma: the shock of a child at the moment when he or she realizes that the parents have a special sexual bond from which the child is excluded, thus forcing an acknowledgment that the child no longer has exclusive possession of the parent.

In tracing the network of these associations, one reaches the conclusion that Ada and Flora share the impulses and reactions of a single personality. We have seen Jane Campion adopt this strategy before—that is, dividing the aspects of a self between different personages, whether for the purpose of counterpoising a persona and its shadow (Kay and Dawn in *Sweetie*), or of suggesting the dual identifications that she invested in

Janet in *An Angel at My Table,* who variously represents her mother and herself. In *The Piano,* the relationship between Ada and Flora begins as one of identification at the start of the movie, but diverges into one of opposition as the action proceeds, with Flora separating from her mother and aligning herself with the "Papa" whom she earlier had thought she would never accept as such.

5 The second stage in the psychic movement that occurs in Ada consists of her liberation from the condition of protective self-containment, in which her libidinal impulses are repressed and displaced into her playing of her piano. This movement takes place, despite her intent, as a consequence of the bartering arrangement that Baines proposes to her, whereby she can regain her piano if she lets him "do things" while she is playing for him. In discussing this central section of the film, I will argue that the representation of Ada's release from repression is more complex and problematic than interpreters to date have tended to recognize, and that Jane Campion is highly aware of the problems she has depicted.

Campion's intentions are fairly clear from her own comments. She wanted, she says, to show "a story about sexual awakening in characters, and particularly in Victorian characters, who aren't talking about their sexuality, or very aware of their sexuality in the way we are now."[42] "The great advantage in setting the story in 1850," she thought, was in the possibility of developing characters "who approach love, sex and eroticism naively, whose first experiences one can observe—there are no more such occasions for us today."[43] The process involved in this experience was what she wanted to "put under the microscope" in order to "comprehend the force of the desire that was involved."[44]

Ada's awakening would be brought about by her encounter with "a man who can empathize and see the woman for who she really is." At the same time, this man was to be "extremely masculine in his masculinity," and his "extreme masculine qualities" were to "bring out" Ada's femininity.[45] Campion is frank in revealing that Ada's reaction to Baines is based on her own experience:

> I find that to be true for myself—they [extremely masculine men] do have an impact on you, and I think the extreme masculinity and extreme femininity, you know, they're interesting ideas, and there's all sorts of fractions in between, but

I did choose Ada and Baines to be at either end of those scales, and when they meet, it's dramatic.[46]

As already noted, the mechanism which enables Ada's erotic passion to become released is the bartering arrangement Baines strikes with her that allows him to touch her—to which she agrees because her desire to recover her piano, as an object in which she is deeply invested at a psychic level, is greater than her revulsion at the idea of being touched. The point that Campion wants to make here—as she will again attempt later in *In the Cut*—is that love can have its origins in eroticism, no matter how it is initiated, in addition to the other way around. Ada is shown, by degrees, as becoming eroticized, first by Baines's increasingly bold touching, then by the sight of his nakedness, and finally by the whole-body sensation of lying next to his naked body. This brings her to the point at which she chooses to give herself to him voluntarily, when he—having realized that the arrangement is making her "a whore" and himself "wretched"—frees her from the bargain by returning the piano to her, without any conditions. The contrast between Baines's "feminized" relinquishing of patriarchal control and the ordinary presumptions of patriarchy is graphically illustrated in the scene following Stewart's witnessing of their lovemaking, when Stewart uses force to try to possess her sexually.

Despite the idealistic intent that informs the vision being presented—that erotic exchange can provide the means of liberating a woman from psychosexual repression, especially when a would-be lover relinquishes his aspirations to patriarchal dominance—the ensuing scenes in this middle section of the film undermine this premise by suggesting that it may amount to no more than a wish-fulfillment fantasy.

The first sign of ambiguity occurs when Ada, faced with the decision of whether or not to return to Baines after he has given back her piano, is shown caressing the keys of her piano, in the same way that she will be shown caressing the surface of the ocean near the end of the movie. At a symbolic level, the suggestion is that she is trying to decide whether she will choose to retreat back into the narcissistic autarky associated with her attachment to her mother, or whether she will relinquish that in order to transfer her libidinal investment to a man. The camera, at this point, focuses on one key, which has an arrow piercing a heart etched into it, linking an A and a D, which refers to the love affair between Ada and Delwar, the father of Flora, which ended in betrayal. By showing us a glimpse of this key, Campion is intimating the fear of masculine perfidy which Ada, based on her own experience of desertion once the man has been sexually gratified, needs to overcome before she can leave her psychic refuge.

She does overcome this fear, returns to Baines, and has passionate sex with him—during which music plays which we have earlier heard her perform on her piano, suggesting that she has indeed transferred her passion from a nonsexual object (her piano) to a sexual object (a man, Baines). When, at the conclusion of their erotic encounter, Baines asks Ada whether she "loves" him, she looks perplexed. Instead of giving him an unambiguously affirmative answer, she instead lifts up his vest and begins kissing his torso—with the implication that erotic gratification is what has been at issue for her, rather than love.

This suggestion is further reinforced by several episodes that take place when Stewart boards up the house to prevent Ada from return-ing to Baines. In the first, we see Ada kiss her reflection in her mirror. Visually, this recalls the moment near the beginning of the movie when Stewart takes out a daguerreotype portrait of Ada and uses the glass that covers it as a mirror in which he can see his own reflection as he drags a comb through his hair. In both instances, Campion presents us with an emblem of narcissism, and the visual parallel between the two episodes implies at a symbolic level that there may be very little, if any, difference between the way Stewart regards Ada as an object and the way Ada regards Baines.

This idea is strengthened further in the two episodes in which Ada eroticizes Stewart in his bedroom, treating him simply as a sexual object, in the way that men have been shown to treat women. As Campion has said, when Ada caresses Stewart, she is thinking "above all of her own eroticism":

> When she caresses [Stewart], she's searching for herself. Usually it's the opposite that happens: women often have the impression of being treated as objects by men. It's perhaps a cliché, but men often want a sexual experience without being involved. The film wants to show, however, that men are vulnerable, and sexually too. They need to be loved and to feel protected.[47]

As is suggested by Ada's kissing of her own image in the mirror, her eroticization of Stewart is really a form of narcissistic autoeroticism.

On the second occasion when she strokes his body, Stewart, sensing the autoerotic nature of her sexual engagement with him, pulls his undergarment back up and discovers that he cannot touch her, despite the desire he has felt.

Commensurately, despite the fact that Ada sends Baines a piano key engraved with the message "Dear George, you have my heart, Ada McGrath," these episodes seem designed to make the viewer wonder whether Ada, who believes herself to be in love, is actually in love or simply confusing the eroticism she has discovered with what she takes to be love. Her flirtation with suicide near the end of the movie, as I will show, suggests that the underlying psychic vulnerabilities that motivated her initial retreat into narcissistic autarky have not been alleviated in the way that one would have supposed had her discovery of "love" been real.

There is a psychological explanation for what Jane Campion is showing through the presentation of these ambiguities—although one does not sense that Campion necessarily had any conscious awareness of it. It has been well established in psychoanalytic theory and practice that when a child has suffered a denial of her intrinsic value as a human being that has led to narcissistic mortification—as in the case of the young Ada as depicted in the novelization of *The Piano*—the child in later life will often seek compensation in a "neosexual"[48] scenario:

> In neosexual organizations the phallus, disinvested of its symbolic oedipal value, becomes divided into a persecuting, sadistic penis and an unattainable, idealized one. The first must be constantly avoided and the second constantly sought after, in whatever imaginary ways the subject has been able to devise.[49]

Both of these diametrically opposed behaviors are responses to the same thing: a need to find some way of protecting the psyche against the unbearable pain of narcissistic mortification. In *The Piano*, the early scenes show that just such a disinvestment of the symbolic oedipal value of the phallus has occurred, and the rest of the movie shows Ada moving from the first of the antithetical responses described in the passage above, to the other. The scenes where Ada eroticizes Stewart show that the eroticization taking place in Ada's imagination—while she "seeks herself" (in Campion's words)—has nothing whatsoever to do with the reality of Stewart as a subject, or as a separate and libidinally invested object in his own right: he is merely a pretext for the eroticization, which in this way becomes a form of autoeroticism, which simply uses another person

An image of Ada's narcissism in *The Piano*.

as the means of personal (and private) excitation. The function of such eroticization is to deal with "the psychic pain of anxiety or depression that might otherwise overwhelm the subject's capacity to metabolise it," so that the erotic engagement "takes the place of containing, feeling, and thinking."[50]

It is not surprising, therefore, to observe that when reality intervenes to disrupt the enactment of this autoerotic fantasy—in the form of Stewart's enraged indignation at what he perceives to be her bad faith—Ada finds that she possesses almost no other sources of psychic strength that can help her to survive the ensuing ordeal to which he subjects her. It is significant that Flora, by this time, has relinquished her identification with her mother and has sided emphatically with Stewart, her father substitute—which suggests that she, more than Ada, has moved ahead in terms of following the usual course of human development.

6 The third stage in Ada's psychological movement is the most ambiguous of all, and the ambiguity is heightened by the fact that, in earlier drafts, *The Piano Lesson* had a different ending.

Stewart's violent mutilation of Ada, in which he chops off the finger with which she had caressed him just a short time before, serves two purposes at the level of fantasy. At the level of the diegesis itself, the mutilation amounts to a symbolic castration that reflects Stewart's rage at the narcissism he has come to realize is the motivation for her erotic approach to him. As such, the brutal mutilation he inflicts on her is as much an act of vengeance as it is a consequence of sexual jealousy. At a deeper level, because the sexual relationship with Baines for which Stewart is punishing Ada has come about because of the bartering arrangement for the piano once owned by Ada's mother, the affair represents an unconscious wish by Ada to take the place of her mother in a fantasy of incest with her father. This helps to explain why Campion transferred to Ada the mutilation that was associatively linked to her mother, Edith, in her imagination. Symbolically, the chopping off of Ada's finger is simultaneously a punishment for her unacknowledged incestuous wishes, which involve taking the place of her mother, and a punishment for her actual adultery.

The existence of the deep, unacknowledged guilt arising from this fantasy also explains why, at the point where she is free to leave Stewart and face the prospect of a happy life with Baines, Ada lapses into a profound depression that is accompanied by a suicidal inclination. As at other key moments in *The Piano*, the representation of Ada's response to the aftermath of her punishment is overdetermined, suggesting that the causes of her depression are far greater than can be explained simply by her attachment to her piano. When Stewart decides to let her depart with Baines, it is because he has heard a desperate plea being uttered by her, in his mind: "'I'm afraid of my will, of what it might make me do, it is so strange and strong.' She said, 'I have to go—let me go. Let Baines take me away, let him try and save me.'" What this passage reveals is Ada's realization that her mind is still "diseased,"[51] that she is at the mercy of unconscious impulses that she cannot control, and that she needs to be "saved" from the self-destructive potential of her own will—already manifest in her muteness—which arises as a consequence of wishes she cannot acknowledge. Ironically, it is Stewart who is sensitive to this aspect of Ada's psychology, rather than Baines, even though it is the latter, in the revised ending, who, having discovered his "feminine side," is depicted as the one who might be able to help her by removing her fear of the phallus.

At first, it looks as if Ada will succumb to her suicidal impulses: she places her foot in the coils of rope attached to her piano when, at her insistence, it is thrown overboard on the voyage to Nelson. Immediately prior to this, Ada is shown caressing the surface of the water with her fingers in the way that she had been earlier shown to caress the piano, which activates a complex collocation of associations linking together ideas of the sea, the piano, the mother, and death. It is therefore not fanciful to detect in Ada's attempted suicide an allusive reference to Edith Campion's attempted suicide during the late 1980s when Jane Campion was shooting *Sweetie,* with the association, through a process of identification, indicating a comparable depth of despair in Ada. Thus, far from having been liberated from repression through the discovery of eroticism, Ada is shown to have plunged herself (metaphorically and literally) into an even greater depth of nihilistic self-negation.

The original ending of *The Piano* reinforced these negative connotations. At a press conference held in New York in 1994, Jane Campion revealed that, in an earlier version of the screenplay, Ada had actually drowned with her piano,[52] and in an interview with Thomas Bourguignon and Michel Ciment, she described how the original ending had been "very traditional, with a violent resolution": "Baines killed Stewart; some fingers were even cut off."[53] The changing of the ending from a tragic to a happy one was undoubtedly motivated, in part, by concerns about what would appeal at the box office, and it is not surprising, therefore, that some critics have found the revised ending—in which Ada, Baines, and Flora constitute a happy family unit in Nelson, marveling "at the grace that had delivered them"—arbitrary and unsatisfactory.

It is likely, however, that Campion did genuinely entertain the possibility of a positive outcome, despite the dark pessimism of her earlier draft, and that the change in ending reflects the oscillations that emerge from an ambivalence in her own thinking. Campion has recorded that, on the occasion when her mother was so depressed that Jane offered to assist her to die, her mother had replied, "I don't want to die, I don't want to die," and that had been a real turning point for Jane: "I realized that my job was not to sort of see her in darkness, but say, 'Oh, it's going to be better, you're going to get better.'"[54] Metaphorically speaking, this is exactly what Campion does in the altered ending to *The Piano,* with the similarity between the process of the fiction and the biographical account reinforcing the idea that the figure of Ada is deeply invested with some of the attributes of Edith Campion, especially as viewed by her daughter. Having initially offered to assist Ada "to die" (by having her drown), Jane Campion realized that her job is to say that Ada is "going to get better." And to achieve this, she has Ada affirm that she wants to live, just as her own mother had done. Just before Ada is pulled back into the canoe, in a sequence that enacts a symbolic rebirth, her voice is heard to say:

> What a death!
> What a chance!
> What a surprise!
> My will has chosen life?
> Still it has had me spooked, and many others besides![55]

Despite this positive affirmation—which has the power to surprise the spectator as much as Ada—Campion could not entirely dispel her own ambivalence about this outcome, even though she had willed it. This is evident in the concluding image of the drowned Ada floating above her piano at the bottom of the sea, and in the recitation by Ada in a final voice-over of a poem by Thomas Hood that leaves the viewer with a powerful image of the silence and death-like emptiness of the void. Significantly, this poem was chosen for the purpose by Edith Campion:

> There is a silence where hath been no sound
> There is a silence where no sound may be
> In the cold grave, under the deep deep sea.[56]

The presence of this image is as chilling as it is sobering. On one hand, it makes the happiness of the trio in Nelson seem fragile in the context of eternity (and, potentially, all the more precious for that) while, at the same time, it intimates the possibility of a nihilistic extinction, devoid of human life, that Ada has only narrowly just avoided—and which, for the filmmaker, may be an ever-present possibility for her mother. It is not without reason that the film is dedicated "For Edith." Once again, Jane Campion, as she had done in her teens, is trying to tell her mother, "Oh, it's going to be better, you're going to get better."

7 Once again, just as she did in *An Angel at My Table,* Jane Campion has shown us a figure, in Ada, who embodies attributes of both herself and her mother, so that the movie becomes a vehicle for the symbolic

exploration of the sources of resemblance, together with their effects. As we have seen, this representation also dramatizes an attempt at self-cure, which is reinforced generically by the conversion of the film from a tragic melodrama into a romantic wish-fulfillment fantasy of the sort constructed by the Brontës in their novels.

Campion, however, remains highly aware of the contrivance that has been necessary to bring about, and sustain, the romance of the film. The Baines character, she says, "is a kind of ideal man for women—he's not interested in forcing anyone," and she admits that, when she made *The Piano,* she had "a very romantic vision of divine mutuality." The whole film, Campion says, presents "a mythic ideal—it's not reality."[57] More-over, she confesses an awareness that there is a destructive element in the vision itself: "'Romantic' means that it is 'diseased,' that it's 'unhealthy,' and I mean that I knew that when I was working into it—because it's a world of, it's an illusory world, and about ideals . . . whereas 'classic' has a kind of truth to it, and honesty."[58] The implication here is that the romantic mode she adopted for *The Piano* was neither honest nor truth-ful, because of its power to propagate illusions, and, as a result, it had the capacity to do harm to the psychic well-being of its viewers. In an apologetic admission—distressing to the reader on account of the sense of culpability it projects—Campion expresses her fear that the film "has probably fucked up heaps of women."[59]

One senses in this statement the disillusionment of a woman who has discovered that the reality of lived experience does not support the idealistic hopes implicit in romantic fictions. In the early 1990s, Jane Campion had entertained such fantasies, but a decade later, her romantic fantasy had crumbled with the end of her marriage. Like Ada, she had discovered that getting married was easy; it was "becoming lovers [that] was the problem."[60] It is not surprising, therefore, that, for her next film, *The Portrait of a Lady,* she would turn to a "classic" mode that is not (in her view) "diseased," and that, in its greater realism and honesty, could provide an antidote to the unattainable fantasy she had come to believe she had presented, in this most popular of all her movies.

6 The Misfortunes of an Heiress: *The Portrait of a Lady*

1 Following the release of *The Piano*, Jane Campion found herself riding the crest of a wave, hailed as a supreme auteur. The film was greeted with acclaim by most critics and with delighted astonishment by audiences—especially women, who viewed it as a unique expression of feminine insights and sensibility. One critic, for example, found herself "entranced, moved, dazed," and "reluctant to re-enter the everyday world after the film had finished."[1] An eminent woman scholar experienced a powerful somatic response to *The Piano*: "Campion's film moved me deeply, stirring my bodily senses and my sense of my body. The film not only 'filled me up' and often 'suffocated' me with feelings that resonated in and constricted my chest and stomach, but it also 'sensitized' the very surfaces of my skin—as well as its own—to *touch*."[2] The film won three Oscars (including one for best screenplay written directly for the screen) and forty-nine other awards internationally. Unsurprisingly, Campion found herself fêted around the world as one of the most outstanding film directors of her generation. In terms of satisfying her childhood urges to create drawings in order to gain attention and to create and enact plays to make the world appreciate her,[3] Campion had succeeded beyond her wildest dreams.

At a personal level, she had also deepened the imaginative exploration—begun in *An Angel at My Table*—of what her relationship with her mother meant to her, in terms of both her deep empathic identification with Edith Campion and the effects of that affinity on the psychic predispositions she recognized in herself. By developing her ideas about the capacity of eroticism to provide a liberating route to self-realization and happiness through a relationship with a man sensitized to a woman's sensibility and desires, she had attempted to construct a vision of how the ills attending psychological dysfunction could be remedied, and she must have felt delighted at the enthusiasm with which other women responded to this vision.

As suggested in the previous chapter, however, Campion had lingering doubts, and they were not minor ones. At one level of her consciousness, she recognized that the vision she had constructed amounted to no more than a wish-fulfillment fantasy that was likely to have "fucked up heaps of women" by generating expectations that, by 1996, she had come to realize were false.[4] In a string of bitter comments issued during the later 1990s, Campion refers recurrently to her own disillusionment with romance: "When I was young and falling in love, I did a con-job on myself, occasionally with very unsuitable people."[5] Metaphorically speaking, by the time she made her film version of Henry James's *The Portrait of a Lady,* she had come to believe that this is what she had done with *The Piano*—done a "con-job" on herself (and others).

She must also have realized that her business in coming to terms with the meaning of her mother's experience and its effect on her was far from complete. She had explored the nature of narcissistic deprivation and a depressive condition she associated with her mother in *An Angel at My Table,* and she had explored certain of its consequences in *The Piano,* but she had not yet begun to probe the causes that could lead a woman to enter into a relationship with a man that could have the power to generate the depth of unhappiness that had led to the divorce of her parents in the mid-1980s. The idea that a relationship in which a woman has invested all her trust and hope could have the potential for disintegration provided yet another source of doubt and insecurity that needed to be explored—in order to be understood, and thus mastered.

It is not surprising, therefore, that for her next film project Campion turned to an adaptation of James's clear-eyed novel *The Portrait of a Lady.* As far as Campion was concerned, this film was meant to provide an antidote and corrective to the romantic vision she had proffered in *The Piano.* In retrospect, one can surmise that it was an attempt to shore up her defenses against any "romantic" vulnerability that she had revealed in her earlier Brontë-esque moment. As she puts it, she was drawn to James on account of the fact that he "is very modern because he's already tearing apart the fairytale. He's saying, 'Be real. Life is hard. . . . No one's going to get the right person.'"[6] Even though the interpretation of James that Campion expresses here would be considered idiosyncratic by James scholars, it does reflect how her adaptation of *The Portrait of a Lady* embodies an attempt to "tear apart" the feminist fairytale she had created in order to get "real" in the light of actual experience as she perceived it.

Owing to this very personal motive, Campion's adaptation of James's novel displays the same mechanisms of appropriation and conversion to her purpose that characterized the adaptation of Janet Frame's *Autobiography* in *An Angel at My Table*. The filmed version of *The Portrait of a Lady*, therefore, illustrates the same process of creative transformation, constituting authorship, that one can observe in every other one of her films.

2 Before considering more precisely the reasons for Campion's selection of James's masterpiece as the vehicle for her demolition of romantic illusions, I want to draw attention to the existence of a closely related screenplay among Edith Campion's papers deposited in the Alexander Turnbull Library in Wellington, New Zealand. The library's catalog lists a manuscript that it describes as "Fourth draft for a screenplay of the work 'The Reef,' by Edith Wharton," attributing this document to Jane Campion and dating the draft circa 1990–1996.[7] It sits in Edith Campion's papers in proximity to the first draft of Laura Jones's screenplay for *The Portrait of a Lady*, dated 1993, and a second draft of this screenplay, dated 1994.[8] The general similarity between Wharton's novel (published in 1912) and that of James, both specifically and generically, combined with the fact that someone in the Campion family was at one time contemplating making a film adaptation of Wharton's work, invites speculation.

As it turns out, the ascription of the screenplay of *The Reef* to Jane Campion is wrong; it was actually Anna Campion who was considering whether she would make a film of Wharton's novel. In the event, Anna decided not to go ahead with the plan, because "at the time . . . [she] found Edith Wharton's unrequited situations difficult to bear and didn't fully appreciate the different mental state a woman of that period would be in."[9]

It is fascinating to learn that both Campion sisters had been planning to make heritage movies, on very similar themes, at around the same time, confirming yet again just how much their activities mirror each other. In the late 1980s, they had each made a movie involving Edith Campion as an actress (Anna's *The Audition* and Jane's *An Angel at My Table*), and in the early 1990s each made a film that was about Edith Campion at a displaced remove (Anna's *Broken Skin* [1991] and Jane's *The Piano*).[10] The similarity of their filmmaking activities attests to a shared preoccupation around this time with issues relating to their mother. That being so, the obvious parallels between *The Reef* and *The Portrait of a Lady*—insofar as they reflect Edith Campion's personal situation in certain respects—allow one to infer the concerns that may have prompted each of her daughters to consider attempting a heritage film of this sort.

3 An outline of Wharton's novel indeed suggests that Anna Campion's motive for considering a film of *The Reef* would have been the same as Jane Campion's motive for making an adaptation of James's novel turned out to be. At the heart of *The Reef* is Sophy Viner, a talented actress who, like Edith Campion, was orphaned at an early age and tricked out of her inheritance by an unethical American trustee. While traveling from London to Paris, Sophy encounters a young American diplomat, George Darrow, who listens sympathetically to her hard-luck story, together with her frustrated yearnings and aspirations, and offers to help her. Drawn to Sophy by her sexual allure and seeing in her face "a darkening gleaming mirror that might give back strange depths of feeling," Darrow becomes sexually obsessed with her, and they enter into an affair in Paris that lasts ten days.[11] After an interval following this initial liaison, Darrow encounters Sophy again in a château at Givré, where she has been hired as governess to the daughter of the widowed Anna Leath, Darrow's fiancée. Sophy has repaired her financial misfortunes by becoming the fiancée of Anna's stepson, Owen. Inevitably, Anna comes to know of the existence of Sophy's affair with Darrow, and when this occurs, Sophy breaks off her engagement to Owen and leaves Givré in order to protect other members of the family group from the suffering that knowledge of the affair would cause. Tragically, even though Sophy is now in love with Owen, it is too late for her to achieve happiness for herself. What to Darrow had merely been a casual interlude turns out to be a "reef" on which the lives of four people have been in danger of foundering.

An awareness of the real-life circumstances of the Campion family allows one to infer what would have interested Anna Campion in this story. In Sophy Viner, she could see shadowy parallels with aspects of her mother's experience: both Edith and Sophy had been orphaned at an early age, both were actresses, and both had lost a fortune through the agency of men who did not work in their interests. The misery and destruction potentially caused to the family group by Darrow's sexual dalliance, which he dismisses as a slight thing, also has its reflection in Richard Campion's sexual adventures. Finally, the fact that Wharton's novel presents a heroine who, in the words of one critic, "is the embodiment of the dark terrain of female sexuality,"[12] associated The Reef with the compulsive power of eroticism that also fascinated Jane Campion, who had depicted it gripping the mother in A Girl's Own Story and who would continue to be preoccupied with it as a theme in all her movies from The Piano onward, until the chaste reversal of Bright Star (2009).

In the light of these autobiographical parallels, it is likely that Anna Campion could see in The Reef the potential for turning Wharton's novel into a vehicle for a vicarious exploration-through-representation of the major issues that were preoccupying both her and her sister around this time. What was it that could lead a woman like her mother into a condition of such misery and loneliness? What are the consequences of a casual sexual dalliance? What is the nature of sexual attraction, and why does it work the way it does? What constitutes the "unromantic" dimensions of affairs such as the one into which Darrow and Sophy enter? A cinematic adaptation of The Reef could have provided a displaced means for exploring some of these questions.

Moreover, filmed adaptations of Edith Wharton's novels were en vogue throughout the 1990s: The Children had been made in 1990, directed by Tony Palmer; both Ethan Frome by John Madden and The Age of Innocence, directed by Martin Scorsese, had been filmed in 1993; and Terence Davies was about to film an incomparably fine adaptation of The House of Mirth (released in 2000).[13] The appetite of audiences for heritage films based on Wharton's novels provided a promising context for such a venture. Anna Campion did not proceed with the project, but the fact she had even contemplated it sheds an interesting light on Jane Campion's decision to proceed with her comparable one.

For Jane, Henry James's masterpiece offered just as much potential for success at the box office as Anna Campion may have felt Wharton's story did. Just as the 1990s saw a flowering of cinematic treatments of novels by Wharton, they saw a positive explosion of adaptations of novels and stories by Henry James. Starting with *The Aspern Papers* (1989), there were filmed versions of *The Turn of the Screw* (1992), *What Maisie Knew* (1995), *The Wings of a Dove* (1997), *Washington Square* (1997), *The American* (1998), *The Haunting of Hell House* (1999), *Nora* (2000), and *The Golden Bowl* (2000)—all, presumably, aimed at satisfying the contemporary popular taste for costume drama. It was to be expected that Campion would feel emboldened to exploit this trend, especially given that, with a $24 million budget at her disposal, she could produce a lavish offering. She was also, by her own profession, "dying for dialogue" after the silence of *The Piano,* keen to work on a movie with "intense dramatic dialogue scenes."[14]

An even more compelling reason for Campion's decision to proceed with the project, I believe, is that she realized that James's story presented an ideal opportunity to explore the same aspects of Edith Campion's relationship with her former husband that Anna Campion may have been interested in exploring through *The Reef.* Apart from lending itself to an identification of the heroine (and, to some extent, Serena Merle) with Campion's mother, Edith, James's *Portrait of a Lady* also allowed Campion to identify herself with Isabel Archer and to see in Gilbert Osmond's relationship with his daughter, Pansy, a reflection of aspects of her own relationship with her father, Richard. It thus held out to her the same opportunity for making personal investments involving multiple identifications that she had explored in her adaptation of Janet Frame's *Autobiography* in *An Angel at My Table.* As such, it reveals the same authoring processes at work that I have identified in the earlier film, with the same coexistence of two levels of identification—one that identifies Isabel Archer with Edith Campion, and another that identifies Isabel with Jane Campion.

4 Campion is frank about her own identification with Isabel Archer: "Isabel was like myself—a romantic addict," she says, adding that "Isabel fantasizes about men like Osmond, and so do I."[15] This strong

personal identification leads her to reconstruct Isabel into a character who is somewhat different from the Isabel presented in the novel. James's Isabel is, above all, curious about the wider world and eager to see and experience it. She has an imagination that is "by habit ridiculously active," and, "like most American girls, is highly and rashly opinionated."[16] As the narrator wryly comments: "It may be affirmed without delay that Isabel was probably very liable to the sin of self-esteem; she often surveyed with complacency the field of her own nature; she was in the habit of taking for granted, on scanty evidence, that she was right; she treated herself to occasions of homage."[17] For James, Isabel represented, in the words of his biographer, "a modern woman whose fate did not necessarily depend on marriage and sex, but on her freedom of choice,"[18] and it is this, rather than any quest to liberate her sexuality, that motivates Isabel to make the injudicious and ill-fated decision that brings about her woe. The novel shows how she is chastened by the consequences of this choice, and eventually ennobled by her decision to live honorably in acceptance of her own responsibility for them.

Campion seems mostly oblivious to this dimension of Isabel Archer, being more interested in how the story could provide her with a vehicle through which she could explore that part of herself which, in the past, had led her to do a "con-job" on herself with "very unsuitable people." People who believe they know Jane Campion well have expressed the view that a similarity exists between Campion and Isabel. Nicole Kidman (who plays Isabel in the film), for example, comments: "I think that all that Isabel has experienced Jane has also experienced at some stage in her life. . . . Isabel said that what she wants from life is chances and dangers. And I think that's also Jane."[19]

The basis for Kidman's observation becomes apparent if one looks closely at the details in James's novel. Campion could undoubtedly see in James's description of Isabel's upbringing a reflection of her own childhood circumstances. Early in the novel, James's narrator comments on Mr. Archer's irresponsibility and neglect of his children:

> He had squandered a substantial fortune, he had been deplorably convivial, he was known to have gambled freely. A few harsh critics went so far as to say that he had not even brought up his daughters. They had had no regular education and no permanent home; they had been at once spoiled and neglected; they had

lived with nursemaids and governesses (usually very bad ones) or had been sent
to superficial schools, kept by the French.[20]

It is not too hard to imagine how Jane Campion would have seen in this
passage a similarity between Mr. Archer and Richard Campion. Like
Archer, Richard had "squandered a fortune"—his wife's inheritance—in
seeking to create a national professional touring theatrical company.
Also like Archer, he had neglected his daughters in pursuit of this obsession, leaving them in the care of a succession of nannies, to their great
distress.[21]

Deprived of her father's attention and interest, James's Isabel Archer is shown to be highly vulnerable to any manifestations of affection between a father and his daughter, as when she observes, with tacit
envy, Osmond's treatment of his daughter, Pansy, when Isabel first meets
them: "He presently sat down on the other side of his daughter, who had
shyly brushed Isabel's fingers with her own; but he ended by drawing her
out of her chair and making her stand between his knees, leaning against
him while he passed his arm around her slimness."[22] Not only does Isabel's implied envy in this scene reflect the similar yearning of the young
Jane for her father's attention, to which Anna Campion attests,[23] but it
also intimates the existence of a sublimated fantasy of incest between
father and daughter that recalls the succession of similar scenes in Campion's earlier movies. In James's novel, this sense of cross-generational
enmeshment is very strong, manifest in Pansy's naïve admission, "If
he [Osmond] were not my papa I should like to marry him,"[24] and in
Osmond's confession, once he realizes the true state of Isabel's feelings
toward him, "If my wife doesn't like me, at least my child does. I shall
look for compensations in Pansy," indicating the degree to which she is
a stand-in for the imaginary *femme* who is missing in his life.[25]

In addition, Isabel's travels through Europe, with their unhappy
outcome, recall Jane Campion's travels, which were equally unhappy. As
Lizzie Franke reports, following an interview with Campion:

> For the 20th-century Antipodean, the experience of coming to Europe has been
> like that of the 19th-century American. Like Isabel, Campion came to Europe as
> a young woman living for a while in England and studying art in Italy. She calls it
> both the best and the darkest time of her early life. She talks of the time she was
> living just outside Venice and a friend was arrested for cocaine trafficking. "I had

Isabel haunted by the image of Osmond's hand around his
daughter's waist, transferred, in her fantasy, to herself.

> no idea that was even going on. I just thought, I'm going to be arrested and put
> in jail, and no one is going to listen to me. I felt that I really had the confidence
> knocked out of me. . . . I think I was close to a breakdown." Her time in Italy, she
> says, helped her understand Europe's "winter spirit," its darkness. It prepared her
> for Isabel Archer.[26]

One senses the metonymic associations that inform this statement by
Campion: the idea of not knowing what was really going on in the drug-
trafficking incident finds its reflection in Isabel's ignorance of the plot-
ting that is going on behind her back in the novel, while Campion's fear
that she would be "put in jail" finds a metaphoric correlative in Isabel's
feelings of imprisonment once Osmond has tried to strip her of her ideas
and her independence. The fact that both the real-life and the imagined
incidents are located in Italy reinforces the association, while Campion's
confession that she came near to experiencing a nervous breakdown
helps to explain the feeling that is being invested, through the acting of
Nicole Kidman, in the later scenes of the movie showing Isabel's distress.

The parallels between James's novel and Jane Campion's life continue. At one poignant moment in the novel, Madame Merle reveals
that Isabel "had a poor little boy, who died two years ago, six months
after his birth."[27] Tragically, this detail provided Campion with another
reflection of her own life, given that her son, Jasper, had died shortly after
his birth in 1994, to the inexpressible grief of his parents. Significantly,
Campion dedicated the movie "In Loving Memory of J. E. C."—that is,
Jasper Englert Campion.

From all these parallels, it is clear that Campion had good reason to feel that in Henry James's *Portrait of a Lady* she had a story with which she could identify to an extent that she had never done before with any of her other sources. The depth and breadth of her personal identification with Isabel Archer alone would have given a sufficient incentive to proceed with an adaptation of *The Portrait of a Lady*, but in addition to that, James's novel also provided her with an opportunity to explore yet another dimension of her relationship with her mother, owing to the identification she could make between Isabel and Edith.

5 Campion's portrayal of Isabel in *The Portrait of a Lady* displays that strange fusion seen in her adaptation of Janet Frame's *Autobiography*, in which the mother's and the daughter's lives appear to be lived interchangeably through the personal identifications with which Campion invests her fictive heroine. Isabel's mother, like Edith's, died when she was a child (just as Ada's mother is reported as having died, in the novelization of *The Piano*). Given her father's neglect and absences, this leaves Isabel virtually an orphan, just like Edith is an orphan, and Sophy Viner in *The Reef* is an orphan. Also, as in *The Reef,* Isabel Archer, like Sophy, is an heiress twice over—first, as we have seen, in the fortune that her profligate father squanders, and second, as a result of the sizable legacy that Mr. Touchett bequeaths to her at the instigation of his son, Ralph. This double legacy strengthens the latent comparison with Edith Campion, who was left a fortune generated by her grandfather's shoe-manufacturing company. The parallel between Edith and both heroines would have been obvious to the Campion sisters, given that both of them, we are told, separately and on different occasions, described their mother as "an heiress," which shows that this fact occupied a significant place in their imaginary.

Moreover, the repetition in James's novel of the loss of a fortune as the result of the actions of exploitative men serves to focus attention on the behavior of the squandering man and the dynamics of the relationship that make it possible for such exploitation to occur. In picking up and foregrounding this theme, Campion was exploring what it might have been in her mother that could have led to such an outcome. At the

Madame Merle stroking a cat in *The Portrait of a Lady.*

same time, Jane's exploration of that issue allowed her to discover the extent to which she had inherited her mother's predispositions—especially concerning her own relationships with men.

Campion appears to have come to a realization that, at the heart of the syndrome she recognized in Edith Campion and herself—and saw reflected in Isabel Archer—was a predisposition toward romance, which in turn sprang from some need to repair an emotional wound caused by neglect and lack of personal affirmation. This longing to find some restorative compensation, Campion intuited, made these fictive heroines particularly vulnerable to the attentions of men, with eroticism seeming to offer confirmation of their worthiness to exist, while at the same time serving as an opiate to palliate the pain arising from what they feel is missing in their inner world. As Campion had shown in her depiction of the mother in *A Girl's Own Story,* even when the relationship between a man and a woman is bad, the force of this narcissistic hunger can lead the woman to surrender her own volition to the man as a result of her need for the affirmation—however fleeting or false—that such eroticism can provide.

In this regard, Henry James's *Portrait of a Lady* proved useful to Campion because of the presence in it of Madame Merle—a woman

Edith Campion with one of her cats, c. 1953, from the Edith
Campion Collection. *Courtesy of the Alexander Turnbull Library,
Wellington, New Zealand (JA-578-07), used with permission.*

who has ruined her life because of yielding to her romantic and erotic
impulses, like Sophy Viner in *The Reef*. The effect on Serena Merle, as
she comes to realize, has been to allow Osmond—far from leaving her
with an enhanced sense of self—to deprive her of an authentic sense of
identity: "You've not only dried up my tears; you've dried up my soul,"
she tells Osmond.[28] In this respect, she is like the female protagonists in
Edith Campion's short stories in their despairing and empty loneliness,
usually following betrayal or abandonment by men—like the protagonist of "Pyramid," who ends up feeling that she "was a moth pinned to
eternity. Nothing was left but the dark, and a sound like the sea in the
ear of the drowned."[29]

A significant detail in the screenplay suggests that Campion also associated Madame Merle, as well as Isabel, with her mother. In scene 54, when Merle is conducting her interview with Edward Rosier concerning his prospects of marrying Pansy, the screen directions read: "Madame Merle strokes one of her three black cats."[30] As demonstrated earlier, cats were one of Edith Campion's obsessions and, as such, recur in Jane Campion's movies as a powerful symbol, usually signifying the danger attending surrender to erotic or passionate impulses. In the movie, one sure sign that Campion was thinking of her mother in this scene is the words that Madame Merle speaks while she is stroking her black cat. In response to Rosier's observation that Osmond "lives like a rich man," Merle answers that "his money's his wife's—she brought him a large fortune." This statement, in combination with the image of the cat, conveys the filmmaker's awareness of the parallel with her parents; Edith also brought her husband a large fortune, and she eventually ended up in the same misery that Isabel is going to suffer, as a result of her surrender to romantic passion. As the exemplification of such ruin, Madame Merle embodies all that Jane Campion mistrusts about the "disease" of romantic infatuation and what it can lead to, as illustrated by the sad story of her mother.

6 If one "reads" the film bearing in mind these autobiographical investments, it becomes apparent that, even though Campion and Laura Jones, her screenwriter, have remained fairly faithful to James's original, they have made significant changes in order to align the story with Campion's personal investments in it. Jones admits as much when she comments on the collaborative process whereby she and Campion developed the script:

> Over a series of meetings, Jane and I talked about why we loved the novel and started to lay the ground for what *kind* of film it could be. I remember our working our way toward understanding Isabel, not only in her world, but for us in our own pasts and in our understanding of what it is to be like a girl like Isabel in any time. We had to do what James had done, to understand Isabel as our "centre of consciousness."[31]

The first and most obvious change is the addition of a prologue, which plays during the credits, in which young women speaking in Australian and New Zealand accents are heard, first in voice-over, discussing their erotic experiences. This is followed by the sight of a group of young women of mixed ethnic backgrounds forming a circle as they lie on the grass, then sitting in trees, and finally dancing expressively in a way that is reminiscent of the young Janet and her sisters dancing in the woods in *An Angel at My Table*. As Kathleen McHugh points out, the ending of this sequence, which shows an "extradiegetic finger" with the words "The Portrait of a Lady" written on it, in the same hand in which Ada wrote her message of love to Baines, recalls *The Piano*.[32] The imagery of this prologue, then, establishes a number of visual links with Campion's earlier films, in order to alert the attentive viewer to the thematic links among them.

The words that the young women speak also tie the film to Campion's concerns. One of them describes how she is "addicted to that being entwined in each other," which echoes the statements given by Campion in her interviews about how she, when she was young and falling in love, was "a romantic addict," with the verbal echo reinforcing the fact that this adaptation is going to be, in part, about the force of erotic desire— one of Campion's obsessions, which she confessed in a French interview given in 1993:

> I have always been intrigued by the power of romantic impulses. I am someone who has often fallen in love, and each time, I adored it. Whenever that happened to me, I experienced a feeling of being completely revitalized. I felt not only in love with a person, but also with life itself. It was a very, very powerful feeling that literally took me over.[33]

The young women of the prologue, therefore, are enacting Jane Campion's own experience of falling in love under the influence of this "very, very powerful feeling." They are also, as their words imply, seeking the narcissistic repair that Ada was depicted as yearning for in *The Piano* when she was shown kissing her own reflection in her mirror. This is intimated in the words uttered by one of the young women: falling in love, she says, "means finding a mirror, the clearest mirror, and the most loyal mirror, and I love that person, and I know they're going to shine that back to me." These girls, in other words, are in the state of innocent and naïve expectation that will be embodied by Isabel Archer at the beginning of the film, just as their creator, Jane Campion, had experienced such expectations in her twenties and thirties, before the disillusionment wrought by the reality of a succession of failed love affairs set in. The

prologue is thus set up to provide a foil that will intensify the failure of
the romantic expectation that the rest of the movie will depict.

A series of significant changes to the settings of the story also shows
Campion subtly adjusting James's work so that it focuses on her personal
concerns and vision of things. The first major change occurs in the scene
in which Osmond declares his love to Isabel. Instead of taking place in
"the large decorated sitting-room" of the hotel in Rome where they are
staying,[34] the exchange takes place in the subterranean gloom of the
Catacombs of Rome—the site where the early Christians buried their
dead. This shift in location allows a layer of symbolism to be introduced
that is not in the novel, but that recalls certain aspects of the symbolic
mindscapes in Campion's earlier films. As Campion revealed in an interview with Michel Ciment, *The Portrait of a Lady,* in her mind, is "truly
a young girl's voyage towards darkness and underground regions."[35]
The new setting for Osmond's seduction of Isabel literalizes this metaphoric concept, by showing Isabel descending into a kind of Hades-like
darkness, associated with death, which symbolizes what the effect on
her will be of Osmond's later attempts to strip her of her identity and
suffocate her spirit. In the same interview, Campion describes how, for
her, Osmond—far from giving a positive reflection that can help to repair Isabel's emotional wound—is "a negative mirror image of Isabel's
spiritual aspirations": "She believes that she's looking for light, when she's
attracted by shadow, by a somber adventure that's going to swallow her
up. When Osmond makes his declaration of love, it's in a place plunged
in darkness, with beams of light. The set seems haunted."[36]

Symbolically, the Catacombs, as a place of darkness, stands in opposition to the darkness of the bush in *The Piano.* Whereas the bush
signifies a fecund place of enchantment, mysteries, and secret rites of
initiation promising liberation into a world of adult satisfactions, the
Catacombs signifies a place of sterility, lifelessness, disillusionment, and
death. Campion has thus inverted the direction of the symbolic signi-
fications inherent in the setting of the love encounter, from one movie
to the next, in a way that is consistent with her intention to debunk the
romantic myth to which she had given expression in *The Piano.*

Further changes to James's original settings occur when Ralph Touchett confronts Isabel over her intention to marry Osmond, and in the
final scenes at Gardencourt in which Isabel sees Ralph on his deathbed

and then finally rejects (or appears to reject) Caspar Goodwood, the most ardent and masculine of her suitors. In the first of these scenes, Campion shifts the encounter between Ralph and Isabel from a garden to the interior of a stable. Again, the shift in location enables Isabel's perversity to be depicted in a scene of shadows, and it also allows Campion to create shots of the bars on the stalls, which symbolically foreshadow the emotional prison in which Isabel will find herself once she has married Osmond. More than that, the stable associatively links Isabel's choice to Edith Campion, by evoking the horses Edith kept at the family's farm in Otaki and the fact that Jane Campion had a mare, on which she joined her mother in horse riding. The setting thus serves as a private symbol that activates the awareness latent in the filmmaker's mind of how similar Isabel's fate was to that of her mother.

In the other of these changed settings, Campion shifts the timing of Isabel's final encounters with Ralph Touchett and Caspar Goodwood from the May of James's novel to winter, depicting Gardencourt as covered in snow and ice. Again, this is a symbol that is familiar from Campion's earlier films, in which young women, like Pam in *A Girl's Own Story*, "feel the cold," signifying an emotional inhibition that arises out of fear of the destructiveness of which men are capable in their relationships with women. By the end of *The Portrait of a Lady*, Isabel has come to join her Campion-esque sisters in this state of chill, in which their experiences of life in general, and of relationships with men in particular, have induced a degree of fear that leaves them craving a comforting source of warmth. This is distinct from, although related to, the mood and tone of the ending of James's version of the story. In the novel, when Isabel informs Osmond of her wish to return to England to be with her cousin Ralph, who is dying, he does not want her to go on the grounds that, because they are "indissolubly united," there is a need to maintain "the honour of a thing" by keeping up the appearance of their marriage. Despite her disenchantment with Osmond, Isabel, when she hears this appeal, realizes that there are values she must observe that transcend the imperatives of the self:

> His last words were not a command, they constituted a kind of appeal; and, though she felt that any expression of respect on his part could only be a refinement of egotism, they represented something transcendent and absolute, like the

sign of the cross or the flag of one's country. He spoke in the name of something sacred and precious—the observance of a magnificent form.[37]

Even though she defies Osmond by going to England, once Goodwood has renewed his suit to her, this sense of the transcendent value of honor impels Isabel, as a married woman, to return to Osmond and Pansy in Rome: "She had not known where to turn; but she knew now. There was a very straight path."[38] As critics have noted, James's Isabel finds freedom and self-realization, paradoxically, by choosing to give up her freedom.[39]

Campion will have none of this, and her discomfort with the assumptions and values that determine the course of James's Isabel is reflected in the changes she made in the ending of her film, which in turn signal the same kind of ambivalence that is apparent in the several different endings she contemplated for *The Piano*. According to Laura Jones, the original ending of the film had Isabel fulfilling her promise to return to Pansy, to show what Isabel (as described by James) does when she takes her "very straight path" back to Rome: "This ending was shot and remained in the first few cuts of the film before Jane decided to draw the circle in tighter than James had."[40] One can see why Campion made this last-minute change. The whole logic of her adaptation worked toward an acceptance of eroticism with a "suitable" man (as against an "unsuitable" one like Osmond) as the idealized fulfillment of the romantic aspirations of a young woman like Isabel. Goodwood had been developed as just such a man, in his ardent, yet considerate (Baines-like) virility, and so it would have been unconvincing for Campion's Isabel to reject his advances outright in the manner of James's Isabel, given the yearning for, and susceptibility to, eroticism that Campion had made Isabel reveal earlier in the movie. Indeed, in the realization of this scene, Campion shows Isabel ardently responding to Goodwood's passion, once she has overcome her initial reticence. By cutting Isabel's return to Rome and by having her appear to hesitate on the threshold of the house at Gardencourt, with her hand on the door handle, Campion allows for the possibility that Isabel will reject the conventional codes of social respectability and will indeed retrace her steps to choose Goodwood. The fact that this choice is not enacted in the film, however, allows for a skeptical mistrust of the romantic ideal of love to be ambiguously perpetuated.

7 Changes such as those I have outlined shift the whole mode, tone, focus, and thematic import of Campion's version of *The Portrait of a Lady,* despite the fidelity that she shows to James's text in terms of the events and dialogue in the novel. This shows once again how the presence of a personal investment can support creative authorship even when the work appears to be merely an adaptation.

One of the most striking shifts was the introduction of explicit eroticism. This new preoccupation is announced in the prologue and resurfaces in a number of subsequent scenes. As Campion has said, she wanted to depict Isabel as "a woman with very strong sexual aspirations, who wants to be loved and who feels frustrated."[41] In this respect, Isabel is turned into a stand-in for Campion, who admits that she has "a deep need for intimacy."[42]

This idiosyncratic reconception of Isabel, which diverges sharply from James's vision, is everywhere apparent in the film. The most notorious instance is the scene Campion invented that shows Isabel writhing in erotic ecstacy at the fantasy of her three suitors making love to her. The scene in which Osmond declares that he is "absolutely in love" with Isabel is also laden with a more explicit erotic charge than occurs in the original. Whereas in the novel, Osmond does not actually kiss Isabel, but rather utters his announcement "in a tone of almost impersonal discretion" which, in Isabel's eyes, makes him appear "beautiful and generous,"[43] in Campion's version Osmond moves in, like an experienced Lothario, to give Isabel an extremely sexually suggestive and prolonged kiss which begins to arouse her erotic impulses. The effect he has on her of releasing her sexual desire is depicted in another fantasy sequence Campion inserts into the narrative of Isabel's travels, when we are shown the naked body of Isabel with Osmond's hand gliding suggestively over her stomach in an action that recalls the image of Osmond's hand encircling his daughter's waist on the occasion when Isabel first visits him. This sequence invests Isabel's experience of sexual desire with suggestions of an incestuous fantasy—of the sort that is evident in several of Campion's earlier movies.

The presence of these incestuous overtones is not accidental. In working with Laura Jones to prepare the screenplay, Campion consulted a number of literary critics and was deeply influenced by Alfred Habegger's reading of James, which she mentions in several of her interviews.[44]

She was particularly struck by Habegger's suggestion that Isabel was looking for a father substitute: "It is because she does not realize how deeply abandoned she feels by her father that Isabel is dangerously responsive to the studied self-portrait of the mutually dependent father and daughter."[45] A quotation from Habegger was even included in a European press kit for the movie. "I love this quote," Campion says: "Freedom and fatherlessness have split the heroine into two disconnected halves—a partly factitious determination to be her own master, and a dark fascination with images of dominance and submission." "The attraction," Campion adds, "is deeper than you can control."[46] In the light of what is known about Jane Campion's family circumstances, especially her need for her father's attention and her grief over his neglect of her, one can see that it is herself as much as Isabel that she is talking about here—which suggests that Isabel's eroticism in *The Portrait of a Lady* has the same origins as Ada's eroticism in *The Piano*, that is, an impulse that is motivated by an irresistible drive to procure emotional repair.

All of this, as I have suggested, makes Campion's Isabel a very different heroine from the one depicted by James, particularly with respect to Isabel's attitude toward eroticism. The differences are highlighted in the scene showing the final encounter between Isabel and Caspar Goodwood. As I suggested above, this scene in Campion's version shows Isabel actively responding sexually to Goodwood's passion. In James's version, Isabel's response is virtually the opposite. Even though she experiences the capacity to respond to Goodwood's love, which she registers as "the hot wind of the desert," she feels equally that "to let him take her in his arms would be the next thing to her dying," because she is the prisoner, one infers, of her powerful moral scrupulousness.[47] When Goodwood actually does take her in his arms and kisses her, with an effect of "white lightning," the force of his masculine sexuality prompts a recoiling in her:

> [I]t was extraordinarily as if, while she took it [the kiss], she felt each thing in his hard manhood that had least pleased her, each aggressive fact of his face, his figure, his presence, justified of its intense identity and made one with this act of possession. So had she heard of those wrecked and under water following a train of images before they sink. But when darkness returned she was free.[48]

As James's biographer puts it, Goodwood is "monotonously masculine; and if Isabel finds his sheer sexual force attractive it is also terrifying. For her, passion, or sex, is not freedom."[49] Thus, by the end of this encounter, James's Isabel, despite her attraction to Goodwood, has mastered herself, and through that self-mastery in the service of values that transcend her own inclination has finally achieved freedom, paradoxically, through a renunciation of freedom that liberates her from the vagaries of passionate impulse. In constructing this ending, James was adhering to the values of the puritanism that the founding fathers imported from Reformation England. Just as John Milton propounded in *Paradise Lost,* human beings are "sufficient to stand, but free to fall," which means that true liberty resides in a freely willed choice to adhere to God's law. In secular terms, Isabel's experience leads her to a felt understanding of this reality (in terms of late nineteenth-century assumptions), and her decision to reject Goodwood reflects her choice to abide by the secular equivalent of God's law. With Campion's Isabel, given that she is conceived as a late twentieth-century proto-feminist, we are left feeling far from sure that this will be the case; indeed, we are almost certain that it will not be.

The filmic mode itself works a significant change that reinforces the personal investment Campion makes in the story of Isabel Archer. In James's novel, the reader's perception of Isabel is guided by the subtle and psychologically nuanced commentary that is provided by James's narrator. Not only does the commentary allow us insight into what the characters are thinking, but it is also imbued with a pervasive irony, in that the reader shares with the narrator knowledge of events that Isabel does not possess. The presence of this irony establishes a rhetorical distance between the reader and the heroine that limits the degree to which we are inclined to identify with her. In Campion's film, this distance largely disappears as a result of the removal of James's authorial commentary. While Jones and Campion retained much of the dialogue in the novel verbatim, they also greatly streamlined and reduced the action by eliminating episodes (such as those involving Isabel's sisters) that do not focus on Isabel and the other main characters. The overall effect is to place Isabel more at the center of her world, in a way that is characteristic of the contemporary woman's film,[50] and to set up Isabel, rather than Ralph Touchett, as the film's center of consciousness.[51] The effect is to bring viewers into a closer relation with Isabel, in order to invite their sympathy.

It is this shift of perspective, I believe, combined with the reconception of Isabel as a "woman with very strong sexual aspirations," that tempered the enthusiasm of many critics and viewers for the film. As one reviewer noted, the governing credo of Campion's movie "adds up to little more than a beautifully embroidered anecdote of a bad marriage."[52] Another commentator observed that, with the removal of the overdeveloped sense of honor that James gave her, "Isabel seems a masochist and a fool—a woman merely afraid of her sexual desires, and therefore someone conventionally victimized by an earlier period's ideas about women" and thus "a cliché."[53] It is little wonder, given the severity of judgments like these, that Campion felt wounded by the reception given to *The Portrait of a Lady*, in which she had invested so much of herself in an attempt to gain the attention and approval she had longed for since she was a child.

8 By the time she had finished her adaptation of James, Campion, through her vicarious exploration of how Isabel could have relinquished her fortune to a man who would leave her miserable, must have attained a greatly deepened understanding of what had taken place with her mother. By working through the complexities inherent in James's depiction of the cross-generational bond between Osmond and his daughter, Pansy, and by registering the link between Isabel's emotional deprivation as a result of paternal neglect and her need for a father stand-in, she had also grown in her understanding of the potential wellsprings of some of her own impulses. Viewed in the context of Campion's overall oeuvre, *The Portrait of a Lady* can be seen as a major turning point—a point at which Campion felt that, for the time being, she had sufficiently exhausted her curiosity about her mother. She was now able to switch her attention again to her father, and in the next two chapters of this book, I will be arguing that *Holy Smoke* and *In the Cut* mark renewed attempts on Campion's part to resolve the equally problematic issues inhering in her relationship with that "damaged man" whom she adored, yet resented.

7 Exacting Revenge on "Cunt Men": *Holy Smoke* as Sexual Fantasy

1 By the time Campion had completed the three films of her middle career—*An Angel at My Table, The Piano,* and *The Portrait of a Lady*—she had gained a deep insight into the psychodynamics involved in the condition of women who are depressed or repressed. She had also, through her representation of the character of Isabel Archer, come to understand what happens when a woman, in Campion's words, "keeps trying to placate the husband who seems to hate her" and "stays on, hoping that by fixing up a damaged man she can heal her own childhood shocks and wounds."[1] Behind both of these explorations, as we have seen, there is a concern on Campion's part to understand her relationship with her mother, and how that relationship might have influenced certain of the predispositions she has recognized in herself.

Nevertheless, the ending of Campion's adaptation of Henry James's great work, as many critics have pointed out, leaves a strong impression that much unfinished business remains to be explored and that the indecisiveness depicted in Isabel Archer may reflect indecisiveness on the part of the filmmaker.[2] On one hand, by her own earlier admissions, she had grown deeply mistrustful of the romantic impulse; on the other hand, she continued to profess her desire for intimacy and a need to be loved. The problem for Campion was to find a way of reconciling these two contradictory impulses, and at the heart of this problem was the nature of eroticism: what role it might play not only in the subversion of romance, but also in the attainment of love—especially in a world in which, in her view, "organized religion had been largely rejected,"[3] meaning that one has to look elsewhere for something that can take its place.[4]

In addition, her exploration of the father-daughter relationship between Osmond and Pansy in James's novel had brought her face-to-face,
yet again, with issues that, one can infer, were inherent in her relationship with her own father, whose attention (according to Anna Campion)
the young Jane constantly sought in response to paternal neglect.[5] In
James's novel, one of the things that renders Isabel Archer vulnerable to
seduction by Osmond is, in the words of McHugh, "her mimetic capti-
vation by an image [of father and daughter],"[6] which is shown to have
arisen out of her father's neglect of her when she was a child. Isabel's
yearning to enter into a relationship with an older man who is capable of
repairing the lack she experienced as a child eventuates in the same kind
of incestuous fantasy that Campion repeatedly depicts in her heroines in
one film after another, implying her ongoing awareness of this syndrome
as a personal problematic to be resolved. *Holy Smoke* and *In the Cut,*
Campion's next two movies, as I will show, were designed specifically to
address the issues inherent in this complex—a classic manifestation of a
disturbed family romance—along with other issues that were important
to Campion in her personal life.

2   As usual, in talking about the genesis of *Holy Smoke,* Jane Campion
    is forthright in identifying the autobiographical roots of the movie,
which was based on an original script written collaboratively with her
sister, Anna. Apparently, Jane wrote "the beginning and the end," while
Anna wrote "the more intimate scenes between PJ and Ruth."[7] Commenting on the character of Ruth in the film, Jane Campion reveals that
"she is a girl pretty close to myself [at that age]":

> I was too cautious to do what she did in terms of going to India and allowing
> myself to be influenced like that at her age. I think I would have been terrified.
>   I had a very close friend who was my flatmate and she joined the Moonies. It
> really threw me that she could so completely change, and she was really working
> strongly to get me to join her.[8]

Campion, then, as a young woman, had become interested in spirituality as a phenomenon that offered hope in a world that seemed to her to
have rejected religion and spiritual values. This interest is reflected in
her decision to attend the Forum,[9] one of the personal growth seminars
conducted by Anthony Robbins (commonly known as the "Mahatma

of motivation") in the late 1980s and early 1990s. Despite her mockery of tantrism and meditation in *Sweetie,* Campion also attended classes in meditation, and in 1999 referred to herself as having "greatly changed" since that time. Even today, she practices meditation each day in accordance with the Vipassana method.[10]

At the same time as Campion was developing her interest in spirituality, she was also trying to come to terms with the power of adult sexuality and was intrigued about how these two powerful realities in life—sex and spirituality—could be reconciled. This is understandable, given that she was born and raised in a country with a deeply rooted puritanical, repressive ethos. As Campion revealed to a French interviewer, "I think that my interest in sex and other forms of relating within a couple led me to the story [of *Holy Smoke*]": "I started to develop the idea in my head of a film on spirituality in our era, by trying to introduce the notion of seduction, complexity, as well as the mundane realities which, in my opinion, are implicated in every spiritual voyage."[11]

For an Antipodean born in the 1950s, the conjunction of sex and spirituality would be a contradiction of terms. At the time she was making *An Angel at My Table* and *The Piano,* Campion expressed her awareness of "the puritan side of the colonists" in New Zealand, together with her opinion that "Anglo-Saxons have not resolved the relationship between what is animal and sexual in themselves and their rationality."[12] One of her main aims in *The Piano* was to depict a revolt against the repression enforced by such an ethos. It is not surprising, therefore, that Campion—especially after her forays into showing the consequences of pursuing an active eroticism—should seek to explore how this powerful, even irresistible, animal reality in the lives of men and women could relate to the thirst in the human soul for spirituality.

Her interest in making a film that addresses these issues, Campion reveals, came from "a two- or three-night romance she had with a much younger man. 'He had cystic fibrosis,' she said, 'and I knew he wasn't going to live very long.'" Campion does not elaborate precisely why, or how, this encounter entered into the movie of *Holy Smoke,* but she does confess, "Sometimes you get touched by someone's spirit and it helps you identify a different path in life that you never forget."[13] The episode obviously left a powerful impression on Campion, as she picked up the topic in her short story "Big Shell," published in *Rolling Stone* in 1988, in which the first-person narrator recounts a one-night stand with a young man in a wheelchair.[14] Even though Campion has not explained how her fleeting romance with a man with a disability prompted the idea for *Holy Smoke,* it can be inferred from a comparison of the movie to this earlier attempt to create a fictionalized version of the encounter. In this chapter, I will identify the thematic continuities that persist between the two works, as well as the complex symbolic displacements that connect the stories in both works to Campion's life story.

3 Campion's initial impulse had been to make a cinematic adaptation of Christopher Isherwood's autobiographical account of his experience in India, *My Guru and His Disciple.* There are many references in Campion's interviews to this ambition. In 1993, she alerted Thomas Bourguignon and Michel Ciment to the fact that she had an adaptation of *My Guru and His Disciple* in sight, along with James's *The Portrait of a Lady.*[15] In May of that year, she revealed that Philip Lopate was working on a screenplay for this project.[16] Early in 1994, she was still working on it, with script editor Billy MacKinnon, with whom she had entered into a fleeting relationship.[17] Soon after that, however, the project faltered, and Campion made *The Portrait of a Lady* instead.

To distinguished French critic and cinephile Michel Ciment, Campion revealed why she had been attracted to the idea of an adaptation of Christopher Isherwood's autobiographical memoir:

> Isherwood's book recounted the story of his friendship with Prabhavananda, one of the first Asian gurus who visited the West. I was fascinated, when I read it, to observe Isherwood's attempts to turn himself into a monk before he had renounced sex—the vow of chastity was too difficult for him! What he wanted more than anything else, in this world, was intimacy, and love. He still remained, nevertheless, friends with Prabhavananda, because he respected the faith expressed in the latter's precepts.[18]

According to Campion, the problem was that she "never succeeded in getting a script that really satisfied [her], despite several attempts by different writers."[19] Campion also felt that, "as much as she loves men," she would have problems making a movie with a man at its center, especially one who was gay.[20] Campion therefore decided to pursue her ongoing interest in how spirituality could be reconciled with eroticism, but this time in a script written by her and Anna.

4 The film that Campion ended up making is strongly marked by the influence of certain movies from the 1970s that she confesses to having admired. Campion is frank in admitting the influence exerted by Bernardo Bertolucci's *Last Tango in Paris,* the hit erotic film of the 1970s (regarded by some at the time as pornographic).[21] Indeed, picking up on this influence, one French reviewer referred to *Holy Smoke* as "Dernier tango dans le bush" (Last Tango in the Bush).[22] What is surprising in Campion's 1999 version of the erotic encounter is the way that she intermingles the explicit, nearly pornographic nature of the eroticism with a search for spiritual enlightenment. As she says:

> It's unfashionable to say you're concerned about what life means. . . . Nobody after they're 40 hasn't examined death closely. . . . The film attempts to prove that an authentic spiritual life is not just about good behaviour, religious theory or even spiritual experience. Far from being isolated from the chaos of life, . . . it occurs as strongly in the midst of your greatest stumbling as it does in nun- or monk-like contemplation in a cave.[23]

The great stumbling to which Campion refers is exemplified, in the film, in Ruth's need to be loved and also in her need for that love to be expressed through the visceral pleasure achieved through sexual lovemaking. In depicting this, Campion was casting off the traces of her repressive upbringing in New Zealand during the second half of the twentieth century and, behind that, the 2,000-year-old tradition of Pauline Christianity—a bold enterprise. In pursuing this ambition, Campion drew upon the resources of the unconscious just as she had done, preeminently, in *The Piano.* Indeed, *Holy Smoke* bears all the hallmarks of a sexual fantasy that has been concretized and made explicit, both in its structure and in the nature of the psychological mechanisms that are depicted as being at work in its action.

In a groundbreaking study of sexual fantasies, drawing on the survey-based findings of a research project conducted over several years, the British psychotherapist Brett Kahr has hypothesized that sexual fantasies almost invariably have their origins in early trauma, whether this be physical, sexual, or emotional: *"one cannot be traumatized,"* he says, "*without experiencing a traumatic consequence*" (emphasis in original).[24] The function of sexual fantasies is to provide psychic relief from the pain of these ongoing consequences—which continue to seek expression throughout the course of one's adult life—by enabling the fantasizer, through the agency of unconscious structures, to transform pain into pleasure "through the act of eroticization."[25] Sexual fantasies achieve this by elaborating scenarios in which the suffering person can either enact a mastering of the trauma that originally affected him or her, or achieve the fulfillment of unconscious wishes, or self-medicate against psychic pain.[26] Often, a mechanism of reversal is involved, which provides "a strategy for reducing mental anguish by switching positions with a perpetrator, especially in fantasy."[27] This reversing of real-life experience is also often accompanied by an element of sadism or deliberate humiliation, which serves to facilitate the discharge of resentment or fear. Whatever the form they take, the purpose of sexual fantasies, in Kahr's words, is to transform trauma "into the triumph of control."[28]

There are plenty of reasons for concluding that the Campion sisters, whether consciously or unconsciously, invoked mechanisms of sexual fantasy in the construction of *Holy Smoke*. In the first place, Anna Campion is a trained psychotherapist. This is reflected in recurrent references to psychoanalytic concepts in the novelization of *Holy Smoke,* such as PJ talking about the "dialogue between the inner and outer selves" in which "we are always chatting away with an internalised other" in a "constant dualism," and his acknowledgment of the need to "monitor the transference, counter-transference situation."[29] In one of her interviews, Anna reveals that the sessions in which she and Jane worked on the script for *Holy Smoke* were "verging on family therapy,"[30] which implies her awareness of a source of trauma within the family that the elaboration of this fictive scenario by the sisters was meant to address.

The presence of strong elements of fantasy prompts one to think of how Jane, as a child, according to Anna Campion, was constantly devising plays in which she would enact all the parts, in an attempt to control the world and make it pay attention to her. Such an activity foreshadows the fully elaborated, complex dramas that constitute certain sexual fantasies. As Anna points out, her filmmaking sister in adult life was merely continuing her practice of compensating for her early lack of parental attention, especially that of her father, through the creation of adult plays in her films.[31]

The possibility that *Holy Smoke* may be the enactment of a concretized sexual fantasy is confirmed, I believe, by the presence in the film of a microcosmic version of just such a fantasy. This occurs in the sequence in which Ruth's sister-in-law, Yvonne, describes to PJ how she is the author of love letters addressed to herself, which purport to be written by lovers, who turn out to be imaginary. In the same scene, she also recounts how, when she is engaged in sexual intercourse with her husband, Robbie, she is actually, in fantasy, having "sex with film stars"—the images of whom she sticks on her bedside drawer, so that she can look at them during the act. Jane Campion has acknowledged that, in addition to closely identifying with the character of Ruth, she also identifies with Yvonne:

> At first I thought I was Ruth, the younger woman, and I still do. Real love seems psychotic most of the time. I haven't been very successful at it myself! I feel myself as Yvonne, too—the complete ditz, who gets manipulated all the time, falls in love, is just a romantic idiot who fantasises sex and love all day long.[32]

Because her obsession with eroticism as a means of gaining attention anticipates Ruth's adoption of eroticism as a form of self-medication, Yvonne's presence in the movie underlines the possibility that Ruth's later actions may be serving the same function as Yvonne's fantasies do for her—and, at another level, the movie as a whole may be serving a similar function for the filmmaker.

Finally, another sign that the fiction of *Holy Smoke* is informed by elements of sexual fantasy is the presence of many of the mechanisms that Kahr has identified as being characteristic of sexual fantasy. I am referring, in particular, to the reversal that takes place when Ruth assumes the dominant role in her encounter with PJ Waters, the exit counselor, and then ritually humiliates and degrades him, becoming an "avenging angel" in the process. This kind of reversal is characteristic of any number of the fantasies gathered through Kahr's research, in which an emotionally deprived woman seeks to reverse the real-life experience of an uninterested father by creating in her mind a man who has a compulsive interest in her and her body, and over whom she can take charge.[33] To my mind, there is no doubt whatsoever that Campion's movie is presenting a fantasy of this sort.

The most compelling evidence of the presence of sexual fantasy, however, is suggested by a comparison between *Holy Smoke* and the earlier short story "Big Shell," which was based on the real-life episode that Campion has said gave her the idea for the film. Because this story is not readily accessible, having been published in the "Summer Stories" section of the Australian edition of the magazine *Rolling Stone* in 1988, I will briefly outline it here, before speculating on how it relates to the film.

"Big Shell" describes the experience of Louise, who has been devastated by the end of an unsatisfactory relationship with her boyfriend, which has caused her to sink into a deep depression when she realizes he has gone: "I went down in a big spiral. Once I felt I was going down I stopped trying to be bright or happy, I decided to go right on down, and down as down could go."[34] Fearing that she is "going to fall apart," Louise takes a job in a souvenir shop selling shells, where she meets a young American man, Dale, who is bound to a wheelchair and who reminds her of her brother, Trevor, who was disabled from birth, got into drugs, and died with a blue plastic bag pulled over his head and tied around his neck. Having decided that Dale "is the most courageous man I had ever met," Louise invites him home in anticipation they might have sex, acknowledging that "I wasn't asleep to the idea that this was some sex ode to my brother." When she invites Dale to sleep in her bed, he comments on the age difference between them (she is "quite a bit older" than he) and mocks aspects of her apartment, offending her, so that she banishes him to the sofa bed in the living room. During the night, however, Dale comes into her room, awakens her, and asks to be lifted into her bed, whereupon he breaks down crying and begins to suck on her breast. This, in turn, releases a flood of grief in Louise:

> I felt a lump deep in my chest, a definite physical presence, that painfully and slowly started to move upwards, until I felt this same lump in my throat. The lump rested there a while, before starting my lips off quivering and my eyes blinking, and then as the lump came into my mouth and finally out into the world my body started shaking and a whole series of little gulps and cries came up out of me. I was panting and blubbering and holding onto Dale, stroking his head, thinking of him as a lame frog who was somehow magically empowered to save me. A sort of medieval witches cure.

In the morning, Dale abruptly leaves, and Louise decides to quit the shell shop. On the night before her final day, she dreams that Dale is inside the giant shell that is on display in the shop, but in the morning she realizes that "nobody could possibly fit in it. Not even a child or a baby."[35]

At first sight, this plot might seem a long way from the story in *Holy Smoke,* but on closer inspection, it becomes apparent that a number of continuities link them: the presentation of a sexual encounter as the pretext and catalyst for an evacuation of painful feelings that are otherwise unspeakable; the idea of a lover serving as a stand-in for a family member; the existence of an age discrepancy between the two main protagonists; and the rendering of the male character into the condition of a child who needs to be comforted by the heroine, who takes on the role of a nurturing, protective mother. The basic thematic configuration in each work is the same, even though the outer details of the stories are different.

The nature of the changes made to the external details from the short story to the film is also highly illuminating as far as Campion's creative process is concerned. One sees the same mixing and matching of the different elements upon which she is drawing, to which she confessed in the composition of *Sweetie.* A character who is a stand-in for the heroine's brother in "Big Shell" is converted into a character who is a stand-in for the heroine's father in *Holy Smoke*—an adjustment that perhaps removes an additional layer of unconscious censorship that had resided in the earlier work. In *Holy Smoke,* the direction of the age discrepancy is reversed between the two sexes, with the male protagonist in the film replacing Louise as the older person who suffers humiliation, while the heroine, Ruth, takes the place of the boy in the short story who asks to be taken into the bed of his older female lover. Such mixing and matching, however, does not obscure the constant factor in both works, which is the grief in the heroine and her need to give that grief expression through entering into an intimate relationship with a man whose vulnerabilities elicit from her a compassion that enables her to discharge her pent-up feelings of grief, which arise from problems in the past. Ruth and Louise end up manifesting the same assumption that Campion attributed to Isabel in *The Portrait of a Lady:* by fixing a damaged man, they can heal their own psychic shocks and wounds.

5   Once one recognizes the lines of connection between Campion's real-life experiences and her successive attempts to create fictive

representations that are designed to address them at a symbolically displaced remove, it becomes easier to see how *Holy Smoke* functions as the concretized, dramatized elaboration of a sexual fantasy relating to an unresolved family romance. To demonstrate this, I will look not only at the film itself, but also at the novelized version written by Anna and Jane Campion, in which certain aspects that are only implicitly suggested in the film are more explicitly delineated, as in the novelization of *The Piano*.

In the first place, one observes that the existence and origins of the trauma from which Ruth suffers are carefully signaled in the movie. The clearest evidence of this occurs in the encounter between Ruth and her father after she has discovered the deceit that has been perpetrated on her, and she upbraids him for his hypocrisy in chastising her for using obscene language in front of her mother. In response, Ruth hurls at him the hitherto unspoken, dark secret of the family:

> RUTH   "You can talk, you hypocrite!
> Where's your little love bomb?"
> FATHER   "I don't know what you're talking about."
> RUTH   "Yes you do! Where's my half sister then, Dad?
> You know, your secretary's secret little love bomb?"
> FATHER   "What love bomb?
> [To the other members of the family] She's in a complete fantasy!"

Gilbert Barron, it transpires from this exchange, is a womanizer who has begotten an illegitimate child, Ruth's half sister. Even though he tries to deflect Ruth's accusation by dismissing her as being "in a complete fantasy," the other members of the family know about this secret at one level, even though on the surface they try to deny its existence. The novelized version of the story is much more explicit on this point, as is revealed in an interior monologue given to Ruth:

> Mum gets me to do this, say the unspeakable, the things that no one wants to bloody well hear, well they do but in secret. She must like the shock, some sort of payback revenge. The thing is, Mum always tells me these things, forgets she's said them or alluded to them, and then feigns innocence when I bring them up. I'm not a good secret-keeper, which is why I'm told. I still don't know much about this half sister, apart from the fact that she's the result of one of Dad's pathetic affairs.[36]

It is not too difficult to discern here a scarcely veiled allusion to Richard Campion's affairs in real life and to the half sister of whose exis-

"Where's your little love bomb?" Ruth confronts her father in *Holy Smoke*.

tence the Campion sisters had recently become aware. Indeed, the effect on Ruth of her father's betrayal of his marital fidelity is to fill her with a sense of the same kind of paternal neglect (experienced emotionally as desertion, and accompanied by a longing for compensatory attention) to which the Campion sisters repeatedly attest in their various interviews. As the movie proceeds, Ruth is shown to be suffering from an acute form of emotional deprivation as a result of this paternal abandonment. It is the pain deriving from this feeling of deprivation that motivates her actions, both in her preliminary search for a compensatory spirituality and subsequently in her trading (or, rather, trade-in) of soul for sex.

Ruth has realized, as she tells PJ (in the novel), that her father and her brothers are "cunt men": "they believe in porno magazines, they just can't get enough smut."[37] In the early parts of the movie, she perceives that PJ is no different in his willingness to use women as sexual objects without making any emotional connection with them. Campion has observed:

> The sex drive is very powerful—so seductive that if there were another drive as strong, we'd never reach enlightenment! And it's PJ's Achilles heel; he's a compulsive seducer. And a joyless one; he's not making love at all to the girls—it's practically a pornographic exercise, he's wanking into them.[38]

Like her creator, Ruth has come to mistrust this sexual drive, not only because it has led her father to commit adultery, but also because of her awareness that it can cause men to depersonalize the women they use to satisfy their lust. As Campion puts it, "Ruth is aware that, for him [PJ], she's just not there, and she needs to be seen as a human being."[39]

The deprivation of love from which she suffers as a result of the dysfunction in the family, we infer, provokes an existential anxiety in Ruth. This is most specifically depicted, in the novelized version, in a description of Ruth's "despair chart." As she lies on her bed in the halfway hut, trying to conjure up a masturbation fantasy that involves Baba, her guru, Ruth recalls an episode from her earlier life. At the age of fifteen, when she had asked her friend Zoey, "What's the point?" Zoey had answered, "It's a black dot that will grow and fester and telescopically enlarge until it will consume you like a dark cave." In response, Ruth had placed a black dot on the wall next to her bed, which she had drawn around each day until it grew to be the size of her fist, and then as large as her head.[40] Ruth's reaction to the sight of this enlarging black mark, and her sense of the meaninglessness it symbolized, had been deep distress:

> I thought I ought to do something to darkly celebrate, like putting a plastic bag on my head and tying it. But instead I sobbed for two days. It began because my hair had been cut two inches too short and I looked very bad, but that wasn't the real reason, the real reason was I hadn't discovered the reason to live.[41]

Underneath Ruth's ironic self-mockery, one senses the existence of a void in her inner psychic space, and the terms in which she describes it are strongly reminiscent of the words given to Edith Campion in Anna Campion's docudrama, *The Audition:* "I can't help thinking that life is meaningless."[42] It is Ruth's paradoxical and contradictory response to this deep existential despair—along with the emotional deprivation and indignation caused by the self-regarding behavior of men that fuels it—that provides the substance of *Holy Smoke,* in both its cinematic and novelistic forms.

6   The pattern of Ruth's response to this underlying trauma is marked by two forms of reversal: an inversion of the direction of Ruth's libidinal investment, in which she comes to realize that she is "trading sex for soul,"[43] and a reversal of roles in her power relationship with PJ Waters. Both reversals represent an attempt to palliate psychic pain through the discharge of perturbing emotions that cannot be brought under control in any other way.

At the beginning of the film, and more explicitly in the novel, an ironic distance is set up between the nature of Ruth's spiritual experience in India, as she perceives it, and what is really taking place. At the same time, the viewer is invited to sympathize with her. This paradoxical invitation to adopt diametrically opposed responses is communicated in several ways. In the first instance, the use of Neil Diamond's song "Holly Holy" in the soundtrack that accompanies the opening credits is highly significant in its contextual implications. This song has struck some reviewers as inappropriately corny and kitschy, and to some degree it is; but if one listens carefully to the lyrics, it helps to explain why Ruth was motivated to join Chidaatma Baba's cult. The song invites an unspecified listener to "dream only of me," while the singer is described as "Wanting only you." The subject of the lyrics also wants to "Touch a man who can't walk upright" and hopes that "that lame man, he gonna fly." As the credit sequence unfolds, we see a procession of happy young women cult members, in pairs (linked as if they were sisters), passing by. During this sequence, the camera focuses on Ruth's wistful gaze as her head turns to follow them, and while this occurs, the words of the song say, "Take the lonely child / And the seed / Let it be full with tomorrow." With characteristic brilliance and imaginative insight, Jane Campion has metaphorically captured all the longing of an emotionally deprived child to find some source of comfort that is capable of consoling and healing her, so that she can move forward into a future that contains hope. Given that, as Kathleen McHugh has pointed out, Baba means "father," one can infer that at the deepest unconscious level (as the words of the song ironically suggest) Ruth's longing for the transcendent spirituality that the cult seems to offer is really an attempt to fill the gap in the internal world of a neglected child, with the guru standing in as a father substitute.[44]

As the credit sequence ends, the film begins a new sequence set in the present, during which Ruth's friend Prue reports to Ruth's parents that their daughter has burned her return airplane ticket and converted to Baba's cult. The representation of Ruth's father, Gilbert Barron, at this point—shown to be provocatively and inappropriately dressed in nothing but his underwear, and directing a lecherous gaze at Prue—illustrates the reference in Neil Diamond's song to the lame man "who can't walk upright." Gilbert's "lameness," metaphorically speaking, resides in his inability to control an addiction to sex that compels him to hit upon

women. For those who know the background of the Campion family, this
sequence will immediately conjure an association with the adulterous
father. Moreover, the presence of a further allusive image—a cat lying
along the back of the sofa on which Gilbert and Prue are seated—also
sets in motion an association between this incident and the sad, real-life
story of Edith Campion. The viewer who is sensitive to the latent overdetermination of these images will be led to infer that Ruth's conversion
owes almost everything to her distress at the dark secret at the heart of
this family, which the film will reveal: her father's sexual compulsion
(which all its members know about, but which no one will mention),
combined with Gilbert Barron's concomitant neglect of his daughter,
which has inflicted on her a painful emotional wound that she is seeking,
through Eastern mysticism, to assuage.

The viewer is warned against taking Ruth's conversion at face value
by the garish, kitschy, sentimentalized Pierre et Gilles explosion of butterflies and flowers that is depicted in the vision Ruth experiences when
the guru touches her on the forehead to open her "third eye."[45] Although
beautiful in its own right, this image recalls the psychedelic pop art
used by the Beatles on posters and record covers when they were going
through their own phase of Eastern mysticism during the late 1960s.
It thus ironically undercuts the audience's ability to believe in Ruth's
conversion—by conveying the naïveté and vulnerability that mark her
at this stage in her life. As Jane Campion has said in her interviews, the
"energy" that Ruth displays at this moment is

> elemental, beautiful, transforming, and it's only available for a short period of
> time. It's a kind of girlshine; as she learns more about life it will be shadowed.
> That is the nature of growing up. *Holy Smoke* begins in joyous mystery, before
> the shadowing. And what a struggle back from there, up from there![46]

As if to demonstrate why there will be a shadowing, Campion undercuts the spectator's ability to believe in the viability of Ruth's belief
that she has found "the way" by having Genevieve Lemon, the actress
who played the "nutcase" Dawn (to use Anna Campion's word), appear as
Ruth's acolyte friend. In this brilliant piece of casting and acting, Lemon
manages to convey the kind of near-moronic, beatific stultification that
Campion, in her skeptical moments, recognizes as inhering in immature
"conversions" of this kind. Campion, as the viewer is invited to do, would
like to believe in this form of so-called spirituality, but is unable to do

so without irony, because (as the mimesis of these sequences shows) she is aware, if only at an unconscious level, that the impulse toward such spirituality can be motivated by a desperate need to find some way of allaying psychic pain.

The novelization of *Holy Smoke* renders more explicitly the presence of the underlying ideas and associations that I have outlined above. In his second letter to Carol and PJ at Pulse Human Resource & Development Center, Stan Mikle, their professional colleague in Australia, reports that Ruth is "up against our old fiend Chidaatma Baba, now you see him— now you don't. Currently re-constructing out of Rishikesh [a holy city for Hindus located in the foothills of the Himalayas in northern India]."[47] This information lets us know that Baba—described a few lines later as "old Daddy"—has been implicated in prior instances of luring young women, which have necessitated intervention using the services of PJ's agency. Indeed, later in *Holy Smoke,* we learn that in the past Baba raped a thirteen-year-old girl, and that the guru habitually rapes his disciples, both female and male.[48] PJ himself was a victim of this kind of abuse, perpetrated by his own guru, Singh: "All was bliss. Then one historic day he [Singh] took me to his private rooms and hugged me. I thought, I'm special, he's chosen me, very happy. Next thing my fly's unzipped, my tool is out, my dick's hanging in his hand and he's rubbing away."[49] When Ruth, fascinated and engaged, asks what this event "means," PJ answers: "It means, well . . . to me it means, uh-oh, I didn't come, he couldn't fuck me." . . . "You don't think he could have loved you?" "Ruth, I thought he was God."[50]

The result, for PJ, was profound disillusionment—and it is this depth of disillusionment that, in the course of their time in the halfway hut, PJ manages to impart to Ruth. And by provoking Ruth's doubt, PJ re-activates her fear—the existential fear, induced by the inability of the circumstances within her family to provide her with a source of security, which she had sought to palliate by seeking refuge in spirituality.

Campion talks about the kind of fear that is involved:

> *Holy Smoke* is as much about fear as it is about power or eroticism or spirituality. "Fear is so enormous. You spend most of your time in your twenties building up some protective surface, and then you feel its inadequacy and how it's going to hold you back and you spend the rest of your life trying to strip it away, or else you end up living a horrible compromise which isn't living at all," says Jane.[51]

The response to this fear that Ruth will adopt is foreshadowed, in the first half of the movie, by that of Yvonne, her sister-in-law.

Yvonne serves to embody the latent reaction to fear that Ruth is shown as seeking to repress by surrendering herself to a willed belief in the efficacy of spirituality. It is for this reason that Jane Campion confesses a strong identification with Yvonne, as well as with Ruth:

> I don't feel so far from Yvonne sometimes. She's honest: "How can anyone resist you? You're a cult in yourself." She senses the possibility of incredible despair: "Don't go there. There's no point in thinking about it. You just have to be cheerful." For Yvonne, PJ is the kind of lover you're so mad about you miss their terrible aspect.[52]

The hypersexualization that causes Yvonne constantly to throw herself seductively at PJ, and which leads her to give him a blow job despite the fact he is entirely indifferent to her, is her way of protecting herself against the "possibility of incredible despair" that lies below the surface of her conscious awareness. It is the arrival of a similar awareness that will lead Ruth to abandon her spirituality and lurch toward sex as an alternative way of palliating the latent psychic suffering that she is desperately seeking to allay and disavow. In this respect, Yvonne stands in a similar relation to Ruth as Dawn in *Sweetie* does to her sister, Kay. Even though Yvonne is presented in *Holy Smoke* as Ruth's sister-in-law, she is really a split-off part of the same personality, representing the shadow side of Ruth's spirituality, just as Dawn in *Sweetie* represented the anarchic obverse of Kay's repression. Ruth's hyper-spirituality and Yvonne's hyper-sexuality, since they both represent attempts to respond to the same threat of despair, are depicted by Campion as obverse sides of the same coin. This means that Ruth's sudden switch from spirituality to an equally intense investment in visceral sexuality is far from surprising; it is the logical outcome of an inability to palliate the psychic pain from which she suffers, as a result of the dysfunction within her family, in any other manner.

7 Ruth is vulnerable to PJ Waters because he, like Chidaatma Baba, is potentially yet another stand-in for her father—whose love and attention she feels she is lacking. This is revealed with particular clarity in the novelized version of *Holy Smoke,* in which we learn that Ruth, when she first encounters PJ, after the rest of the family have brought him in

to "de-programme" her after her return to Australia, perceives him as "an old time jock my father's age."[53] Even though the enforced situation prompts her to "hate him" at first sight, she discovers that "pathetically I didn't want him to hate me."[54] This internal reaction in Ruth to PJ reflects her deep need for paternal interest and approval, which she believes is lacking in the dysfunctional circumstances of her family. As her sequestered contact with him lengthens, she experiences an irresistible need to attract his attention: "The crazy shit is I can't leave him alone, I have this craving to go on and on talking and saying things. Anything I want, being anything. Bad, terrible, I don't care."[55] When she finally succeeds in seducing him, she reveals (in the novel) that she has done so largely for the sake of preventing him from walking through the door:

> If he walks through that door it's finished. It's all over. I scream, "Stop! Stop!" thinking, I will have you, I will! Then when I'm just about on him I let it go, it's loud, he stops in shock. I'm shocked too; that I can do it, have pee running down my legs. I give him a long full kiss, tongue deep inside. He's gasping, mouth panting at me.[56]

The naked Ruth uncontrollably voiding urine is one of the most striking scenes in the history of cinema, for it indicates the intensity of her emotional need which, at that moment, cannot be expressed adequately in any other way. Commenting on this scene, Campion has said: "Children wet their beds when they can't cope with trauma. It's a fantastic expression of distress."[57] The trauma that causes Ruth to regress to this childlike state is the fact that PJ has successfully destroyed the protective ramparts that, at an unconscious level, she felt she had erected by converting to a mystical religion. When her faith in that religion is destroyed by PJ's demonstration of its hypocrisy, the pain inherent in the trauma against which she has been protecting herself comes flooding back, and the distress causes her to pee uncontrollably—like a frightened child in her dreams.

This renewed vulnerability leaves Ruth with a need to find an alternative form of psychic self-protection, and we see her turning her earlier impulse inside out. She now seeks to allay the grief she cannot express verbally with the opiate of sex—just as her sister-in-law, Yvonne, had earlier been shown to do.

Ruth is facilitated in doing this by the fact that PJ, who is also emotionally needy, is an easy victim. Ruth recognizes him at once as a "cunt man," like her father and brothers, not only because of his vanity—reflected in his habits of dying his hair and of wearing ironed jeans and snakeskin boots—but also because she sees him spraying breath freshener into his mouth before their first encounter, just as Yvonne, another sex addict, sprays perfume into her crotch before her nighttime assignation with PJ in the cattle yards.

In the course of their encounter, PJ comes to recognize that his compulsive womanizing and his need to dominate arise from his own deep neediness.[58] Her awareness of this neediness allows Ruth, before her breakdown, to intuit the nature of his defendedness: "You can't stand the fact that I've got faith, can you? Because you're so frightened and dried up, defending yourself with your textbooks and all your bloody sources, that feeling, just trusting your heart is beyond you and without that you can't love, you can't know anything."[59] Just as Ruth's factitious faith is ripe to be deconstructed, PJ's factitious refuge in womanizing is equally ripe to be demolished.

8 The demolition comes when Ruth exploits their mutual vulnerabilities to effect a transposition of roles in the power relationship between them, and it is here that the movie most clearly comes to resemble the enactment of a sexual fantasy. Prompted by the destructive side of her mind, which tells her, "It's all lost, it's all over, your faith is fucked, there is nothing out there, all there is is fantasy and the grand no-purpose reality," Ruth decides to show PJ "the true face of his pussy religion."[60] In doing so, she is seeking to achieve two contradictory things. On one hand, she is trying to secure confirmation that she is loved, while, on the other hand, she is trying to punish him for the self-regarding lecherousness that his sexual objectification of her implies.

At the level of fantasy, both these impulses represent an attempt on Ruth's part to discharge the feelings she has toward her father, for whom PJ, in her unconscious, is a stand-in. This is most clearly revealed, in the novel, during the scene outside the disco when PJ intervenes to prevent the drunken Ruth from having sex with two "dog boys." Seeing PJ approach, Ruth says, "Hi Daddy. . . . I want to fuck you, Daddy. Come on Daddy. Daddy FUCK ME!!!"[61] At one level, then, Ruth's desire to have sex with PJ represents the fulfillment of an incestuous fantasy arising out of a need to repair the narcissistic mortification she has experienced as a result of her father's neglect and sexual perfidy. At another level, she wants to make him suffer by inflicting on him the treatment he metes out to others. As Jane Campion puts it:

> She [Ruth] . . . throws back at PJ a reflection of his chauvinism and his sexual vanity. She acts towards PJ out of the full force of knowing what it is to be sexually objectified: to only be seen in terms of one's beauty—which in some ways, is not to be seen at all. This is why she dresses him up in the red dress, so that when he looks at himself he is seeing a woman his own age, someone sexually undesirable. She wants to appal [sic] him with his own double standard.[62]

Ruth's sexual engagement with PJ, therefore, expresses a combination of loving hate, resentment, and yearning.

Ruth's desire to punish PJ and, in him, her father reflects an element of sadism, which, like role reversal, is characteristic of certain types of sexual fantasy. In order to feel vindicated and in control, she ritually degrades and humiliates him. At the nightclub, she arouses his jealousy by provocatively sharing a lesbian kiss with Meryl, the sister of Yani, who is the boyfriend of Ruth's oldest brother, Tim, and by making out with the two "dog boys." The effect on PJ is to make him "want to hurt her" out of jealous anger, because he "couldn't take anyone touching her."[63] This shows that Ruth, through projection, has successfully managed to arouse in PJ the same negative feelings she was shown earlier to have toward her father. In this way, she evacuates her own psychic pain by transferring it to a stand-in for the perpetrator.

She also tries to undermine his confidence in himself as a lover by ridiculing the idea that their sexual encounter has any worth, by mocking him on account of his age, and by telling him that she wants "a young man." In a scene strikingly reminiscent of *A Girl's Own Story* (when Gloria and her brother, Graeme, have sex while pretending to be cats), Ruth pretends to be a cat, crawling on all fours to PJ, "flopping [her] . . . big paws onto his knees," and saying "Meow," in order to satirize the presumption she imagines he might have that their lovemaking was meaningful to her. As she takes control, Ruth starts to act like a dominatrix, heaping ever more hurtful abuse on him until she makes him over into "a same-age fun-loving woman" in order to present him with a mirror image of his undesirability. PJ's humiliation is complete when she forces him to recognize that he is a "dirty old man." By the time PJ is

"You look lovely"—a fantasy of role reversal in *Holy Smoke*.

moved, pathetically, to protest that he was "young once, and handsome too," Ruth realizes she has beaten him: "I won didn't I? I'm on top, aren't I? I'm the winner."

The problem for Ruth is that, in the face of the breakdown of the defensive carapace she had constructed through adherence to the supra-rational certainties of a mystical spirituality, the course of action she has adopted in erecting a new defense has made her "ruth-less"—that is, she has become emptied of the compassion that her name literally signifies.[64] This becomes apparent to her when Ruth asks PJ to tell her what she is, and he replies by writing on her forehead, in reversed letters, the words "BE KIND." It is significant that Ruth has to look at a reflection of herself in a mirror to be able to decipher what PJ has written. This motif of looking at one's reflection in a mirror, as we have seen, is one of the filmmaker's favorite symbolic devices. Here, it suggests that Ruth needs to recognize the wound in her psychological makeup that is causing her to act in a way that is diametrically opposed to love, which her earlier conversion to spirituality indicates is the true object of her search. The sudden realization that she has betrayed her own core values by seducing and humiliating PJ provokes a bitter self-attack in Ruth. Gripped by "dark, heavy thoughts," she confesses the return of her fear: "I'm scared that, despite all my strong feelings, I'm really heartless." Later, when they are in bed, this self-attack continues, as she professes to PJ that "no one can be close to me" and wants to know "if you even like me?"[65] What the viewer observes in these exchanges is the return in Ruth of a deep-seated fear that she is unlovable, a conviction emanating from her early emotional wound. Ironically, whereas Ruth thought that, by gaining mastery over PJ, she would end up being on top, she has actually become the biter bit.

He, on the other hand, in the course of the humiliation she has inflicted on him, has fallen deeply in love with her because, by giving over dominance, as Baines (played by the same actor, Harvey Keitel) does in *The Piano*, he feels personally connected to a sexual partner for the first time. She, however, has lost faith in her ability to love anyone at all and is full of self-loathing: "Look. Look, it's all gone, I'm ashamed of myself. I tortured you, it was all a defilement." Ruth now feels "lost" in what has become, for her, "a bloody wilderness."[66] Ironically, they have traded their needinesses in the course of trading their roles. Whereas initially Ruth was the one who was craving love and intimacy, while PJ protected himself against it by engaging in sex of a sort that is "kind of pornographic," "wanking into his partners," as Jane Campion puts it, it is now PJ who cannot imagine living without the intimate connection with Ruth that he imagines they have formed. Indeed, he has become so dependent on this fantasy of fusion that, when she declines his proposal that they get married and attempts to run off, he knocks her out (with a punch to the jaw in the film and by hitting her on the back of her head with a log in the novel) in order to prevent her from leaving him. The needy dependency that hitherto in his life he has been denying and disavowing, and against which he has defended himself through womanizing and meaningless sex, has resurged with a vengeance.

9 The denouement of the film attempts to retrieve something positive from this wreckage of human need and aspiration. Ruth comes to realize, "that old disgusting sex manic slob IS the only person who has ever truly loved me!!!"[67] Consequently, when she has been rescued by her brothers and Yvonne and sees the semi-delirious, wrecked PJ lying abjectly in the bed of their truck, her compassion and pity (her "ruth")

are reawakened, and she joins PJ to cradle him comfortingly in her arms. This is a complex moment, just like the moment in "Big Shell" which it recalls, when Louise cradles Dale in her arms as he suckles at her breast, in that it translates the heroine from her former roles—seductress then avenging angel—into the role of a comforting, nurturing mother, indicating that yet another reversal has occurred. At the deepest level of fantasy, therefore, it seems as if the film has been contrived simultaneously to serve different functions: on one hand, to express resentment and enact revenge, and, on the other, to administer comfort to the traumatized heroine by having her discover the idiom of care, expressed in the tenderness with which she holds the damaged PJ, that she longs to receive for herself. At a more superficial level, both PJ and Ruth are shown as attaining some form of spiritual redemption: he by releasing his ability to love, and she by discovering her capacity to experience pity and understanding. Even though there is no future for them in an ongoing intimate relationship with each other, they both come to realize, as Ruth later writes to PJ, that "[s]omething did happen, didn't it?" He, in return, wears the distant love she professes "like a blessing."

The epilogue to the film shows that the whole experience has had a profoundly transformative effect on both of them. Ruth reports, "My Dad finally did run off with his secretary" (reflecting the actual breakup of Richard and Edith Campion's marriage in real life), which has resulted in Ruth's mother joining her daughter in India, where they both work in a refuge for wounded animals, putting into practice the compassion Ruth has learned. Ruth now has a boyfriend, suggesting that she *has* developed the capacity to love and be loved. For his part, PJ has married Carol, his assistant, and they are the parents of twins. He is also writing (like Jane Campion) his second novel, which is about "a man who meets his avenging angel." PJ has also undergone a regenerative transformation as the result of his experience.

The ameliorative regeneration depicted in both Ruth and PJ serves to illustrate Campion's central thesis: in the contemporary world, spirituality emerges out of the mundane realities that are implicated in every spiritual voyage, including eroticism and love. In propounding a fictive exemplification of this vision in *Holy Smoke,* Campion along with her sister, Anna, were seeking, I believe, to resolve the lingering issues they had with their own father—in what was, in Anna's words, an act of "family therapy."

Campion, however, in her customary way, appears not to have been fully satisfied with what she depicted, for as *Holy Smoke* appeared, she was preparing the screenplay for yet another film that would deal with fathers, eroticism, and issues of sexuality and relationships: the erotic thriller *In the Cut*, to which I will now turn.

8 "That which terrifies and attracts simultaneously": Killing Daddy in *In the Cut*

1 Jane Campion's *In the Cut*, which appeared in 2003, is inextricably intertwined with *Holy Smoke* and appears to be part of the same preoccupation that is apparent in the earlier film, that is, to work through the lingering effects of a trauma that is associated with the father, particularly in terms of the effects of his misdeeds on his wife and, through her awareness of them, on his daughter. Even more than in her earlier movies, Campion grounds the movie explicitly in the complexities of a family romance that she shows her heroine trying to resolve.

For her vehicle, Campion chose an erotic thriller written by Susanna Moore, *In the Cut*, that had been published in 1995. Campion was responding to the success of a number of films in this genre, such as *Malice* (1993), *Se7en* (1995), and Almodovar's *Live Flesh* (*Carne trémula*; 1997). She first read Moore's book—a runaway bestseller in the United States—in 1996, at the instigation of Nicole Kidman, who had starred in *Malice* and who expressed a desire to act the part of Frannie should Campion decide to make a cinematic adaptation of it. Moore's novel is a highly shocking tale of a single woman (Frannie) who, disenchanted with her inability to find any man who can live up to her romantic ideal, takes refuge in her academic pursuits; she is an academic teaching English literature at New York University. In particular, she has thrown herself into a research project to compile a lexicon of New York street slang as an alternative to engagement in relationships with men, which she has come to regard as futile. Frannie's retreat into a withdrawn inwardness is shattered, however, when she sees a woman giving a blow job to a man in the darkened cellar of a bar, which releases in her the sexual desire she has repressed. Thereafter, she is drawn into a relationship with a New York cop, James A. Malloy, that is grounded in visceral sexual attraction, leading her to transgress all the prohibitions of her earlier conventional propriety. Eventually, after having come to the conclusion that her lover is the killer of a number of young women whose bodies have been gruesomely "disarticulated," Frannie discovers, too late, that she has accused the wrong man, and ends up being murdered by her lover's partner, Rodriguez, the cop she thought she could trust, who turns out to be the psychotic serial killer. As the novel ends, we are presented with the thoughts of the dying Frannie as she succumbs to the razor of the madman who is killing her.

The chronology of Campion's encounter with this novel suggests that she read it while she was developing the script for *Holy Smoke,* following the release of *The Portrait of a Lady.* It is not surprising, therefore, to find that there are strong traces of the influence of Moore's novel in *Holy Smoke*—especially in terms of its explicit depiction of visceral sex emptied of romantic sentiment and in the presence of a strong element of sadomasochism. Indeed, the sheer physicality of the sexual fantasy found in *Holy Smoke* can probably be traced to Moore's *In the Cut.* Campion describes, for example, how fascinated she was by the first love scene in the book, which she found erotic because there was no kissing in it, with the encounter following "rules that are unfamiliar to us."[1] Moore's de-sentimentalized, deliberately pornographic approach to the depiction of sex (in that it is calculated to titillate by being transgressive and shocking) thus provided Campion with a template for her representation of the sexual fantasies that Ruth and Frannie enact in the two movies.

Equally, certain of the preoccupations of *Holy Smoke* invade (and transform) the adaptation of *In the Cut* that Campion eventually made, especially the idea that Campion first propounded in *The Piano:* love can grow out of eroticism. Campion developed the screenplay for *In the Cut* during several months spent at her writer's hut near Glenorchy—a tiny hamlet set in the spectacular mountain scenery at the head of Lake Wakatipu, in the South Island of New Zealand. This sojourn occurred between the wrap-up of the filming of *Holy Smoke* and its international release, so it is not surprising that her head would have been full of the notions that she had been pursuing in that movie. As a result, the filmed adaptation of *In the Cut* ended up being much more optimistic about the possibility of finding love than the original source had been.

Bearing the concerns of *Holy Smoke* in mind, it is easy to see what might have appealed to Campion about what one reviewer described as Moore's "obnoxious" story.[2] First, it contained many elements of sexual fantasy, including the subject's release from repression through a fanta-sized reversal of customary inhibitions, and the eventual punishment that answers to the guilt of the fantasist for entertaining the possibility of such a breakout. In Moore's novel, this punishment takes the form of "mortification" in a literalized sense: death. Second, Moore's story en-gaged unapologetically in a form of eroticism that the author admitted was "pornographic" in its inspiration and intent.[3] Campion, as we know, had been strongly attracted to pornography as a mode of transgression in her youth, making pornographic paintings while still a student, put-ting on "little plays about women and sex," and even considering a career making pornographic films.[4] For Campion, pornography and eroticism are ways of challenging the repressive mores entrenched in the two Antipodean societies she has experienced, and it is not surprising that she identified *In the Cut* as a potential vehicle for her resistance against conventional taboos, which she considers prudish and dishonest. Third, Campion's personal experiences of failed love relationships have led her to become disillusioned with what she calls the "mythology" of romance, which she sees as kindling hopes in women that are doomed to end in disappointment. As she has said in her interviews, her "understanding of love" as she has matured "is that it's all about being able to see who's there with you and not be blinded by your own fantasies and projections on to that person." Women should not, she says, go looking for their masculine ideal "out there in the world," because "it is a complete fantasy" that does not exist.[5] Campion's concern in this film was to reveal how the romantic model falls short for women, creating enormous amounts of grief—or, as Meg Ryan, the actress who eventually played Frannie, reported, "Jane said, 'We are going to kill romance and give birth to love.'"[6] For this pur-pose, Susanna Moore's de-sentimentalized depiction of a relationship grounded solely in sex suited Campion admirably, providing a salutary antidote to her earlier romantic "addiction," as she has described it.

Despite being drawn to Moore's novel, Campion nevertheless found *In the Cut* "incredibly disturbing" on account of its nihilism, leaving her feeling initially that she could never touch it. After discussions with Susanna Moore and Nicole Kidman, however, she decided "to do something different with the material." Even though Campion faithfully reproduced most of the actual events (apart from the ending) and much of the dialogue of the novel in the film, other changes she made caused Moore to feel that the tone and vision of the work had become so radically altered that it had become "more her story now than mine."[7]

2 What are the changes Jane Campion made to the original? In the first place, she completely altered the ending, allowing Frannie not only to survive the murder attempt, but also to find love. As Susanna Moore later observed, she could understand why Campion felt a need to do this: "she's more optimistic than I am. The ending had to manifest her vision."[8]

The contrast between Moore's original ending and Campion's revised one is highly instructive and is crucial to an interpretation of the film. Moore had set out with the explicit intention, as she explains, of writing a book about "sex and murder."[9] This identification of sex with violent death is inherent in the core metaphor of the novel—the police officers' slang phrase "in the cut"—which, apart from referring literally to the gash left by a knife, also means, in Moore's words, "in the cunt" and "a safe place to hide." All these associations are brought together in the horrific final scene of the novel, which shows the psychotically deranged cop, Rodriguez, in a brutally perverted parody of lovemaking, progressively slicing Frannie with a razor until she bleeds to death. In Moore's vision, the very attraction of sex resides in its potential to "fix" and "unseal" what is closed within one's psyche and body,[10] but the cost of that surrender is the extinction of one's sense of identity, and in this sense it is, metaphorically speaking, death dealing. The allure of this extinction, the thought of which repels at the same time as it attracts, is its ability to provide a truly "safe place to hide," which is why, when the sex-death-cut combination is literalized at the end of the novel, Frannie, in her dying moments, longs for her "Scallop shell of quiet."[11] As Campion realized, by propounding such a death wish, Moore's novel is "quite nihilistic."[12]

In contradistinction, Jane Campion's vision, despite her disillusionment with the mythology of romance, is ultimately life affirming. Her aim is to depict a totally different psychic economy at work, in which the heroine, driven by a desire to find love, seeks to resolve the issues that are causing her psychological inhibition, so that she can move forward in her life. As Campion has confessed: "I honor what Susanna did, but I . . . [didn't] want to leave people in such despair. Movies are different from books. They're a dream you live with forever, and I couldn't make people live with this."[13] For this reason, she substituted a new ending in order to reverse the thematic direction of the work: Frannie does not die, but kills her would-be murderer, and returns to Malloy in the hope of finding genuine love.

This change in thematic direction was reinforced by another major change to the source: the addition of a backstory, centering on Frannie's parents, that illustrates both the attractions and danger of romance. As Kathleen McHugh has observed, this backstory, along with an expansion of the role of the double, achieved through the development of the character of Pauline, is intertwined in a family romance that Campion added to the film:

> Pauline becomes Frannie's beloved and abject half-sister, her double, their familial and psychic bond to each other forged in the traumas suffered by their mothers at the hand of their father. Whereas he impulsively proposed to, married, and suddenly deserted Frannie's mother, killing her with grief as he moved on to another of his four wives, he didn't even marry Pauline's mother. Their mothers' experiences have left them differently damaged; while Pauline sleeps with and stalks married men, wanting to marry just once "for her mother," Frannie is shut down, repressed; her desires incline to words, to imagination, not to romance or marriage.[14]

For McHugh, these added elements in the backstory locate In the Cut "in the industry tradition of noir/family melodrama hybrids," such as Mildred Pierce, Strangers on a Train, and It's a Wonderful Life. She also notes that the added subplot "infuses" the film with "Campion's long-standing creative interests in sisters, daughters, and mothers." The overall effect, McHugh suggests, is to recast the focus of this noir thriller "from single urban woman in peril to mothers and daughters at risk, the 'freedom to make poor choices' endemic to the crime narrative . . . and here set in the context of romance, family genealogy, trauma, and repetition."[15]

While McHugh's suggestions concerning the significance of the added material are valuable, they do not begin to suggest the full import of the backstory because McHugh does not step outside the film to make the links between Campion's changes and the circumstances of her personal background that impelled them. The shaping influence of those links is intimated by the reiteration of motifs found in her earlier films: Pauline-as-double recalls Yvonne-as-double in *Holy Smoke,* while also becoming the literal embodiment of the half sister referred to in that earlier film; the trauma suffered by the mothers recalls the distraught and depressed mother in *A Girl's Own Story,* as well as the grief of Isabel in *The Portrait of a Lady;* the allusions in the backstory to the father's multiple wives evokes the image of Bluebeard in *The Piano's* shadow play, with the severed heads of his wives similarly intimating the tragic suffering caused by a husband; Frannie's initial repression evokes the closing down of Kay's sexuality in *Sweetie;* and so on. Altogether, the added elements, considered in the context of Campion's overall oeuvre, attest to a consistency of thematic preoccupation that arises out of the filmmaker's personal background. In the rest of this chapter, I will demonstrate how that is so.

Most strikingly, the presence of the backstory serves to invest the characters of Frannie and Pauline, her half sister, with a psychic economy that they did not possess in the original, and helps to establish how events in the past are influencing the two sisters' predispositions in the present. By showing this link between past and present and by grounding the sisters' psychic troubles in a disturbed family romance, Campion is able to transform the viewer's perception of them—of Frannie, in particular. Instead of being a repressed woman who seeks to convert shame into pleasure, and then courts death in a supreme act of self-punitive sadomasochism, Frannie is turned into someone who is desperately seeking, in Campion's words, to "confront her shadow, her demons, her fears, in order to have a chance of redemption."[16] Because of the backstory, the viewer is able to infer that Frannie has been traumatized by events in her childhood that haunt her in the present through the lingering existence of traumatic memories that condition her attitude toward men and romance.

Campion conveys the story of Frannie's parents through a series of dream-like fantasy sequences, shot in sepia tones in the style of "WW 1

The opening skating sequence in *In the Cut.*

[*sic*] newsreel images,"[17] in which her mother and father appear as skaters on a frozen pond. The first of these episodes occurs at the end of the opening credit sequence. Frannie, lying drowsily in bed, looks out the window at a shower of petals falling, which she mistakenly thinks is a snowstorm. This association with snowflakes, and hence the "cold"— always a powerful symbol in Campion's movies—leads Frannie to drift into a dream in which she sees "the image of a woman in a 50's style skating skirt ice skating."[18] In the foreground, the camera focuses in close-up on the clenched fist of a man wearing a leather glove—an image familiar to the viewer from *A Girl's Own Story,* in which the man who invites the young Pam into his car is also wearing a glove. The man then skates off energetically in the direction of the dancing woman, as if in pursuit of her as an object of prey. As he passes across the foreground again, in a wide arc, blood surrealistically wells up from where the blades of his skates have made incisions in the ice, bleeding into the title, *In the Cut,* until it turns red.

Through the symbolism, displacement, and condensation present in this little episode, Campion firmly establishes her personal investment in the story. By setting it in the 1950s—a decade earlier than the time when Frannie, who is forty, would have been born—Campion is associating Frannie's mother with her own mother, Edith Campion, at the time when Jane was born (1954). The choice of an actor with a striking physical resemblance to the young Richard Campion to play the skating suitor-husband further reinforces the autobiographical frame of reference, as does the visual intertextual allusion to *A Girl's Own Story*. In this regard, Campion is repeating her practice in *Sweetie*, in which the actor who was cast to play Louis had an uncanny likeness to Gerard Lee, upon whom the character of Louis was based.[19]

The song that accompanies the opening credit sequence—"Que Sera, Sera" (originally sung by Doris Day in Alfred Hitchcock's movie *The Man Who Knew Too Much*)—foreshadows the ironies that will unfold as the inset skating sequences progress and also the tragic outcomes that will result from the action set in the present:

> When I was just a little girl
> I asked my mother, what will I be,
> Will I be pretty, will I be rich,
> Here's what she said to me.
>
> Que sera, sera
> Whatever will be, will be,
> The future's not ours to see,
> Que sera, sera.
> What will be, will be.
>
> When I was just a child in school
> I asked my teacher what should I try,
> Should I paint pictures, should I sing songs,
> This was her wise reply.
>
> Que sera, sera,
> Whatever will be, will be
> The future's not ours to see
> Que sera, sera,
> What will be, will be.

In the earlier stages of the credit sequence, when Pauline, who has spent the night at Frannie's apartment, sharing a bed with Frannie, is walking through the latter's garden, sipping her coffee, the first two stanzas are sung (in a deliberately low-key way, as if it is an ordinary person, like Frannie or Pauline, singing with an untrained voice) to a piano accompaniment marked by a sinister, jarring discordance. When the scene switches to the skating episode set in the past, however, the melody of the song is taken up by the orchestra and expanded into a lush, swelling, romantic reprise while the parents are skating. This contrast between

the subdued discordance of the song in the present and its swelling romanticism in the past underlines an ironic gap between the romantic
expectations of the skating mother and what eventually is shown to have
happened to her. The juxtaposition of the past and the present at the
beginning of the movie primes us to watch for the connections between
the experience of the parents and the effects of that experience on their
daughters.

This link between past and present is developed in the second inset
skating sequence, when Pauline tells Frannie how she fantasizes about
marrying her doctor, whom she is stalking. Pauline's confession prompts
Frannie to tell "how our father proposed to my mother." Their father,
Frannie recounts, was very handsome when he was young, and although
he was already engaged to someone else, he could not take his eyes off her
mother. Finally, his fiancée got jealous and threw her engagement ring
back at him, which he then used, that same day, to propose to Frannie's
mother. At the moment when he, down on his knee, slipped the diamond
on her finger, it began to snow. Whereas Pauline finds this story "very
romantic," Frannie is frozen by her awareness of its destructive outcome:
"That's my mother's story—the way she always told it. He killed her.
When he left, she just went crazy with grief, you know, she didn't understand it, couldn't believe it."

Frannie's father, we learn, has married four times and is already plot-
ting the fifth—to which Pauline replies, "He never married my mother."
Apart from activating autobiographical allusions to the story of Edith
and Richard Campion, including the breakup of their marriage and the
existence of a half sister, this little episode neatly exemplifies the contrasting reactions of each of the daughters to the original trauma. The
main action of the movie will work through the consequences in the lives
of the two daughters of their father's treatment of their mothers, showing
the death-dealing outcomes for Pauline and the life-and-death struggle
for Frannie. As I will show, both daughters represent projections, at the
autobiographical level of reference, of Campion, manifesting the contradictory impulses that she recognized in her own psychological makeup
as a result of her parents' actions.

The third skating sequence takes place after the murder of Pauline
and is imaged as a nightmarish hallucination on the part of Frannie who,
out of grief, has become drunk on vodka. The screenplay of the movie

contains a description of this episode that differs somewhat from the version in the final film and is therefore worth quoting in full. According to the screenplay, the scene shows:

> Her young father skating on the tree-fringed lake from the engagement story, except he is no longer an expert but comically out of control.
>
> Her mother—but it's not her mother, it's Frannie—has fallen over and the comically out of control father, now older, now younger, is heading towards her. He doesn't stop, he can't stop, his skates slice through her legs.
>
> Once more Frannie's father merrily and more expertly skates on one blade towards Frannie. This time aiming directly for Frannie's neck. She puts her hand up to protect herself and screams.
>
> She opens her eyes just before her head is decapitated. . . . The apartment bell is ringing.[20]

In another instance of brilliantly imaginative displacement and symbolic condensation, Jane Campion has conceived this episode as an allegory of her parents' story, which she then projects as that of Frannie's parents. The "comically out of control" skating of the young father suggests the compulsiveness of the disturbed sexual pathology that has caused him to progress through a series of women. It is this behavior that has literally, as the expression goes, "cut" her mother "off at the knees." The fact that Frannie becomes substituted for her mother at the moment when the father is about to slice through her neck signifies the effect that her father's devastating betrayal and abandonment of her mother has had on his daughter. Her fear and mistrust of romance and men have led her, metaphorically speaking, to the verge of being "decapitated," that is, she has lost her ability to engage in a normal, healthy relationship with a man, because of her empathic identification with her mother.

Even though the substitution of Frannie for her mother, as specified in the screenplay, did not find its way into the final version of the movie, it nevertheless remains implicit in the film. Campion also decided not to show the father as "now older, now younger" (which would have signified the long-standing duration of his womanizing), as she had specified in the screenplay. Most probably, the filmmaker concluded that to include these details would make the episode too obviously personal, and she decided to maintain its generic quality, without having a comic sequence disrupt the pervasive romantic tone she was trying to create.

The final recurrence of the fantasy sequence involving the young father takes place when Rodriguez, who has imprisoned Frannie behind the bars of the (phallic) lighthouse to which he takes her after having asked her to marry him, kisses her. This action prompts a flash of recall of her father kissing her mother on the frozen lake of the skating sequences. This juxtaposition suggests that, in order to save herself, Frannie has to sort out the impact that her parents' failed romance has had on her before she can free herself from the damage it has caused to her psychic well-being. The final version of the film depicts the process through which that working-out is achieved.

3 For those who know about Jane Campion's family background, it is clear that she made these major changes to the source novel in order to turn her film into a vehicle for the exploration of her personal problematic. Once this fundamental conversion and the reversal of thematic direction are understood, many other aspects of Campion's approach to the adaptation make sense.

The film is full of Campion's private symbols that indicate the autobiographical associations inhering for the filmmaker in what is being shown on-screen. In the opening sequence, for example, showing the East Village of New York at dawn, when the camera pauses to show a pile of rubbish, a black cat appears in the background. The same conjunction of images occurs when Frannie pours some milk into a cup for a cat (white this time) as she goes to put a bag of rubbish in a garbage container outside her apartment. Similarly, a white cat appears under the $5 Psychic Reader sign in the time between the discovery of Pauline's murder and Frannie's near-fatal encounter with Rodriguez, the psychopathic cop. That same Psychic Reader sign has already been seen in the background during Frannie's encounter on the street with John Graham, a highly disturbed medical trainee who earlier slept with Frannie before being jilted by her, and hence appears as a suspect for the killer in the viewer's eyes. During their exchange, Graham describes how he suffers from panic attacks, and asks Frannie, "Doesn't that ever happen to you where you get these funny images from the past, like you saw something, or you knew something, weird memories of childhood ... ?"[21]

This fluid, recurrent collocation of images suggests a nexus of associations. Cats, as we have seen with respect to Campion's earlier movies, are closely associated with Edith Campion in the filmmaker's lexicon of personal symbols. They are also associated variously with sexuality (as in *A Girl's Own Story*) and with a disillusioned view of romance on the part of a woman who has been betrayed (as with Madame Merle in *The Portrait of a Lady*). By depicting a cat in the vicinity of rubbish, Campion is making an implicit comment on the delusory nature of romantic expectation—brutally illustrated in the experience of Frannie's mother (and her own)—owing to the force of masculine sexual desire. These imagistic associations are even more strongly marked in the screenplay than the film, with the screenplay specifying that the Baby Doll Lounge has as its sign "a giant winking cat, biting its tail."[22] Further, by showing a cat under the Psychic Reader sign that had earlier been associated with John Graham's admission that he is troubled by "funny images from the past," Campion links the idea of traumatic memory to the thought of Frannie's mother (alias Edith Campion) as the victim of male conduct that has been impelled by a compulsive sexual urge. In this way, Campion "thickens" the latent meaning of the representation by adding images that, as she has said, "arise" from her unconscious—illustrating her claim that she cannot let herself know things "in a direct way," but needs to "read it in signs," through metaphor, as happens when one visits a psychic.[23] Her acknowledgment of this intuitive process involving the release of images from the unconscious is signaled in *In the Cut* by the reiterated inclusion of the Psychic Reader sign, which becomes another private symbol for Campion.

The motif of rubbish as an image associated with the destructiveness wrought by self-regarding male desire returns in a further episode added by Campion that is not in the source: the trip undertaken by Frannie and Malloy to the countryside, where they visit a secluded lake with rubbish floating in it. As they walk through the trees toward the lake, Frannie recites lines from Keats's poem "La Belle Dame sans Merci": "Oh, what can ail thee, knight at arms ... " Again, the poetry associates the scene with Campion's mother, with her passion for poetry, while the words evoke the idea of a "damaged man," which, by implication, refers to the young husband in Frannie's fantasy memories and, through him, to the husband who deserted Edith Campion. The lake itself recalls the image of the frozen lake in Frannie's fantasy, except that the rubbish floating in it undermines the romantic ambience of the earlier scene.

Through characteristic symbolic suggestion, Campion shows both Malloy and Frannie as wanting to reject what the rubbish in the lake signifies—indicated by the way they each explode a bag of rubbish by shooting into it. The suggestion here—that, at the deepest level of their unconscious, they are each seeking love, rather than mere sex—is reinforced by the fear Malloy expresses, at the moment when Frannie starts to initiate lovemaking, that she is "only there for the sex." By zipping him up again, Frannie confirms that she, too, is looking for more than that—a condition of mind that is absent in Moore's treatment of the heroine. Malloy, for his part, wants Frannie to get engaged to him. In contrast to Moore, Campion thus shows herself to be a romantic, in spite of her inability to believe in romance.

4 Campion's reworking of Susanna Moore's novel is also apparent in her changed conception of the main characters. As she had done in *Sweetie,* Campion doubles the characters to make them seem to be the split-out parts of a single personality, and thereby makes them serve a different function than that of Moore's characters. In the novel, for instance, Pauline—who has been friends with Frannie since they met in London fifteen years earlier, when Frannie was studying Middle English—is an art dealer who is described as "an aesthetic snob."[24] She is a highly sophisticated woman who "sees the diminished side of most things," referring to herself as a "slut" who ascribes her inability to find true love "as if it were a congenital weakness or fair punishment for some feminist principle that she mistakenly espoused in late adolescence and cannot now abandon honorably."[25] In Moore's version, Pauline affects a blasé ennui, claiming "completely disingenuously to fuck only married men because she prefers to be alone on the holidays."[26]

Campion's Pauline is very different, being presented as a romantic dreamer—"a war veteran of romance,"[27] as the filmmaker describes her. Whereas she was merely a friend in the source, Pauline is turned into

Frannie's half sister in Campion's reconceptualization. This change in relationship serves two purposes: it not only activates an autobiographical allusion to Campion's half sister in real life, but also strengthens the conception of Pauline as Frannie's double. As the screenplay specifies, Frannie and Pauline "look like sisters,"[28] and the similarity of their appearance to one another (and to Jane Campion at that age) reinforces the idea that they embody the contradictory impulses of a single personality, just as Ruth and Yvonne in *Holy Smoke* had done. They are shown to have adopted modes of behavior that are designed to protect them against the possibility of suffering the fates of their respective mothers at the hand of their father. Pauline incessantly seeks love through serial affairs, often with married men, out of a needy obsessiveness that arises from desperation. In the movie, this is illustrated by Pauline's pursuit of her doctor, with whom she has made eleven appointments in one week in her efforts to seduce him. She even goes to the length of stealing a suit that his wife has left at the dry cleaners, saying, "This is what I do to get a dick inside me." Her pursuit of men, Pauline reveals, is motivated by a desire to repair the wrong done to her mother: she expresses a desire to get married, at least once, "just for my Mum." The tragic irony of her response to the trauma of her mother's desertion is that she seems moved unconsciously to set herself up for failure—by pursuing men in situations that will ensure she will not be able to marry them, thus dooming her recurrently to reexperience her mother's rejection.

Frannie, on the other hand, while having initially shared some of Pauline's romantic inclinations, has moved in the opposite direction. In Moore's novel, she is a divorcée and describes herself as "spinsterish," as possessing "a certain rigidity, a certain prudishness," which she hates in herself.[29] Following her divorce, her relationships with men have become highly delibidinized, which is why she is able to maintain a relationship with the medical trainee, John Graham. When she has sex with Malloy, she does so in the hope that what is sealed and closed in her can be "opened" through his forceful possession of her. This is what Malloy understands when he says "Give it up," as he penetrates her anally.[30]

As with Pauline, Campion's Frannie is turned into someone whose attitude to men and sex is somewhat different than in the original source. Frannie's problem, in Campion's reconceptualization, is not that she suffers from an involuntary repression from which she has to be liberated through an overpowering act of mastery and possession, but rather that she "quite simply, has been greatly deceived, and ... has never found what she was looking for in a man."[31] As a way of protecting herself against this disappointment, Campion's Frannie has retreated from the world into a self-protective, repressive inwardness. Nevertheless, as Campion remarks, "In her heart, Frannie is really longing for love—despite the fact she is brave and ironic towards the world."[32] Both sisters in Campion's reworked version, therefore, are depicted as longing to find love, even though it seems to evade them.

On the other side of the gender divide, Malloy and Rodriguez similarly look like one another—to the extent that Frannie understandably confuses their identities. Like Frannie and Pauline, they are closely bonded, having had an identical sign tattooed on their wrists, the three of spades, following their first successful mission together. And just as Frannie and Pauline embody contrasting responses to a common experience—their father's abandonment of their mothers—so too do Malloy and Rodriguez share a common experience—the breakdown of their marriages—that has prompted two radically divergent responses in them. Malloy has emptied himself of sentiment in an attempt to protect himself against his disillusionment with romance, and has replaced it with an addiction to sex as a form of self-soothing. Rodriguez, on the other hand, incessantly searches out women on whom he can exact revenge, in a sadistic inversion of romantic courtship.

In Campion's *In the Cut,* then, there are two sets of doubled characters who are mirrored across the gender divide: Frannie and Pauline on the feminine side, and Malloy and Rodriguez on the masculine one. In both pairs, each of the doubled characters is paralleled with a counterpart in the pair of the other gender—Frannie with Malloy, and Pauline with Rodriguez—creating a symmetry through which Campion constructs a thematic paradigm consisting of opposites. A parallel is established between Malloy and Frannie (in their initial recoiling from romance, followed by their hope that it can arise out of the erotic interchange they share), while a second parallel is established between Rodriguez and Pauline (in their incessant search for love—however perverted in the case of Rodriguez). The parallel between Pauline and Rodriguez is underlined by the fact that both have had restraining orders taken out against them. While some of the cues for the doubling of these characters were latent in Susanna Moore's original, Campion's reworking greatly bolsters the incipient patterning.

If we stand back from the doubled pairs and view them as the split-out attributes of a single personality, it becomes apparent that both Frannie and Pauline, on one side, and Malloy and Rodriguez on the other, represent contrasting responses to the failure of romance that turn out to be the obverse of one another; in other words, they embody the alternative impulses that are potentially available to people who are responding to the same experience. Malloy, as Campion has observed, "medicates . . . himself with sex," meaning that he eschews romance altogether in his approach to women.[33] This makes him attractive, in Frannie's eyes, as he manifests what she has come to repress in herself: the registration of the self through the gratification of sexual desire, without the need for romance. When she first encounters him, he overturns her presuppositions about romance, which she had assumed to be illusory and hypocritical, because of the directness and sincerity of his approach, which is purely sexual. In Campion's words, Frannie's encounter with Malloy perturbs her because "he is totally confident, at a physical level, which both terrifies and attracts her."[34] When he makes love to her, he does so at a purely visceral level, which obviates the possibility for the kind of deception that can lead to the undermining of romantic expectation.

Rodriguez, in contrast, embodies the death-dealing potential of the masculine sexual drive. Far from being direct and sincere like Malloy, he is a deep dissimulator, impelled by motives that are vengeful and sadistic. We learn that he has had his gun taken away from him after he tried to kill his wife when she discovered he was having an affair with another woman and in response threw his fishing trophy out the window. Having been turned into a "housemouse," he has nothing: "no wife, no gun, no shield, not even his letter from the police shrink to say he's normal."[35] Rodriguez's response to this deprivation and his feeling of impotency, symbolized by the substitution of a water pistol for his real (phallic) gun, is to seek compensation in perverted relationships with women. For him, the women he stalks are, at one level, surrogates for the love object that is missing in his life—signified by the diamond engagement ring he presents to his victims. At another level, they are stand-ins for the agent of his misfortunes, and thus become an object of hatred whom he must kill. Rodriguez thus personifies all that is treacherous in men whose attitude toward sex and romance has become driven by motives that are distorted as a result of psychological disturbance.

Taken as a whole, then, Malloy and Rodriguez, in their contrasting responses to romantic disillusionment, embody two of the motives driving masculine sexuality that Frannie unconsciously recognizes as being inherent in the sexual behavior of the handsome young father of her fantasies. We could say that, if Malloy represents the attractive side of the father's sexuality, Rodriguez represents the shadow side of the handsome skater. Frannie's job will be to sort out the difference between the two, and to work out her relationship to each, so that she can free herself from her fear of the latter in order to liberate herself into love through the former and thereby find redemption.

5 The alterations Campion made to the source for *In the Cut* create a symbolic context that illuminates Frannie's confrontation of her own fears. In the rest of this chapter, I will examine the process through which she encounters and attempts to resolve them.

As in *Holy Smoke*, the events that unfold in the course of *In the Cut* can be viewed as the enactment of a fantasy, grounded in unresolved incestuous yearnings, on the part of the heroine. The backstory, with its explanation of the father's serial sexual relationships, imparts a whole new significance to the major elements in the narrative. When Frannie enters the cellar of the Red Turtle bar, her descent is more than literal. As Campion puts it, "Frannie goes down the rabbit hole [as in *Alice in Wonderland*] . . . and finds herself in a different world, an underworld."[36] What she encounters there is the world of visceral sex, exemplified in the sight of a woman with blue fingernails giving a blow job to a man with his face in shadow. Not only does this sight confront Frannie with the sexual impulse she has been repressing in herself, but it also presents her with an image of the illicit sexual activity of her father that, in conjunction with her own disappointments in love, has helped to bring that repression about.

There is, indeed, a sort of primal fantasy taking place in this episode. Several commentators have remarked on the voyeuristic quality of the cinematographic style Campion uses for much of the movie: "voyeuristic long lenses drift in and out of focus." This creates "a complicity in the audience because, like Frannie, we feel as if we are spying."[37] What Frannie is spying on, in fantasy, is the sight of her "father"—identified with the faceless man—engaged in one of his sexual affairs, from which she is excluded. This episode makes one think of the scene in *The Piano* in which Flora spies on Ada and Baines when they, too, are engaged in an adulterous affair. In her director's commentary, Campion describes the romantic mythology with which Frannie surrounds her father, which she inherited from her mother: "[it is] on the one hand so attractive because it's so heightened and beautiful, and he's this gorgeous, handsome skater, and the romance of it is so attractive."[38] The little girl in Frannie still retains her infatuation with her father: she longs to be the object of his attention, to reinsert herself as the object of her father's love, to repair the neglect of her brought about by the redirection of his (sexual) attentions elsewhere. A lingering trace of Frannie's grief at this neglect may be detected when, after Pauline's murder, she tells Malloy how, "when I was 13, my father left me in Geneva for five days: he said later that it never occurred to him that I wouldn't be all right." This recalls the similar episode in James's *Portrait of a Lady* that left Isabel Archer with a similar incestuous yearning for the attention and affection of her father.

In the context of this unresolved incestuous fantasy, Frannie's subsequent affair with Malloy serves several purposes. On one level, having sex with the detective provides a means of eroticizing the trauma she has experienced at being excluded from her father's love life. Engaging in sex, in such circumstances, is a means by which, in fantasy, she is able to remain in contact with her father, through turning Malloy into a stand-in for him, insofar as he is propelled by the same compulsive sexual urge that Frannie recognizes in her father. To the extent that Malloy *is* a stand-in, he also represents the forbidden, which means that by surrendering to him, Frannie is engaging in transgression. The transgressive aspect of their encounter, for Frannie, is reflected in displaced form in the nature of the sex they have, which involves anal kissing and anal penetration, thus transgressing the personal boundaries that the repressed Frannie had previously set for herself. Moreover, because Frannie thinks that Malloy may be the man she saw in the cellar of the Red Turtle, and hence the murderer, he also represents her father in his destructive aspect, being motivated by compulsions that led to the behavior that, metaphorically, killed her mother. In these circumstances, sex with Malloy is also a means of eroticizing Frannie's fear of her attraction toward what she knows is dangerous. It is for this reason that, in Campion's words, Frannie is both "terrorized" by and "drawn" toward Malloy. Because it is serving these functions, sex is just as much a form of self-medication for Frannie as it is for Malloy. This is particularly evident in the scene near the end of the movie, following the murder of Pauline, in which Frannie chains Malloy to a pipe and then makes love to him, in what Campion describes as "a grief fuck"—in other words, an attempt to alleviate the pain of grief by eroticizing it.[39]

By the end of the movie, it becomes apparent that the pattern of Frannie's responses in *In the Cut* is very similar to that of Ruth in *Holy Smoke,* but with a significant difference. Both Ruth and Frannie have retreated into a form of withdrawal at the time when the story begins— Ruth into mystical spirituality, and Frannie into an obsession with words. In each case, this withdrawal has been prompted by a desire to defend themselves against the pain of knowledge that perturbs them at an unconscious level and that they can scarcely allow themselves to admit: Ruth's awareness that her father has had a love child from one of his "pathetic affairs," and Frannie's awareness of the terrible damage her father's sexual behavior inflicted on her mother. As the movie proceeds, both are shown as succumbing to the force of the sexuality that they have repressed, and in each case, the surrender is impelled by a longing to be the love object of a figure who stands in for a transgressive father who has neglected them.

Following this return from repression, both Ruth and Frannie seek to avenge themselves on the man who represents the agent of their fears and grief, but it is here that differences emerge in Campion's treatment of the two heroines. In *Holy Smoke,* because the masculine predispositions that both repelled and yet drew Ruth were combined in one father figure, PJ Waters, the revenge she exacts upon him in her quest for psychic relief involves the complete repudiation of him. In *In the Cut,* however, because the attributes of the young father are split out into two men who resemble him, both physically and in their womanizing, Frannie can elect to stay with one and repudiate the other, who is made to embody the sinister aspects of the father so that they can be "killed" and evacuated without Frannie having to reject love and sexuality altogether.

Frannie's difficulty is in discerning which of the two, Malloy or Rodriguez, is trustworthy and which is not. In this respect, she embodies the perplexity of the filmmaker, which Jane Campion whimsically intimates by making two brief appearances in the film. The first occurs on Frannie's first date with Malloy, when Campion appears as a barmaid directly behind her; the second occurs when Malloy is telling Frannie how Rodriguez tried to kill his wife, at which moment Campion is shown dancing with Rodriguez. These two episodes alert the viewer to Jane Campion's personal investment in this story: Frannie's difficulties are her difficulties, as is her need to resolve them. As Campion has said: "My life and my cinema reflect one another, even though my own life is much less intense. I live through my films."[40]

Discerning the difference between Malloy and Rodriguez is not easy for Frannie, given that both police officers appear to help her at significant moments. Following the murder of Pauline, when Frannie's student Cornelius becomes enraged at her rejection of him as he starts to make out with her, Rodriguez intervenes by throwing pebbles against the window, causing Cornelius to flee. Soon after this, Malloy "tenderly" bathes and cleans her, suggesting the same kind of solicitude. At first, she makes a near-fatal mistake when she decides that Malloy murdered Pauline. It is only when she sees the matching tattoo on Rodriguez's wrist, after he has led her into the enclosure of the lighthouse under the George Washington Bridge, that she realizes her mistake.

Frannie's confrontation with her would-be murderer during this episode is full of symbolic allusions that suggest the nature of the inner psychic process taking place. When, with a frisson, she realizes that Rodriguez, not Malloy, is the murderer, she looks upward through the bars of the fence surrounding the lighthouse with a gaze implying her awareness that she is a prisoner in this symbolic structure. Earlier in the movie, we saw an image of the red lighthouse on the blackboard of the classroom in which Frannie is giving instruction on Virginia Woolf's novel To the Lighthouse. In her director's commentary, Campion admits that she drew the lighthouse on the blackboard as a blatant phallic symbol—the one thing she "regrets" about the film.[41] However embarrassed Campion might subsequently have come to feel about it, the earlier graphic iteration of the red lighthouse confirms its importance as a symbol of the force of male sexuality that both attracts and terrifies—from the idea of which Frannie, as her entrapment at the actual lighthouse suggests, cannot escape.

Then, in a major divergence from the source novel, Frannie puts on Malloy's jacket, instead of hanging it up as Rodriguez invites her to do. This is not merely for the sake of expediency, as Frannie knows Malloy's gun is in the pocket, but also for a symbolic reason. When Rodriguez asks Frannie whether she "is cold," after a long pause, she says, "No." In terms of the metaphoric structure of the film, the putting on of Malloy's jacket even though she is not physically cold signifies her new desire to be warmed by what he represents—a loving sexuality that is devoid of distorted motives.

Further symbolism occurs when Rodriguez begins to dance "romantically" with Frannie. In the course of doing so, he executes the exact same moves he performed while dancing with Campion-as-barmaid in the earlier scene, which signals the personal level of reference for the filmmaker of what is taking place. The presence of this autobiographical dimension is reinforced by the backstory at this point. Although the action does not appear in the movie, the screenplay specifies that Rodriguez, when he asks Frannie to marry him, "goes down on one knee," just as the young father did in the earlier skating sequence.[42] As he proposes to her, he holds out an engagement ring on a dagger, which, in a frozen close-up shot, appears tilted at the angle of an erect penis, yet another striking phallic image. The symbolic suggestion here is that Rodriguez represents the death-dealing potential that the superficial appearance of romantic gestures can disguise when these are motivated by a sexual impulse that is the product of emotional disturbance. Rodriguez confirms this when he describes to Frannie how he has been dreaming for his whole life about one girl he met, but does not know if she loves him. In other words, he is just as much the prisoner of an obsession with a fantasy image of what is missing from his inner world as Frannie is, with the difference that his failure to find it has caused him to act outward—murderously—whereas her failure has, up until this point, induced her to turn inward.

In the context of these symbolic associations, Frannie's action in shooting Rodriguez through the heart takes on a special significance.

The phallic dagger on which Rodriguez offers a ring to Frannie in *In the Cut*.

After pinning her against the bars of the fence, half-strangling her, Rodriguez then kisses her "tenderly" (as the screenplay specifies), as if to act out his fantasy of finding his missing beloved. At that moment, an image of Frannie's young father kissing her mother while the snow is romantically falling flashes onto the screen, suggesting the association in her mind between what is happening to her and the traumatic memories that have haunted her all her life. It is this association, combined with her awareness of the threat of her imminent death, that triggers her to shoot him through the heart.

Symbolically, at one level, by killing Rodriguez, Frannie is finally freeing herself from any attachment to the romantic illusion associated with the story of her mother and father, which leaves her free to discover the nature of real love. In doing so, she has attained the understanding of love that Jane Campion professes: "it's all about being able to see who's there with you and not be blinded by your own fantasies and projections on to that person. So much of the time we spend looking for the person to fulfil the fantasy that is inside ourselves."[43] In the future, one senses, Frannie will no longer persist in attempting to find in her partners the materialization of a romantic illusion that is produced by impossible wishes that derive from the past—in Frannie's case (as, one suspects, in Jane's), a desire to be loved by a "gorgeous" but neglectful father who is driven by sexual compulsions.

At another, and possibly even more important level, Frannie's killing of Rodriguez represents a killing off in Frannie of the fears about the untrustworthiness of men she developed as a result of her father's marital perfidy and the devastation it wrought on her mother. This, more than anything else, has been the cause of Frannie's repression, in Campion's redaction of Moore's story, and Campion, in the references to "Daddy" in her director's commentary, is explicit about this:

> Rodriguez kisses Frannie as he goes to kill her, and as the image of her father comes to her it's like the big wake-up call, you know, he's the guy, shoot Daddy, you've got to do it, you've got to do it, you know, quite literally. Bang! And she's like, you know, undoing her mythology as the film is in process—enough, I guess, to at that moment get it, you know, and save herself. I mean that's the conceit of the film's, you know, psychology, I guess, or mythology.[44]

"Getting it," for Frannie, means not only ceasing to look for what she will never find, because it does not exist, but also ceasing to fear what she can attain, which is the kind of honest and direct love that a man like Malloy can offer. It is this realization that moves Frannie to put on Malloy's coat and then, when she has killed Rodriguez (and all that he represents), to return to Malloy and lie in his arms, without a word.

6   It will be clear from this exposition that *In the Cut* represents a major effort on Jane Campion's part to bring together the different aspects of the personal family romance with which she had attempted to deal in her earlier films—even to the extent of killing off the rival sister, Pauline, as she had done with Dawn in *Sweetie*. What strikes one, however, is that the solution arising from the synthesis she proposes is depicted as being far from secure. As Campion says, "you don't know what is going to happen to Frannie and Malloy in the future—something's possible, but you don't know if it will work out."[45]

Campion had good reason to feel ambivalent about the prospects for her protagonists. By 2003, her marriage to Colin Englert had unraveled, and she was reported as living alone with her daughter, Alice, in Sydney.[46] The marriage had always been tenuous. In 1993, Campion had described her entry into this relationship as a "risk." When the interviewer asked her whether by this she meant "getting married," Campion replied: "Oh, no. . . . I wanted to get married. Colin and I had been best friends for six or seven years. The big emotional risk was in becoming lovers."[47] By the time she made *In the Cut,* therefore, Campion had good reason for being skeptical about the longevity of love, based on her own experience. The ending of her marriage makes particularly poignant the quotation of the penultimate stanza of "Que Sera, Sera" (in a version emended by Campion to fit her circumstances) on the soundtrack as the closing credits roll:

> When I grew up and fell in love
> I asked my sweetheart what lies ahead
> Will there be rainbows, day after day
> Here's what my sweetheart said.
>
> Que sera, sera,
> Whatever will be, will be
> The future's not ours to see
> Que sera, sera,
> What will be, will be.

But Jane Campion has shown herself to be a person who never loses hope, and it is in this spirit, I believe, that she dedicated the film to her daughter, "Alice Allegra Englert." Accordingly, the quotation of the final stanza of "Que Sera, Sera" on the soundtrack—emended to make it apply to a daughter, rather than a son, through the substitution of "pretty" from the first stanza to replace the "handsome" of the fourth—has a special relevance to Campion's personal situation and to her investment in her daughter's well-being, in particular:

> Now I have children of my own
> They ask their mother, what will I be
> Will I be pretty, will I be rich
> I tell them tenderly.
>
> Que sera, sera,
> Whatever will be, will be
> The future's not ours to see
> Que sera, sera,
> What will be, will be.

Thus, while an element of skepticism is built into the ending of *In the Cut,* this remarkably insightful and resilient filmmaker has allowed for the possibility that we, like Frannie and, in real life, like Campion's daughter, Alice Allegra (whose name means "happiness"), and even like herself, may be pleasantly surprised by what might eventuate in the future.

9 Lighting a Lamp: Loss, Art, and Transcendence in *The Water Diary* and *Bright Star*

1 By the time she finished *In the Cut,* released in 2003, Jane Campion had become aware that she was beginning to repeat herself. As she puts it, "I was starting to work with a bit of a full suitcase, and the same old suitcase, and that's why I stopped working for a while, because I wanted to chuck the whole lot out and see what came up."[1] After a "sabbatical" of several years, during which she found herself "doing things like embroidering pillow slips and very crafty simple stuff, like horses and stuff for my daughter; doing like my mum and my sister and friends,"[2] Campion's attempt to rediscover herself bore fruit in three films that show her going in various new directions. The first was a short film, *The Water Diary* (2006), made as part of a United Nations Millennium Development Goals project about water and global warming. The second was *The Lady Bug,* a surrealistic three-minute segment in a compilation of thirty-three short films, *Chacun son cinéma; ou, Ce petit coup au coeur quand la lumière s'éteint et que le film commence,* shown at Cannes in May 2007, in which Campion satirized the attitude of men toward women in the world of filmmaking. The third was a new feature-length film, *Bright Star* (2009), dealing with the tragically truncated love relationship between the Romantic poet John Keats and Fanny Brawne, the seventeen-year-old daughter of his neighbor at Hampstead Heath.

The Lady Bug was a fanciful, one-off *jeu d'esprit* which protested the position of women directors in the cinema industry, but, given that the plans for *Bright Star* were announced in mid-2006, soon after the completion of *The Water Diary,* it is not surprising that the latter two films bear a close relationship to one another—not only stylistically, with Campion using the same cinematographer (Greig Fraser) and composer (Mark Bradshaw), but also thematically. The second, longer film picks up from the point where the earlier one leaves off, that is, with characters who wait, metaphorically speaking, for "the rain" after the literal drought depicted in *The Water Diary* and the spiritual drought depicted earlier in *Holy Smoke* and *In the Cut*. Both of the newer films reveal a further development in Campion's vision, in which "the rain" can only be found as the consequence of a cathartic response to a beauty that is fleeting and transient; being experienced under the sign of death, it is unable to survive for long the brutal realities of the actual world. Both films, moreover, are closely associated with Campion's daughter, Alice Englert, who in various ways is both the incentive for, and the instrument of, Campion's exploration of her new understanding. Campion's casting of Alice as the main character, Ziggy, in *The Water Diary* and her use of her daughter as the inspiration for her realization of the character of Fanny in *Bright Star*,[3] makes for a complex set of imaginative projections and identifications. Indeed, in terms of autobiographically driven associations, these two films are as richly overdetermined with latent meaning as any of Campion's earlier movies. That being the case, it is useful to examine them together.

2   On the face of it, Campion's *The Water Diary*, only eighteen minutes long, tells the simple story of the grief that a girl, Ziggy, and her friend Sam suffer at the deaths of two favorite horses, killed by Ziggy's father to save them from starvation during a drought. Following this incident, the children of the area attempt to induce the rain to come back by having the most beautiful and talented girl among them play her viola on the top of a hill. The film, however, is laden with visual images deriving from Campion's personal mythology that invest this simple narrative with an extraordinary depth of symbolic condensation. The deep attachment Ziggy and Sam display for their horses recalls not only Edith Campion's lifelong passion for horses and horse riding, but Jane Campion's childhood enthusiasm for that sport. As Campion has revealed in an interview, she moved to the countryside when she was thirteen—the age of Ziggy in the movie—and owned a mare.[4] Indeed, a photo survives of the young Jane dressed in exactly the same kind of horse-riding outfit

in which Ziggy appears during the "gymkhana without horses" in *The Water Diary*. It is not fanciful, therefore, to see in Ziggy's story a fictive projection of Jane's experience, with the fact that Ziggy is played by Campion's daughter reinforcing the association between Ziggy and a version of Jane's earlier self. Such a level of autobiographical association is reinforced, as it was in *Sweetie*, by recurrent images of horses, including the collection of toy porcelain horses that is arrayed along the windowsill of Ziggy's bedroom, the poster of a horse that hangs on one of its walls, and the toy horse that is placed on Ziggy's desk.

This complex layer of autobiographical identification is progressively deepened as the film proceeds, with a number of details suggesting that the story is being constructed as a displaced version of Campion's own history with her parents. When Ziggy, not yet understanding what has happened, asks who made the two mounds of earth that have appeared in the back paddock, her brother answers: "Dad made them." Immediately following this, observing the two empty bridles, Ziggy avers, "When it rains, Poppy and Snow [the horses] will come back—I've kept their halters." At a symbolic level, the father's act in killing the horses stands for the destruction of something his daughter holds to be precious but which they both hope will be regained in the future. Just what that something is becomes apparent in the next scene in which the two girls "search for buried bodies" in the dam that is now "completely dried up." Sam finds in the dirt a gold wedding ring, upon which the camera focuses in a close-up shot. Sam decides that she will wear the ring on a string around her neck (in a gesture that foreshadows the way Fanny will wear a key around her neck in *Bright Star*), keeping it "for when I meet my dream man." From this, one can infer that the destruction of the horses is symbolically associated with the destruction of the marriage between Richard and Edith Campion, and, as a consequence of that, the destruction of the likelihood that a girl (Ziggy, Alice, Jane) will be able to come into possession of an idea of masculinity in which she can invest sufficient trust to find emotional assurance and security. The ring—another motif that recurs repeatedly in Campion's movies—when the girls find it, is encrusted, literally and metaphorically, with "dirt," which draws attention to the same kind of danger attending romance as was signified by the dagger on which Rodriguez extended a ring to Frannie in *In the Cut*. Yet the ring

The wedding ring that the children find in the dirt in *The Water Diary*.

itself is gold, it is beautiful, and it provides the basis for a hope that might be realized in the future, the arrival of the "dream man" who, symbolically, will have the qualities that will be able to cancel out the damaging effects of the past.

At another level, as so often in Campion's movies, this episode involving the wedding ring conflates one level of reference with a second one that superimposes her mother's experience upon her own. Metaphorically speaking, the idea of a lost marriage, evoked by the discarded ring, is likely to allude to the disintegration of not only Edith Campion's marriage, but Jane Campion's marriage to Colin Englert. The fact that the ring is discovered by the two girls, one of whom is being acted by Campion's daughter from her failed marriage, serves two symbolic functions: on one hand, it evokes the disappointment that can be experienced by a woman who has committed herself to a relationship with a man; on the other hand, it intimates the possibility of a romantic ideal to which the girls can aspire.

Once one starts to apprehend the logic of the metaphorical and metonymical meanings latent within the manifest story of *The Water Diary*, it becomes apparent that the drought is a symbol for the absence of something in the psychic structure of one's being that is capable of nurturing and sustaining a flourishing emotional life. The possibility of such an *épanouissement* is what the longed-for rain symbolizes, as does the ring, and both are associated with romance and beauty. Furthermore, in Campion's imaginary, these things are associated with her mother, as we learn when Ziggy describes how her mother believed that she heard rain on the roof: "she really believed it." This is likely to allude to Edith Campion's inextinguishable belief in a romantic ideal and in the great art and literature through which creative minds over the centuries have been able to communicate a vision of it.[5]

In the second half of *The Water Diary*, one can see Campion's focus shift to the search for a way of recovering the lost ideal. The potential for art to provide the means is signaled in the "water dream" experienced by Pam (played by Genevieve Lemon, one of Campion's favorite actresses), in which Felicity, the most beautiful and talented girl in the area, was playing her viola on top of a hill. Her music, Pam reports, was so beautiful that clouds gathered from miles around, weeping at the beauty of her playing, "and it rained and rained." This prepares the way for the children, led by Ziggy, to attempt to enact this dream literally—by assembling on the top of a hill with jars of water, each containing one of their teardrops, while Felicity stands on a water tank and plays her viola. By giving the redemptive agent of this attempted restoration the name Felicity, Campion was once again covertly acknowledging her hopes for her own daughter, as "felicity" is a translation of Alice Englert's second name, Allegra, which means "happy" in Italian.

By including this allegory, Campion seems to be saying that art that is stimulated as a response to the acknowledgment of emotionally painful experiences in life has the power to actualize a catharsis that, metaphorically speaking, can bring back the rain and, in so doing, provide some form of redemptive consolation in a world that is prone to drought in the form of those things that cause our anxiety or suffering. Significantly, however, even though at the end of *The Water Diary* we see dark (presumably, rain-laden) clouds gathering, and we see one of the children open an umbrella, we do not actually see any rain falling. An exploration of that possibility is the great theme that Campion would pick up in *Bright Star*.[6]

3 Whether or not she was fully aware of it, given her professed willingness to follow the impulses of her unconscious, with *The Water Diary* Campion had begun to shift the locus of her personal investments yet

again. Whereas her previous films showed her preoccupation swinging between issues relating to her mother and issues relating to her father, including the consequences of both in her own life, after her break from filmmaking, her new ventures attested to an investment in her daughter, Alice, along with a concern to explore simultaneously the hopes that Campion might have had for herself and the hopes she could entertain for a young woman on the threshold of adulthood.

The effects of this shift in focus are immediately apparent in *Bright Star,* which is about as far from the explicit eroticism of *Holy Smoke* and *In the Cut* as it is possible to be. As Campion has affirmed in an interview, even before she had completed the making of *In the Cut,* she "was heading towards this Keats vision of life, more about sensitivity, honouring things like that, tenderness. I find that more powerful and moving for me than anything else."[7] In another interview, she confessed that what appealed to her about the story of Keats and Fanny was "something about their purity and their innocence."[8] Gone is any assumption that love can arise out of a relationship with a man that is grounded in carnal eroticism; instead, there is a new emphasis on a transcendent, ideal love that is hardly accompanied by sexuality at all, apart from a few chaste kisses that the lovers in this film share. It is as if the pendulum has swung to the opposite extreme—glimpsed earlier in the repression of physical sexuality by Kay in *Sweetie*—a phenomenon not unknown to psychoanalysts when dealing with analysands who have been subjected to childhood traumas of the sort that are implicit in Campion's cinematic representations. This change in focus is signaled in one of *Bright Star's* opening shots of masses of white cotton sheets flapping in the wind —an image that, at a symbolic level, suggests something from which the dirt has been cleansed, with the wind bringing a refreshment that foreshadows the many other images of wind entering confined spaces through open windows that will appear recurrently in the rest of the film.

The choice of subject for *Bright Star* is significant. By Campion's own account, backed up by the testimony of her sister, Anna, the great romantic in the Campion family was their mother. Edith was not only a champion of romantic fiction, such as the gothic melodramas of the Brontë sisters that provided part of the inspiration for *The Piano,* but

Fanny in front of a curtain billowing with wind at Elm Cottage in *Bright Star*.
Courtesy of Pathé/Photofest.

was also passionate about poetry and suggested the magnificently ap-
posite poem by Hood that provides the epilogue to *The Piano*. She also
ensured that poetry—especially by Shakespeare—was frequently re-
cited in the Campion household and was an accomplished poet in her
own right, with a number of her poems, including several on the subject
of her cats, being published in *Landfall*, the leading New Zealand literary journal of the time. There can be no doubt that the selection of the
romance between Keats and Fanny Brawne on Jane Campion's part was
influenced by an awareness of her mother's twin passions for romance
and for poetry.

Another clue is provided by *In the Cut*—a film in which Campion
explores through her fictive surrogate, Frannie, the effects on her of the
betrayal of her mother's romantic expectations by the sexual infidelity
of an adulterous husband. When Frannie and Malloy are walking beside
a lake—symbolically filled with floating rubbish, associated with the
attempt Frannie will make to initiate sex with the detective, which he
rejects—she recites the opening lines of Keats's "La Belle Dame sans
Merci":

O what can ail thee, Knight at arms
  Alone and palely loitering?
The sedge has withered from the Lake,
  And no birds sing!

The poem is associated with the psychic sickness in Malloy that impels him to seek self-medication in sex—an addiction into which, with partial success, he has inducted Frannie. Malloy's rejection of Frannie's offer to fellate him, on the grounds that he wants something more—love—in association with the famous lines by Keats sets up the pretext for *Bright Star*. Having explored what eroticism can offer, only to find, with Malloy, that it is not enough, Campion flips the coin over to reveal its other side: a love which, although intensely passionate, is transcendent, nonphysical, and romantically idealized. So, for her next venture, she dramatized one of the most famous love affairs in English literary history, made all the more poignant by its tragic outcome.

The close association of this story with Edith is made palpably evident by the filmmaker's reiteration of several private symbols associated with her mother. The first, the motif of a ring, occurs when Keats places a ring on Fanny's finger, telling her it was his mother's. The information that the ring belonged to the poet's mother is Campion's invention, because in her source, Andrew Motion's biography of Keats, there is no suggestion that this is the case: we are told simply that Keats "probably . . . [gave] her a garnet ring."[9] The added detail, however, recalls *In the Cut*, which Campion had made six years earlier, in which the psychotic killer, Rodriguez, gives Frannie an engagement ring immediately before he attempts to murder her. We can see in the carrying over of this symbol from one film to the other that the two episodes in which the heroine is given an engagement ring stand in strong contrast to one another: the ring Rodriguez gives Frannie signifies the death-dealing potential of romance associated with the inconstancy of her father, while the ring Keats gives Fanny signifies the purity of the romantic ideal associated with his mother. The important point is that, in Campion's imaginary, both the positive possibility and the negative outcome are closely associated with the real-life story of her mother.

A second sign that this is so is evident in the presence of a cat, used here again as a symbolic motif in the way that it recurs in virtually all Campion's movies at moments when the action resonates with Edith

Campion's passions, her predispositions, her artistic commitments, or her fate in the director's imagination. In *Bright Star,* this symbolic motif appears in the foregrounding of the Brawne family's cat: it appears in most scenes that deal with poetry, and its role is often combined with the image of a nearby fire. Keats holds the cat on his lap as he sits before the fire, fondling its ears, in an early scene in which he explains the nature of poetry to Fanny; the cat appears when Fanny, alone, is reading poetry; and it is also present when Fanny, seated before an open window with billowing curtains, is impatiently awaiting a letter from Keats during his sojourn on the Isle of Wight. The cat is such a powerful presence in this movie that it is even acknowledged in the closing credits as if it were a character. What the presence of the cat in *Bright Star* connotatively signifies is that the story told by the film has relevance both to Edith's idealistic view of the romantic love that she would like to believe is capable of redeeming human experience, and to her sense that the forces in this world are likely to frustrate it.

A manuscript poem by Edith Campion given to me by Jane Campion in June 2008 suggests the imaginative collocations inhering in the image of a cat for the director, and also how they were present in her mind during the genesis of *Bright Star:*

> We walk out, my cat and I
> Into the bite of wintered morning
> And stand, under a cloud silvered sky
> Under a sun, watered down
> By the month of May.
> Our nostrils take the cold air
> And expel it in white wraiths.
> We look with disapproval
> At trees surrendering leaves
> At earth sulky under frost
> Our hearts sad, sullen and cockled.
> Suddenly
> We are expanded and released
> My cat and I,
> Over whelmed by the Bush Warbler's
> Sweet, wild cry.[10]

Not only does this poem, with its evocation of a desolate winter scene to suggest, metaphorically, a state of emotional depression, illustrate the romantic cast of Edith Campion's sensibility, but it also suggests that the

```
We walk out, my cat and I
Into the bite of wintered morning
And stand, under a cloud silvered sky
Under a sun, watered down
By the month of May.
Our nostrils take the cold air
And expel it in white wraiths.
We look with disapproval
At trees surrendering leaves
At earth sulky under frost
Our hearts sad, sullen and cockled.
Suddenly
We are expanded and released
My cat and I,
Over whelmed by the Bush Warbler's
Sweet, wild cry.
```

Typescript of a poem written by Edith Campion. *Courtesy of Jane Campion.*

encounter with beauty—here identified (in a very Keatsian manner) with the song of a bird—has, for Edith, a power to countermand the destructive imperative of that depression. Significantly, it is the poet's beloved cat who, assuming the role of an intimate subjective object, shares Edith's experience of this cathartic emotional expansion that releases her from what would otherwise be a suffocating spiritual entrapment.

The imagery in this poem, I would suggest, is picked up and elaborated in the mise-en-scène of Jane Campion's redaction of Keats's story in *Bright Star*. The equivalent in the film of the poem's birdsong is the purified love between Keats and Fanny, expressed in the sonnet from which the film takes its title. The possibility of this love being a solution for life's ills, however, while entertained, is undermined by a foregrounding of a destructive mutability that renders love fleeting and transient, and attainable only as an ideal whose beauty can be glimpsed and captured in art. The film's thesis is announced near the beginning, when Fanny recites the opening lines of Keats's poetic romance *Endymion*, which is presented in *Bright Star* as having been recently published:

A thing of beauty is a joy for ever:
Its loveliness increases; it will never
Pass into nothingness; but still will keep

A bower quiet for us, and a sleep
Full of sweet dreams, and health, and quiet breathing.

Some shape of beauty moves away the pall
From our dark spirits.[11]

The optimism of this idealistic effusion, however, has already been undermined by the arresting striking image that opens the film: the action of a needle, seen in extreme close-up, as it penetrates cloth that is being embroidered, bursting through the resistance with a violence that tears the fabric through which it is being pushed. It is hard to think of a symbolic image that could more powerfully suggest the ability of a brutal reality to destroy the integrity of things, even while an attempt is made to embroider an image that will constitute a compensatory beauty.

Such is the paradox that Campion explores in this profoundly suggestive film. At one level, the love affair that develops between Keats and Fanny Brawne, the beauty of the sentiments and the passion of the emotions with which Keats invests it, which are answered by the equally intense feelings of Fanny, seems to supply all that was lacking in the carnal couplings of PJ Waters and Malloy in Campion's two preceding feature films. In case the viewer misses this fact, the inadequacy of a relationship grounded primarily in sexual desire is figured in the parodic relationship between Keats's friend Brown and the serving girl Abigail Donohue, which, being devoid of love, prompts Keats to observe of Brown, "with what ease you help yourself."

Keats, in Campion's film, does not "help himself"; rather, he experiences love with an intensity that he confuses with the sensation of dying. At one point, he declares his desire to possess Fanny's loveliness and death simultaneously, and at another he feels that his love of her is so intense that it is causing him to be "absorbed" and "dissolved." Inevitably, this association of love with death is accompanied by a realization of the "impossibilities" in the world that will prevent the love between the couple from being fulfilled in terms of mundane life. Chief among them are Keats's illness, which soon kills him, and his poverty, which means that the lovers cannot marry. The transience that this imposes on the lovers' happiness is displayed proleptically in the movie by images of flowers, which fill the meadows in spring—as when Fanny reads a letter from Keats in a field of bluebells, and when Keats approaches the

Brawnes' house through a field of daffodils. Transience is also symbolized by butterflies: Fanny wears butterfly clips in her hair in one of the
opening scenes; she starts a butterfly farm in her bedroom as the love
between her and Keats deepens; and with her younger siblings, Toots
and Samuel, she captures butterflies in the spring meadows. The problem
is that spring is followed by winter, which kills the flowers and strips the
trees of leaves, while butterflies live for only a few days—a somber reality
that is imaged by recurrent shots of bare tree trunks, fallen leaves, and
dead butterflies lying on the floor.

The passion of the lovers, therefore, although beautiful in its intensity and selfless purity, cannot survive the encounter with the reality of
mundane life, with its threats and imperfections. As Keats tells Fanny,
as his imminent mortality becomes apparent, "We have woven a world
of our own invention" that is "attached to this world by threads; we must
cut the threads." The tragic frustration of their relationship caused by
Keats's death, therefore, carries with it a feeling almost of bitterness,
bitterness at a world which seems to offer the possibility of hope, but
which, as soon as that possibility becomes visible, cruelly whips it away.
The hope is entertained, but as Fanny observes at one point in the film,
"hopes are different from results."

The film concludes with imagery that the viewer recognizes from
Campion's earlier films—*The Portrait of a Lady,* in particular—as the
final scenes are imbued with images of coldness that signify awareness
of a chilling impediment to the fulfillment of hope, at least at the level
of personal psychic aspiration. Following the news of Keats's death in
Italy, we see an image of Fanny outside, from Brown's perspective looking through a window, with a snowball in her hand. Our final glimpse
of Fanny is of her walking alone through a snow-covered winter scene
on Hampstead Heath, reciting, with a painful awareness of their irony,
the lines of "Bright Star"—the sonnet that Keats had written for her. As
well as recalling the solitude of Isabel at the end of *The Portrait of a Lady,*
these images recall the chill of the ice with which Campion ended the
short film she made at the commencement of her career, *A Girl's Own
Story. Bright Star* appears, in this reading, to be "a woman's own story,"
recording a vision that articulates not only the good that Campion would

like to believe possible in this world, but also the unlikelihood of that good ever being attained because of the world's imperfections. The best one can hope for, the film seems to be saying, is for the vision itself to be captured through the beauty of art, an art that is born out of the suffering that, ironically, will destroy the possibility of the solution that art is prompted to contemplate.

4 Campion, in the press kit released when *Bright Star* was shown at Cannes, suggested that she conceived of the world of Keats and Fanny as "light filled, literally leaking light." Even though the film ends with Keats's death, she continued, "the lamp lit by his poetic genius and unique spirit cannot be extinguished. It is *Bright Star*'s ambition to sensitize the audience, to light the lamp."[12] This strikes me as disingenuous— as an attempt to put a positive spin on a film that is ultimately ambivalent at best, and pessimistic at worst. Campion would like to believe in the ideal she has tried to capture, but is fearful it cannot be realized.

This underlying ambivalence is registered by the appearance of almost all of the personal symbols that have recurred through her earlier films, leaving the impression that *Bright Star* is almost a summative retrospective. Most of the imagery that appears has been seen before. The still lake to which the melancholy Fanny comes was seen in *In the Cut*; the bare trees and concluding scene set in snow appeared in *The Portrait of a Lady*; the butterflies and flowers appeared surrealistically in *Holy Smoke* in an aura around Ruth's head, to suggest the naïve idealism with which she was seeking security through spirituality; images of hands caressing surfaces appeared in *The Piano*, as did the idea of a hole in a garment that was capable of being "fixed"; the wind that enters through windows, causing curtains to billow with fresh air, was prefigured in *The Piano* with the story Ada tells Flora of the wind that invites the child to play, suggesting an invitation to heterosexual romance as the solution to emotional repression; the ring that Keats gives to Fanny recalls the rings that appear in *Sweetie* and *In the Cut*; the marked contrasts between dark and light recall the similar symbolic contrasts in *The Portrait of a Lady*; the idea of a world of invention as a refuge from the pall cast by the real world recalls *An Angel at My Table*; and the bough of cherry blossoms Fanny presents to Keats recalls the petal shower in *In the Cut* and suggests the sordid reality that may succeed the hope that is implicit in Fanny's innocent gesture.

Campion, in her interview, appears to be distancing herself from the kind of personal engagement she formerly pursued, as if some kind of renunciation of her struggle were taking place in *Bright Star.* Whether or not this is the case will become apparent in any movie that Campion makes, which cinephiles eagerly await.

Conclusion: Theorizing the Personal Component of Authorship

1 This book has shown how the contents and representational strategies of each of Jane Campion's films are determined largely by the nature of the filmmaker's personal investment in her creations. That personal investment, in turn, arises out of and is informed by familial situations that the filmmaker seeks to address through a complex process of condensation and displacement involving metaphor and metonymy. Underlying the superficial appearance of disparateness that has troubled some critics, the personal preoccupations I have revealed in Campion's films attest to a striking continuity that imparts a remarkable degree of unity to her oeuvre, despite shifts in style, genre, and mode. All of these aspects of her cinematic practice have implications for a theory of authorship.

2 The most significant attribute of authorship that Campion's example illustrates is the ability of an auteur-director to implant a metonymical system in a film that works, in conjunction with other elements in the representation (metaphor, plot, character, setting), to establish a subtext of latent signification that the viewer perceives as having meaning for the author.[1] Whether the scenario is an original script written by the director, or is based on a script written by someone else, or constitutes an adaptation of a work by another author, the implantation of this metaphorical and metonymical system will convert the material to the personal purposes of the auteur-director. Moreover, the symbolic suggestiveness generated by such a system will not only embody the meaning that the material has for the director, but also condition the way in which attentive "readers" will respond to the material, whether or

not they are aware of its personal relevance for the filmmaker. The filmic texture that is operating with this level of investment will be conveyed through an impression registering in viewers that the image or sequence is *overdetermined,* that is, that there is a degree of condensation at work in the representation that carries more than one latent signification.[2] The means by which this overdetermination is communicated can be nuanced and subtle. As Kaja Silverman has aptly suggested: "Insofar as a filmmaker can be said to function as one of the enunciators of the works that bear his or her name, those works will contain sounds, images, patterns, and/or formal configurations which provide the cinematic equivalent of the linguistic markers through which subjectivity is achieved."[3] Indeed, stylistic devices are one of the main ways in which the presence of overdetermination is revealed: the positioning of an object in the frame; the duration of the shot and what it lingers on; striking camera movements; unusual angles; the selection of the type of shot in relation to its content; and so on. Such devices alert the reader to the presence of a latent meaningfulness which may not be explicitly articulated but which is felt nevertheless, being registered in the unconscious of both the author and the responsive viewer.

Campion's practices exemplify many of the strategies that are available to an auteur-director who wishes to invest material with metonymical significance. These include the use of symbolism to provide the equivalent of an unspoken meta-commentary on the significance of what is being depicted at a given moment. Her settings, for example, are invested with an archetypal signification that has psychological relevance. One thinks of Campion's use of dark subterranean places, such as the catacombs in *The Portrait of a Lady* and the cellar in *In the Cut,* which symbolize both the sinister nature of the unknown and also the strange mixture of attraction and dread that Campion's heroines feel when they confront an eroticism that is forbidden yet exciting. Similar use is made of settings involving the symbolism inherent in heat or cold, as in the desert of *Holy Smoke* (associated with sexual desire and spiritual thirst) and the snow at the conclusion of *The Portrait of a Lady* (symbolizing the emotional chill that has settled into Isabel as a result of her experience of a dysfunctional marriage).

Another device Campion frequently uses is a nondiegetic insert that provides a hint as to the symbolic significance of the diegetic material that surrounds it. One striking instance occurs in *The Piano* when Flora is offering her fanciful explanation of how her mother came to be mute. As she is describing how a great storm blew up as her parents' voices rose for the final bars of their duet, with "a great bolt of lightning" coming out of the sky, striking her father so that he "lit up like a torch," the image of a child's animated drawing of a father going up in flames is inserted for a brief second or so. The effect is to intimate the homicidal resentment toward her father of a hurt, adoring child who wishes to annihilate him to requite his neglect of her. In other words, at a suggestive symbolic level, this nondiegetic insert encapsulates the filmmaker's motivation for the whole film. Another instance of this strategy can be found in *Sweetie* in the sequence of time-lapse photography showing seeds germinating, which similarly intimates, at a symbolic level, the motivating personal investment of the filmmaker.

Other aspects of the mise-en-scène are chosen for their potential to be invested with metonymical overtones. These include props and features of the decor, such as the heaters by which Campion's heroines literally and metaphorically seek to warm themselves, the bars or boards that signify the heroines' sense of entrapment, and the mirrors that suggest either the heroines' narcissistic self-investment or the nature of their relationships with others.[4] The use of color, too, is important for the generation of symbolic meaning (for example, the autochrome blue of the bush scenes in *The Piano*, suggestive of the claustrophobic effects of emotional depression and sexual repression, and the repetition of red lights in *In the Cut*, signifying danger). Structural oppositions are equally important, such as the contrast between Kay and Dawn in *Sweetie*, and between Frannie and Pauline in *In the Cut*, which represent diametrically opposed attributes of femininity, or the contrast between Stewart and Baines in *The Piano*, which opposes a repressed puritanical masculinity against a liberated androgynous masculinity.

Finally, symbolism is evident in the presence of recurrent iconic elements that serve as motifs—or "cinethemes," as Richard O'Neill-Dean has called them.[5] In Campion's movies, flowers, for example, are repeatedly used to represent innocence, along with other images conveying the idea of fragility or transience, such as wings, petals, and butterflies. Other reiterated images are associated with sexuality and the loss of innocence, such as rings and ring shapes that serve as vulval symbols, and the various phallic images that suggest penetration—the most striking instance being the engagement ring that Rodriguez holds out to Frannie on a dagger just before he attempts to murder her in *In the Cut*. Critics have often noted the repeated images of hands and fingers, which variously suggest sexual desire and interest (as in the repeated shots of Ada's fingers in *The Piano*) or a quality in men that is perceived to be threatening and dangerous (as with the gloved fist at the opening of *In the Cut*). The list of such metonymical cinethemes is virtually endless, encompassing the image of severed women's heads, which suggests the dangerous consequences of sexual knowledge (as, for example, in *The Piano*, where women's bleeding heads are displayed in the Bluebeard play, and in *In the Cut*, where Frannie is shown nursing her half sister's severed head), and the repeated images of women's feet in shoes, which also seem to have a sexual connotation (as in the shot of Frannie with one of her red shoes on and the other off, which suggests the divided nature of her attitude toward sexuality, which is marked by the antithetical impulses of desire and fear).[6] Such motifs are repeated not only within Campion's individual films, but also across her films, creating the impression of a dense metonymic and symbolic system that extends through her work as a whole—even though Campion, by her own admission, has not always realized this.[7]

One's sense of the existence of this personal level of reference is further enhanced by the way Campion handles the cinematography and focalization.[8] Although her heroines are viewed from the outside, with the camera serving as a kind of third-person narrator, the manner in which shots are composed and juxtaposed blurs the boundaries between an external and an internal focalization. A classic instance of this, as Dana Polan and others have pointed out, occurs in *The Piano* in the scene where Ada gazes with longing at her abandoned piano on the beach. The scene begins with a high angle shot taken from behind Ada's shoulder, which suggests the narrative perspective of a nonfocalized story. The camera then does a slow zoom to focus on the piano, and then cuts to Ada's face in close-up before it begins to glide slowly around her, maintaining a focus on the depth of inner emotion that is conveyed in Ada's eyes as she gazes at the piano.[9] The effect is to shift the focalization from the external perspective of the narrative camera to the internal perspective of the character who is its subject. As a result, the implied perspective of the director becomes closely identified with that of the heroine. Camera work of this kind achieves a similar degree of identification between the filmmaker and her fictive surrogate in each of Campion's feature films, reinforcing the idea of their personal relevance.

Another example occurs in *The Water Diary* in the scene in which Ziggy's friend Sam discovers a gold wedding ring in the dirt at the bottom of a dried-up dam. After an establishing shot showing the two girls descending into the depression, the film cuts to a close-up shot of Sam's fingers on the ring as she pulls it out of the dirt—from a side angle that could not reflect Ziggy's perspective, as she is standing behind Sam. Then there is a cut to a medium shot over Sam's shoulder that seems to reflect an omniscient point of view associated with the filmmaker in her communication to the spectator. Immediately after that, however, the viewer is invited to identify with Ziggy's perspective, when Sam turns her head back over her shoulder to speak to Ziggy, saying that the ring is "for when I meet my dream man," after which there is a cut to Ziggy tying the ring on a string around Sam's neck, followed by a voice-over from Ziggy that anchors the episode back into the narrative. This manipulation of the intercutting between shots is subtle, but it does serve to make the "reader" experience a shift in the focalization that indicates the presence of overdetermination in the image, and when that occurs, as it frequently does in Campion's movies, it is almost invariably a sign that an autobiographical level of associative reference is being activated.

Taken altogether, techniques and strategies such as those described above have the effect of making the movie function as if it were a dream. The same mechanisms of dramatization, displacement, condensation, and symbolism enable the filmmaker to create a representation that allows psychic perturbations or preoccupations to be addressed vicariously at a displaced remove. Such processes and effects, I would argue, constitute an essential aspect of the authorship of an auteur-director such as Campion.

3 The personal investment present in Jane Campion's cinema, interpreted in the light of our awareness of its origins in the filmmaker's life circumstances, also allows us to see what motivates an auteur to

make films in the first place. As I have demonstrated, Campion's film-making derives from an impulse to use creativity to address a problematic that originates in the circumstances of her earlier life. For her, fictive creation—in this case, through the medium of film—serves to activate a process of self-exploration, self-experience, and self-repair.

The psychology motivating this kind of engagement has been well described in contemporary psychoanalytic theory. As Danièle Flaumenbaum and others have argued, when a person is suffering from the lingering effects of childhood trauma, such effects will not be allayed until the individual has been able to construct an accurate representation of the sources of the perturbation. Until one has been able to grieve past miseries and "accept things as they are," by distancing oneself from any unspoken truths, omissions, or falsehoods, one will remain trapped within a "crypt" in which one is tyrannized by "fantasmal pathologies" that will seek expression "in one way or another."[10] This is what Kaja Silverman, following Laplanche and Pontalis, has termed "the authorial fantasmatic," which is a scene of authorial desire that comprises "that unconscious fantasy, or cluster of fantasies, which structure not merely dreams and other related psychic formations, but object-choice, identity, and 'the subject's life as a whole.'"[11] When traumatic feelings originating from "the familial reserve" are able to be brought into some form of mental representation—which can take the form of "endless secondary productions"[12]—this can have the effect of releasing the troubled subject from being bound in "unconscious fetters," leaving him or her free to "move forwards into the future."[13] Inevitably, the process whereby past traumas are brought into mental representation will involve what Heinz Hartmann has called a "regressive adaptation," which is "a mental achievement (whose roots are archaic) [that] gains a new significance both for synthesis and in relation to the external world, precisely because of the detour through the archaic."[14]

As Campion's case illustrates, this "detour through the archaic" is precisely what cinematic creation offers to the auteur-director, through making possible the construction of a representation that allows access to what Daniel N. Stern has called "a narrative point of origin."[15] Such access is achieved through the setting in motion of an affectively loaded version of the original experience—through a loading of metaphorical and metonymical investments in the representation—that the individual found troubling or traumatic in the past, but at a safely condensed and displaced symbolic remove. As Stern points out, even when this narrative point of origin is known, it can nevertheless remain affectively inaccessible to the individual if the key experiences are unable to be recreated.[16] Fictive representation enables the creator to gain affective access to the experience that perturbed him or her, while making it possible for this experience to be shared with an audience. At the same time, it allows the original trauma to be addressed indirectly, thus shielding the psyche from the direct confrontation of a pain that may be consciously or unconsciously perceived to be too threatening or unbearable.

4 Once this function of a work of art is recognized, it becomes possible to see how a film can be constructed to serve as a "transformational object"—both for the filmmaker in the first instance, and subsequently for the responsive viewer, who "may be captated by the authorial system of a given text or group of texts."[17] I would suggest that this concept points to an important dimension of cinematic authorship that has not received sufficient attention in the debates over auteurism to date, and will therefore briefly elaborate on it.

The notion of a "transformational object" derives from Donald W. Winnicott's discoveries concerning the use of "transitional objects" in the play of children, which serve as mechanisms to help them negotiate the gap between subjective reality and the external environment:

> From the beginning the baby has maximally intense experiences *in the potential space between the subjective object and the object objectively perceived,* between me-extensions and the not-me. This potential space is at the interplay between there being nothing but me and there being objects and phenomena outside omnipotent control.[18]

The play that occurs in this potential space, Winnicott proposed, is facilitated by the use of transitional objects, which are things that function as reassuring symbols for the union between mother and child *"at the point in time and space of the initiation of their state of separateness"* (emphasis in original).[19] With maturity, after the preverbal affect has become married to the self-reflexivity made possible by the acquisition of language, an individual can use language and other forms of symbolic representation to construct more sophisticated transitional objects as a means of negotiating between his or her inner psychic world and external reality. Because of this, Winnicott believed, the use of transitional objects resides at the heart of all cultural experience, with the artistic creativity of adults serving the same function as the play of children.

Building upon Winnicott's insights, the contemporary psychoanalytic theorist Christopher Bollas has extended the idea of a "transitional" object into that of a "transformational" object by recognizing the transformative effect that the process of negotiation involved in the use of transitional objects can have. There are two human aesthetics, Bollas argues, that inform the choice and use of objects. The first human aesthetic involves the infant's choice of an object that can assist him or her to tolerate the state of being separate from the mother. The second human aesthetic concerns the child's discovery that it is possible for objects to "speak the self."[20] In adulthood, therefore, we are constantly selecting objects that "disperse the objectifying self into elaborating subjectivities."[21] Such objects can be anything that the mind selects: a particular piece of music, a perfume, a taste, a person, an event. When such objects become invested with subjective connotations, they acquire the status of "subjective objects," which, in turn, function as "potential forms of transformation" because of their ability to elicit "new psychic textures that bring us into differing areas of potential being":

> Certain objects, like psychic "keys," open doors to unconsciously intense—and rich—experience in which we articulate the self that we are through the elaborating character of our response. This selection constitutes the *jouissance* of the true self, a bliss released through the finding of specific objects that free idiom to its articulation.[22]

Through the reflexivity of the process involved, the individual gains an enhanced sense of who she or he is:

> The simple experiencing self and the complex reflecting self enable the person to process life according to different yet interdependent modes of engagement: one immersive, the other reflective.... the aim of this position is to objectify as best as possible where one has been or what is meant by one's actions.[23]

At such moments of self-experiencing, Bollas surmises, we project meaning into objects at an unconscious level, so that the selection of objects often becomes a type of self-utterance: "This idiom of self expression is a potential means not only of representing unconscious phantasies but of conjuring dense psychic textures that constitute a form of thinking by experiencing."[24] Subjective objects, therefore, "can be said to have a lexical function when we employ them to 'speak' our idiom through the 'syntax of self experience.'" Over time, we can build up a "lexicon" of such subjective objects that are capable of triggering self-experience, owing to the projective associations that inhere in them. The final goal of this process, Bollas concludes, is to achieve a symmetry, or symbiotic harmony, between the inner self and external reality, and to make the environment "symmetrical to human need."[25]

The purpose of representations that are created as transformational objects, such as films (or any works of imaginative creation), can be explained, I would suggest, in terms of the various functions of the fantasies that all human beings experience at least from the time of birth. Based on the findings of an extensive research project conducted in Britain on sexual fantasies, the psychotherapist Brett Kahr has identified fourteen different functions of fantasies:

(1) wish fulfillment
(2) self-comfort and self-medication
(3) trial action
(4) elaboration of childhood play
(5) establishment of object relations
(6) identification of transitional objects and transitional phenomena
(7) communication of inner conflict
(8) indulgence in masochistic punishment
(9) defense against intimacy and merger
(10) discharge of aggression
(11) avoidance of painful reality
(12) evacuation of sadistic strivings
(13) mastery of trauma
(14) equilibriation of the self[26]

When one looks across the span of Campion's films in the light of the personal identifications, projections, and emotional investment that I have shown to be embodied in their fictions, one finds that most, if not all, of these functions are present. Wish fulfillment is reflected in the desire of her heroines to be the object of attention from a father (or father figure); to be free of the destructive effects on them of paternal disapproval or neglect; and, simultaneously, to detach themselves from a sense of emotional dependency on, or fusion with, or abandonment by, a mother who is also felt to exert a harmful influence. Self-medication is equally apparent in the eroticism in which Campion's heroines engage, especially those in her films from *The Piano* onward (Ada, Isabel, Ruth and Yvonne, Frannie and Pauline). Transitional objects play a prominent role in the psychic life of these heroines, such as the piano itself in the film of that name, which stands in for Ada's dead mother, having once belonged to her and being the means whereby the daughter can sustain a sense of connection with her now inaccessible mother. Similarly, *The Piano* and other Campion films, such as *In the Cut*, can be viewed as attempts to establish an important object relation in their search to find ways in which the heroine can relate without fear to the masculine. An impulse to indulge in masochistic self-punishment is seen in the experiences of heroines like Ada, Ruth, and Frannie, who are subjected, respectively, to mutilation, violence, and the threat of murder as punishment for their attraction toward the impossible and the forbidden (eroticism that entails a fantasy of incest). Usually, a number of the different functions identified by Kahr can be seen working in Campion's movies simultaneously. The discharge of aggression and the evacuation of sadistic strivings are both present in *Sweetie,* as seen in the killing off of the resented sister (presented in the form of an accident), while the half sister in *In the Cut* is similarly disposed of, but in a more explicitly brutal manner. Likewise, the mastery of trauma and an avoidance of painful reality are accomplished through the retreat into artistic creation into which Janet withdraws in *An Angel at My Table* in a move that simultaneously addresses the source of pain in the filmmaker's relationship with her mother, while also depicting one aspect of its resolution: engagement in fictive creativity itself. Generally, all of Campion's films attest, in one way or another, to attempts to attain and maintain the equilibriation of the self through the processes of self-experience that are made possible by the construction of the film to serve as a transformational object capable of rectifying the potentially damaging effects of trauma that occurred earlier in the filmmaker's life. On the evidence of research conducted over many years, Kahr concluded that fantasies are "extensions of our capacity for creativity."[27] The practice observable in Campion's filmmaking, I think, proves the symmetry of this conclusion: creativity arises equally from our capacity to fantasize. As I hope I have by now demonstrated, all of Campion's films represent an attempt to give these fantasies fictive embodiment.[28]

5 While Campion's films provide an extreme example of this psychological dimension underpinning cinematic creativity, it is likely to be present to a greater or lesser degree in the work of most, if not all, directors. Truffaut, for example, in *Les 400 coups* (1959) and in the other autobiographical films he made with Jean-Pierre Léaud playing Antoine Doinel, his fictive surrogate, displays the same kind of personal investment as Campion, and for similar reasons: to repair the emotional damage caused by parental neglect in his earlier life. All of Truffaut's films, but particularly the Doinel series, display desperate attempts to find some substitute for the missing maternal object in the hero's imaginary. As Anne Gillain has shown, drawing upon Winnicott's theory of transitional space:

> The maternal body for which Antoine yearns, which both fascinates and frightens him, remains absent and seemingly inaccessible. . . . Cinema, as the ultimate representation of transitional activities in Truffaut's own personal development, will compensate for parental neglect and allow for an approach of external reality.[29]

Thus, in *Les 400 coups*, "the city is a maternal space which shelters the child, protects his games, hides and feeds him,"[30] providing the same function that the movie, by extension, performs for the director.

Truffaut's method differs somewhat from Campion's, in that rather than relying upon a dense layer of metonymical symbolism, as Campion tends to do, Truffaut projects the autobiographical elements through a narrative process of transcription that is much more direct, involving a far lesser degree of displacement. In the first movie of the Doinel sequence, Antoine, a youth on the threshold of puberty, stands in for the young Truffaut and reenacts the events that Truffaut experienced in real life.[31] As well as representing this dimension in the action of the film, Truffaut makes Doinel deliver a verbal summary of the traumatizing circumstances of the childhood he shares with his creator, during the session he spends with the psychotherapist who questions him in the reform school to which he has been sent.

In comparison, Campion interposes a much greater degree of symbolic displacement between her real-life experience and her fictionalized response to it. While it is possible through painstaking archaeology to identify elements that correspond directly to events or objects in Campion's past experience, as she has warned us, everything is "mixed and matched," with elements being transposed and reassembled, so that the lines that connect the fiction to the reality are obscured. Her habit of drawing upon archetypal symbolic imagery and structuring her material in binary oppositions also places an additional layer of signification between the director and the filmic representation. Campion's personal investment thus works through a process of what I would call "embodied symbolism," which, because of the displacement involved, is much more oblique and indirect than the more simple symbolic transcription to be found in Truffaut's overtly autobiographical films.

With Tsai Ming-liang, a contemporary Malaysian Taiwanese auteur who was greatly influenced by Truffaut, the director's personal investment is materialized both directly and indirectly. In *Ni na bian ji dian* (*What Time Is It over There?* 2001), through which Tsai projects his response to his father's death, he follows Truffaut's practice of having a specific actor stand in for his earlier self. In every film Tsai has made, the Taiwanese actor Lee Kang-sheng bears the same relationship to the director as Jean-Pierre Léaud did for Truffaut. Tsai Ming-liang also thickens his cinematic fictions with personal symbolic images in the manner of Jane Campion: watermelons, associated with sexual desire, are especially evident in *Tian bian yi duo yun* (*The Wayward Cloud,* 2005); dividing spaces, such as corridors and stairways, suggest isolation and alienation; and, above all, water is shown in all its forms: leaking, upwelling, raining down, flooding, flowing as a river, stagnant, putrid, thick with fecal matter, and refreshing. As Tsai has admitted, water for him means a lot of things: "It's my belief that human beings are just like plants. They can't live without water or they'll dry up. Human beings, without love or other nourishment, also dry up. The more water you see in my movies, the more the characters need to fill a gap in their lives, to get hydrated again."[32] One of the most striking instances of this occurs in *He liu* (*The River,* 1997), when the lead character, Hsiao-kang (played, as always, by Lee Kang-sheng as Tsai's stand-in), floats lifelessly in the Tanshui River, imitating a corpse. Water as a personal symbol for Tsai thus functions in its variant forms in his movies as an allegorical commentary upon the psychic condition of his characters at any given moment, projecting a search for spiritual respite and emotional nourishment that reflects his construction of each of his films as a personal transformational object.

Other auteur-directors use the capacity of a film to function as a transformational object in a manner that is closer to Campion's more oblique practice. Alfred Hitchcock, for example, as Donald Spoto has shown, repeatedly made movies that allowed him to indulge his "dark fantasies about killing, and of unfulfilled sexual daydreams," and at the same time to exorcise his guilt over the deep divisions and dual drives he recognized within himself.[33] His strategy was to contrive or adapt plots that transposed his repressed impulses into literal actions within the narrative, as in *Shadow of a Doubt* (1943), in which the charming Uncle Charlie turns out to be an evil strangler who seduces and kills rich widows. Another example occurs in *The 39 Steps* (1935), in which Hitchcock adapts a thriller plot based on John Buchan's novel to illuminate his awareness of the gap between the persona of respectability he fostered and the dark secrets he harbored within, together with his fear of a bad reputation.[34] Similarly, the action in *Vertigo* (1958) may be interpreted as a displaced projection of his secret romantic impulses and of the attraction and repulsion he felt about the object of those erotic impulses: "the idealized blond[e] he thought he desired but really believed to be a fraud."[35] In terms of its function as a transformational object, therefore, one suspects that cinematic creation for Hitchcock served as a form of confession (he came from a Roman Catholic background), whereby he sought to evacuate the unwanted parts of himself by exposing and projecting them at a displaced remove, and to receive absolution in the form of the audience's acclaim. The existence of a deeply personal motive of this kind helps to explain why Hitchcock betrays his authorial presence so unmistakably through the enunciative strategies he employs in his movies, just as Campion does.[36]

Hitchcock's practice, like Campion's, demonstrates that the more complex the personal problematic of the filmmaker is, the more complex and resonant will be the fantasies that are embodied in the fiction of the film. We can see this again in Steven Soderbergh's *Sex, Lies, and*

Videotape (1989), another striking example of personal cinema. Soderbergh has admitted that, in the several years before he made this movie, his own life was a lot like that of the unfaithful husband, John Mullany, in *Sex, Lies, and Videotape:* "It was a real problem for me because I was beginning to feel very unhappy and I had to put an end to my behavior and begin thinking about the effects it was having on other people. I was living with someone I really liked but at the same time I was behaving miserably and I wanted to know why."[37] Soderbergh made *Sex, Lies, and Videotape,* therefore, as "both an act of liberation and remorse."[38]

Soderbergh's comments point not only to the operation of several of the functions of fantasy identified by Kahr, but also to the complexity of the process whereby the real-life situation is addressed through a fantasy, fictive creation. A key to the nature of Soderbergh's representational strategy is provided by a further comment he made to Michel Ciment, admitting that "at that point in my life I was closer to the James Spader character," that is, to Graham Dalton, who has withdrawn into a self-protective inwardness in an effort to prevent himself from "scaring others" (in particular, the girlfriend he loves), which has left him unable to relate to women in a sexual way other than vicariously, via the videotaped interviews he makes of them. Confessing that the other male character, the husband, was "just a sketch," Soderbergh adds that "[i]n treating him like that I was punishing myself for what had happened."[39] In other words, Soderbergh, in a move that recalls Campion's choices in *Sweetie,* split out the two sides of his contradictory impulses in order to embody them in two separate male characters, who are then put into a complex set of interactions with two female characters whose characters and relationship to one another mirror those of the men: Ann parallels Graham in her frigidity, and Cynthia reflects John in her unscrupled libidinousness. The purpose of Soderbergh's strategy, in terms of the function of the film as a transformational object, was thus simultaneously to inflict a masochistic punishment on himself—by showing one side of himself (John) as crass and despicable, and the other (Graham) as abject and impotent—while envisioning the possibility of a redemptive solution, by showing Graham moving toward a relationship with Ann (whose own actions mirror his movement) that is grounded in honesty and genuine relating. As a result, the fiction of the film, for Soderbergh, is designed to accomplish not merely wish fulfillment, but also an imaginative equilibriation of the self that could enable such an outcome to be achieved. To my mind, this illustrates the primary function of personal cinema: through the construction of the film as a transformational object, the director creates an imaginative fiction that is capable of making the environment, as Bollas put it, "symmetrical to human need."

Most directors, one suspects, make films for similar reasons. Roman Polanski once said disparagingly of director John Cassavetes that "[h]e's not a filmmaker—he's made some films, that's all. Anyone could take a camera and do what he did with *Shadows*."[40] It may be possible, hypothetically, to imagine a director who functions merely as a *metteur en scène* who has no motive arising out of any concern with issues relating to the self, but even then the decisions of such a director regarding the mise-en-scène would inevitably reflect the influence of his or her psychological formation. The influence of this personal element may be so banal that there would be no point in excavating it, but it would exist nevertheless, even if it were to amount to no more than an unthinking reiteration of the most commonplace discourses of the day. If such were the case, we would be confronted by a hack, not an auteur, but some element of authorship would still be present in the work of such a director.

6 An understanding of the motives and strategies involved in personal cinema puts one in a position to speculate on the implications of the practices of an auteur-director like Campion for a theory of cinematic authorship at large.

The most obvious implication is that the status of the auteur in the authoring process must be reasserted—but in terms that avoid the exclusive and excessive claims for the auteur made by the "young firebrands," as André Bazin called them, who espoused the *politique des auteurs*.[41] In this regard, Bazin's position seems right: while he saw the auteur as playing the most noticeable function in the production of a film's meaning, he believed that the auteur, nevertheless, was simply one function within "a system of forces."[42] Furthermore, as Dudley Andrew rightly points out, the global commercialization of culture "places even the most intentional auteur . . . inside a system that is larger than he, a system that quickly and crudely exchanges his value on the market in its own way."[43]

Despite the need for these qualifications, the nature, motives, and effects of the creative process I have outlined show that a director like Campion still exerts by far the most powerful influence on the meaning of a film, even though there may be other forces involved. The manner in which she shapes her original material and reworks the material she derives from other sources attests to a creative input that is far more substantial than simply that of a catalyst for the activation of meanings outside the author's control. Also, even though no one would question the idea that latent meaning inheres in the codes, genres, and discipline of the filmic system of representation, the manner in which an auteur like Campion treats these elements is liable to convert them to an application that generates new meaning, thus constituting a process of original authorship. This can be seen in the genre films Campion has made—*An Angel at My Table* (a biopic), *The Piano* and *The Portrait of a Lady* (heritage films), *In the Cut* (an erotic thriller)—which are no less idiosyncratic and personal than her films that are less heavily generically marked, such as *Sweetie* and *Holy Smoke*.

Similarly, the example of Campion shows that even though the economically driven concerns of production companies may exert an influence on the meaning of a film, the scale of this influence is likely to be nowhere near as great as the influence exerted by the filmmaker. Campion is frank in admitting the power of production companies to shape the films they fund, out of their concern to create a product that will have box-office appeal. *The Piano*, for example, originally had a more violent ending in which Baines killed Stewart and Ada drowned. Campion would also have preferred to keep the original ending of Susanna Moore's *In the Cut*, in which Frannie is murdered by Rodriguez. In each case, she felt obliged to change the ending in order to get her project funded.[44] Even so, the substitution of positive endings for the alternative nihilistic ones does not significantly alter the character of the films concerned, because the nature of Campion's thematic concerns and her cinematic strategies mean that her personality is manifest in every aspect of her movies—*tota in toto, et tota in qualibet parte* (whole in the whole, and whole in every part of it), just as the soul was considered in medieval and Renaissance philosophy to be dispersed throughout the body as an animating power (*prima potentia*).[45]

No one would dispute that a filmic text can embody or solicit other types of meaning—such as those inherent in preexisting discourses that a critic or viewer might associate with the representation, or the meanings that specific cultural or social subgroups might discern through the lens of their particular perspectives and preoccupations—but all this shows is that any critic must be careful to differentiate between these different types of meaning and then to identify the kind of meaning with which he or she is concerned. The determining influence of an auteur-director like Campion, or any other filmmaker who is involved in the creation of personal cinema, cannot be denied or overlooked if the film is to be comprehensively apprehended. To do so would be perverse.

On the evidence of Campion's practices, together with the examples provided by other practitioners of personal cinema such as those I have discussed above, one must conclude that, in films that are constructed to address deeply personal concerns on the part of the director, the extent of the director's influence will fully justify the claim that such a filmmaker is indeed an auteur, in the same way that a poet or novelist is. Furthermore, it may even be that *no* filmmaker is entirely free of the shaping instincts that arise from the "authorial fantasmatic" that resides in us all. In that case, even movies that appear to be entirely conventional in terms of genre and appeal, such as the romantic comedies of Garry Marshall or Nancy Meyers, may reflect the kind of personal investment that one would associate with authorship as I have been describing it. Meyers, for example, has confessed that Erica Barry in *Something's Gotta Give* (2003), played by Diane Keaton, is a reflection of herself (which is why Keaton is made up as a Meyers look-alike) and that Erica's story is based on her own experience.[46] The fact that even such an apparently conventional genre film such as *Something's Gotta Give* can be inspired by a director's own experience suggests that authorship may be a given if filmic representation is serving as a transformational object for the filmmaker. The question then becomes, not whether such authorship is present beyond the nonconventional films of independent filmmakers, but whether it can ever be absent from a director's engagement with his or her film, given that no director's practices are ever likely to be free from the influence of the emotional economy that is a legacy of his or her personal experience.

7 A critical friend, upon reading these conclusions, queried whether the approach I have advocated could be applied to any filmmaker other than Campion in the absence of an equivalent amount of information about the filmmaker's personal background. In response, I would suggest that, even though Campion is somewhat unusual in the degree to which she has talked about the connections between her life and her art, she is far from unique. Comparable evidence exists for others whom one would judge to be auteurs according to the criteria I have suggested. Such evidence resides in the form of interviews, director's commentaries, press releases, and other biographical material, all of which are capable of yielding many insights—providing one knows that there is good reason to look for it. Apart from illuminating the genius of Jane Campion's filmmaking art, therefore, I hope that this book has made a convincing case for the worth of applying this kind of approach to other filmmakers whose work might be considered to constitute a personal cinema.

There is, indeed, a great need for additional case studies of this kind, because the kind of evidence I have been discussing helps to explain why certain films strike the viewer as having depth, texture, and resonance that transcend the merely stereotypical. Because of the degree of personal investment, the filmic representation, through the unconscious conversation between director and viewer, strikes the members of the audience as having a greater depth of latent signification than the ostensible narrative would superficially appear to suggest. Furthermore, future case studies of this sort will, I predict, confirm the status of the auteur-director as a prime source of the meaning of a film that one cannot afford to ignore. Such studies will help to illuminate the nature of creativity, the connection between trauma and creativity, and the process whereby creativity transforms experience into art. When this is achieved, our understanding of the complexity and richness of cinema as a signifying system will be greatly enlarged. To neglect it would greatly impoverish the understanding of audiences as to what a film may have to offer them.

Notes

INTRODUCTION

All translations throughout this book are mine unless otherwise indicated.

1. See Wexman, *Film and Authorship*; Grant, *Auteurs and Authorship*; and Gerstner and Staiger, *Authorship and Film*.

2. Grant, *Auteurs and Authorship*, xi.

3. For a gesture in this direction, see work by Catherine Portuges, who, drawing upon the theories of D. W. Winnicott, suggests that the object relations theory of creativity "holds as yet unrealised possibilities for elaborating the intersections of autobiography, gender and film theory." Portuges, *Screen Memories*, 59.

4. Metz, *The Imaginary Signifier*, 84n10.

5. See Gillain, *François Truffaut*; and Gillain, "Script of Delinquency," 142–57.

6. Silverman, *Acoustic Mirror*, 202.

7. I would number among these some of the excellent studies of Alfred Hitchcock's films, such as Raymond Bellour's essays on *The Birds, Marnie, Psycho,* and *North by Northwest* in Bellour, *Analysis of Film*; and Spoto's *Dark Side of Genius*.

8. For commentary on the backlash against the excesses of structuralism and poststructuralism—in particular, their suspension of reference—see Stam, *Film Theory*, 327–78.

9. Laplanche and Pontalis, *Language of Psycho-analysis*, 354.

10. I am drawing here upon psychoanalytic concepts explored by Christopher Bollas in "The Aesthetic Moment," 40–48. See also Bollas's *Shadow of the Object* and *Being a Character*.

11. See Truffaut, "Une certaine tendance du cinéma français," reprinted in translation as "A Certain Tendency of the French Cinema," 224–37, esp. 230.

12. Throughout this book, I use the term "mise-en-scène" in its broader sense of referring to *all* elements of visual style, including cinematographic technique and the elements that appear in the film frame (settings, props, costumes, lighting, and the placement and behavior of the actors), rather than in the more narrow sense given by Bordwell and Thompson in *Film Art*, chap. 6.

13. Hoveyda, "Les Taches du soleil," 8–9.

14. See Rivette, "Notes sur une révolution," 94–97, esp. 97n2. Rivette points out that Truffaut used this quotation as an epigraph for a collection of his critical writings, *The Films in My Life*.

15. Astruc, "Naissance d'une novelle avant-garde," 17–23.

16. Sarris, "Notes on the Auteur Theory in 1962," 35–45, esp. 43.

17. Kael, "Circles and Squares," esp. 49.

18. Barthes' essay "The Death of the Author" (1967) is reprinted in his *Image/Music/Text*; Foucault also proclaimed the author dead in his 1969 essay "What Is an Author?"

19. Caughie, *Theories of Authorship*, 201.

20. Barthes, "Death of the Author," 145.

21. Ibid., 147.

22. For a trenchant critique of Barthes' theory, see Silverman, "The Female Authorial Voice," in her *Acoustic Mirror*, reprinted in Wexman, *Film and Authorship*, 50–75.

23. Wollen, *Signs and Meaning in the Cinema*. See also Stam and Miller, *Film and Theory*, 123.

24. Wollen, "From *Signs and Meaning in the Cinema:* The Auteur Theory," esp. 561.

25. Hillier, "Auteur Theory and Authorship."

26. See, for example, Petrie, "Alternatives to Auteurs"; and Vidal, "Who Makes Movies?"

27. Wood, "Ideology, Genre, Auteur."

28. Stam and Miller, *Film and Theory*, 6.

29. Verhoeven, *Jane Campion*, 22–25.

30. Staiger, "Authorship Approaches."

31. Ibid., 34–36.

32. Ibid., 43.

33. For an example of the former, see Yacowar, "Hitchcock's Imagery and Art" (1977). For an example of the latter, see Bellour, "Hitchcock the Enunciator," reprinted in Bellour, *Analysis of Film*, 217–37.

34. Petrie, "Alternatives to Auteurs," 110–18, esp. 113.

35. Sarris, "Notes on the Auteur Theory in 1962," esp. 43.

36. Wollen, "From *Signs and Meaning in the Cinema:* The Auteur Theory," 167–68.

37. Polan, *Jane Campion*, 160–67.

38. Ibid., 12.

39. McHugh, *Jane Campion*, 17–18.

40. Ibid., 18.

41. Ibid., 50.

42. Ibid., 63–64.

43. Sarmas, "What Rape Is," 14.

44. See Martin, "Losing the Way," 89–102.

45. See Gordon, "Portraits Perversely Framed," esp. 22; and Ciment, "The Function and the State of Film Criticism," 41, who shrewdly foresaw such a reaction.

46. McKee, *Story*, 9.

47. Timothy Corrigan, *A Cinema without Walls: Movies and Culture after Vietnam* (New Brunswick, N.J.: Rutgers University Press, 1991), 106.

48. Verhoeven, *Jane Campion*, 11.

49. I am alluding here to the instructions Hamlet gives to the players who are about to perform *The Mousetrap* in Shakespeare's *Hamlet* (III.2.29), and the words of Vindice in Cyril Tourneur's *The Revenger's Tragedy* (III.5.202–205).

50. Geertz, "Thick Description," 3–30.

51. Gillett, *Views from beyond the Mirror*.

52. Mackenzie, "Beloved Rivals."

53. Campion, "Director's Commentary," *Sweetie*.

54. Campion, "Director's Commentary," *An Angel at My Table*.

55. "Quand je les enfile, c'est comme un souvenir corporel, une sensation extraordinaire. Quand je serai très vieille, je me vois très bien dans une ferme avec des *gumboots*. Je ne suis pas sure que Janet en ait eu vraiment. Mais, j'ai voulu qu'elle en porte." Colmant, "Jane et Janet."

56. Campion, "Director's Commentary," *An Angel at My Table*.

57. Sampson, "Carry on Campion."

58. Verhoeven, *Jane Campion*, 15–16.

59. Ibid., 36, quoting Lewis, "Wholly Jane."

60. Gillain, "Script of Delinquency," 142–57.

61. Vanoye, *Scénarios modèles*, 207. I am indebted to Michel Marie for bringing the work of this scholar to my attention. It is a great pity, in my view, that Vanoye's work is not better known among English-speaking film scholars—a consequence of the fact that his books have not been translated.

62. "Il suffit que l'un de leurs films soit directement autobiographique ou personnel que cette qualité s'étende implicitement, à des degrés divers, sur l'ensemble de leur production aux yeux du spectateur" (ibid.).

63. "[C]elle d'une recréation plus complexe dans laquelle le 'je' diffuse en divers éléments du film: narration, voix-je, personnage plus ou moins fugitif ou stable, point de vue, etc." (ibid., 208).

64. See Spoto, *Dark Side of Genius*.

65. I am indebted to Hilary Radner for pointing out this parallel between Isabel Archer and Edith Campion.

66. See Gaitanos, *Nola Millar*, 148–49.

67. "Seule une approche génético-biographique peut nous permettre d'apprécier justement le contenu, le degré d'autobiographie dans un film ou une oeuvre cinématographique." Vanoye, *Scénarios modèles*, 209.

68. Noël Salathé, *Aperçus sur les caractères (Éléments pour une nosographie gestaltiste)* (1988), quoted in Vanoye, *Scénarios modèles*, 213.

69. Vanoye, *Scénarios modèles*, 213.

70. Ibid.

71. Hartmann, *Ego Psychology*, 76.

72. Stern, *Interpersonal World*, 266.

73. Mackenzie, "Campions Enjoy a Rich Friendship."

74. Ibid.

75. See Radner, "In extremis."

76. Williams, "Portrait of an Artist."

77. Campion, "Director's Commentary," *Sweetie*.

78. Ibid.

79. Campion, "Director's Commentary," *In the Cut*.

80. Freud, *Standard Edition*, 16:376.

81. McHugh, *Jane Campion*, 44, 46, 64, 107, 113, 126.

1. ORIGINS OF A PROBLEMATIC

1. For this and much of the information that follows, see the obituary for Edith Campion: Dekker, "Creator of Professional Theatre."

2. Edith Campion published this information on the dust jacket of her volume of short stories, *A Place to Pass Through*.

3. See Cheshire, *Pocket Essential Jane Campion*, 9.

4. Gaitanos, *Nola Millar*, 91.

5. Dekker, "A Man of the Stage."

6. See Wilson, *The Social Dimension of Sectarianism*, 87–102.

7. Mackenzie, "Beloved Rivals."

8. Dekker, "Creator of Professional Theatre," B7.

9. For the psychology of religious addiction, see Vanderheyden, "Religious Addiction."

10. McDougall, *Plea for a Measure of Abnormality*, 300–301.

11. Ibid., 301–302.

12. Bollas, *Being a Character*, 17.

13. Gaitanos, *Nola Millar*, 98.

14. Ibid., 100, 104, 111.

15. Ibid., 91, 111.

16. Ibid., 141, 114.

17. Richard Campion, interview with Sarah Gaitanos, 24 September 1998, reported in Gaitanos, *Nola Millar*, 143.

18. "Mes parents ont eu une vie irréelle. Par example, gagner de l'argent était pour eux un mystère complet." Colmant, "Jane et Janet."

19. Gaitanos, *Nola Millar*, 149. Gaitanos bases this account on conversations and interviews with several people who were close to Nola Millar and involved

with the New Zealand Players at the time
(see 350n52).

20. Mackenzie, "Beloved Rivals."

21. See Verhoeven, *Jane Campion*,
57–58.

22. Mason, "Richard
Campion—Producer."

23. Jane Campion, interview in *Premiere Women in Hollywood Special* (1997),
quoted by Cheshire, *Pocket Essential Jane
Campion*, 16.

24. Harcourt, *A Dramatic Appearance*,
113.

25. Millar, "Theatre."

26. Ibid.

27. Sargeson, "Review."

28. Campion, *A Place to Pass Through*,
4.

29. For an account of this fascinating
but little-known film, see Margolis, "The
Campions Indulge in *The Audition*."

30. Campion and Sargeson, *Tandem*, 5.

31. Ibid., dedication.

32. It is interesting to note that another
New Zealand writer, the Maori novelist
Witi Ihimaera, also uses the image of a
spider to suggest the persecutory aspects
of a cross-generationally bonded relationship involving emotional incest. See Ihimaera, *The Matriarch*, 265.

33. Firestone and Catlett, *Fear of Intimacy*, 123.

34. See Fox, *Ship of Dreams*.

35. Again, there exists a fascinating
parallel with Witi Ihimaera's sequel to *The
Matriarch*, *The Dream Swimmer*, in which
Tamatea, the hero, evacuates and exor-
cises his loving hate for his grandmother
through having violent sex with Tepora,
who serves as a younger stand-in for the
matriarch. See Ihimaera, *The Dream
Swimmer*, 318.

36. Dekker, "Creator of Professional
Theatre," B7.

37. Freud, *Collected Papers*, 5:74–78.

38. Ibid.

39. Ibid.

40. On family systems theory, see
Bradshaw, *Family Secrets*.

41. Mackenzie, "Beloved Rivals."

42. "J'aime l'aspect irrational de
l'érotisme. Cette énergie sauvage qui s'en
dégage et qu'on ne parvient pas à maî-
triser. Il peut ainsi arriver qu'un couple
merveilleusement marié détruise sa vie
parce que soudain la passion folle fait
irruption." Attali, "La leçon érotique de
Jane Campion."

43. Campion, "Director's Commentary," *In the Cut*.

44. Hessey, "Campion Goes Out on a
Limb—Again," 28.

45. Ciment, "Red Wigs of Autobiography," 67.

46. "Metonymy" is a rhetorical strategy whereby something that is not named
directly is evoked by reference to other
things that suggest it through association.
For an account of metonymy in filmic textuality, see Christian Metz, "Metaphor/
Metonymy; or, the Imaginary Referent,"
in his *The Imaginary Signifier*, 149–203.

47. Campion, "Interview," *La leçon de
piano*.

48. Campion, "Director's Commentary," *Sweetie*.

49. See Bollas, *Shadow of the Object*.

50. Campion, "Director's Commentary," *Sweetie*.

51. Polan, *Jane Campion*, 1–3;
McHugh, *Jane Campion*, 49–50.

52. "En fait mes parents étaient surtout
absorbés par leur histoire, ils étaient très
amoureux et les enfants venaient en second." Colmant, "Jane et Janet."

53. McDougall, *Plea for a Measure of
Abnormality*, 303.

54. Colmant, "Jane et Janet."

55. "Dans les premiers temps, quand
j'étais à la fac, j'étais assez malheureuse,
très seule. Je n'arriverais pas à m'insérer
dans un groupe, en fait, je suis assez tordue et ça m'a pris un certain temps pour

trouver des gens qui partageraient mon sens d'humeur" (ibid.).

56. Campion, "Director's Commentary," *Sweetie*.

57. Mackenzie, "Campions Enjoy a Rich Friendship," 70.

58. *Guardian Weekend*, 5 June 1999, quoted by Cheshire, *Pocket Essential Jane Campion*, 11.

59. Taubin, "Jane and Anna Campion."

60. McHugh, *Jane Campion*, 46, 126.

61. Cheshire, *Pocket Essential Jane Campion*, 11.

62. Mackenzie, "Campions Enjoy a Rich Friendship," 70.

63. Dekker, "Creator of Professional Theatre," B7.

64. Campion and Campion, *Holy Smoke*, 187.

65. For further comment on this topic, see Fox, "Puritanism and the Erotics of Transgression."

66. See Polan, *Jane Campion*, 53.

67. Ciment, "A Voyage to Discover Herself," 177.

68. See Winnicott, *Maturational Processes*, 245–46.

69. For example, Polan, *Jane Campion*, 57–58, 72–73.

70. Williamson, "The New Filmmakers," 9.

71. "Ruth a une force très australienne, et je me sens foncièrement liée a l'Australie, ce sont mes paysages, ma vie." Tranchant, "*Holy Smoke*."

72. Taubin, "Jane and Anna Campion."

73. For further comment on the influence of New Zealand puritanism on Campion, see Fox, "Puritanism and the Erotics of Transgression."

74. "The Making of *An Angel at My Table*," a documentary created by Bridget Ikin and Tiara Lowndes (2002); Franke, "Jane Campion," 208.

2. THE "TRAGIC UNDERBELLY" OF THE FAMILY

1. Hessey, "Campion Goes Out on a Limb—Again," 28.

2. Ibid.

3. McHugh, *Jane Campion*, 139.

4. "À l'âge de 25 ans, j'ai commencé à travailler d'une manière un peur particulière, et a déveloper, une relation avec mon subconscient. C'était le moment où j'écrivais mon premier film. Au bout de trois pages, c'était fini, je ne pouvais pas aller plus loin. Alors, je passais le relais à mon subconscient. Mais pour que ce processus opère, il faut croire qu'il y a des réponses possibles." Colmant, "Jane et Janet."

5. Ciment, "Two Interviews with Jane Campion," 43.

6. See Jane Campion's interview with Lynden Barber, "Angel with an Eccentric Eye," 61.

7. This information is imparted by Michel Ciment in an interview included in disk 3, *Jane Campion: Le coffret*.

8. Abramowitz, "Jane Campion."

9. Stiles, "Jane Campion," esp. 4–5.

10. McHugh, *Jane Campion*, 23.

11. The only items published from 1980 onward are three short pieces: "To Black Cat"; "Matador"; and "Rider Waits."

12. McHugh, *Jane Campion*, 23.

13. "The Making of *The Portrait of a Lady*."

14. McHugh, *Jane Campion*, 126.

15. Polan, *Jane Campion*, 60–61.

16. Ibid., 62.

17. "The Grass Is Greener: Interview with Jane Campion."

18. Polan, *Jane Campion*, 57–64.

19. Ciment, "Two Interviews with Jane Campion," 33.

20. Urban, "Contradictions of Jane Campion," 14.

21. Reported by Wexman, *Jane Campion*, xv.

22. Stiles, "Jane Campion," 7.

23. Campion, "Director's Commentary," *In the Cut*.

24. Stiles, "Jane Campion," 7.

25. Campion, "To Black Cat," 238.

26. Campion, "Director's Commentary," *Sweetie*.

27. Taubin, "Jane and Anna Campion."

28. Ciment, "Two Interviews with Jane Campion," 35.

29. Polan, *Jane Campion*, 77–79.

30. Bourguignon and Ciment, "Interview with Jane Campion," 102.

31. Ciment, "Two Interviews with Jane Campion," 35.

32. "Ma mère était très pauvre, et elle m'a raconté que les seuls vêtements qu'elle possédait, quand elle était enfant, c'était son uniforme d'écolière. Et quand elle était invitée à des goûters d'enfants, elle y allait en uniforme alors que toutes les filles portaient de jolies robes." Colmant, "Jane et Janet."

33. Ibid.

34. I acknowledge my debt to Hilary Radner for this insight.

35. "Jane Campion on Jane Campion," in Verhoeven, *Jane Campion*, 200.

3. LIVING IN THE SHADOW OF THE FAMILY TREE

1. "A Conversation with Director Jane Campion," included in the press kit for the release of *Sweetie*, 5, in author's possession.

2. Hawker, "Jane Campion," 21.

3. See McHugh, *Jane Campion*, 64, 58.

4. "A Conversation with Director Jane Campion," press kit, 6.

5. Ciment, "Two Interviews with Jane Campion," 43.

6. McHugh, *Jane Campion*, 63–64.

7. Ciment, "Two Interviews with Jane Campion," 43.

8. Forsberg, "'Sweetie' Isn't Sugary."

9. Ibid.

10. Campion, "Director's Commentary," *Sweetie*.

11. This newspaper headline is shown in the documentary "'Sweetie' la folle: Entretien avec Michel Ciment," disk 1, *Jane Campion: Le coffret*.

12. Ciment, "Two Interviews with Jane Campion," 38.

13. Campion, "Director's Commentary," *Sweetie*.

14. Ibid.

15. Matthews, "Leaving Sequence."

16. Ibid.

17. Ibid.

18. Ripoche, "Fleurs de soufre," disk 1, *Jane Campion: Le coffret*.

19. See, e.g., Canby, "'Sweetie,' a Wry Comedy"; and McHugh, *Jane Campion*, 64–65.

20. Ciment, "Interview," in *Jane Campion: Le coffret*.

21. Stevens, *Jung*, 63.

22. Jung, "Psychology and Religion," 11:131.

23. Stevens, *Jung*, 65.

24. Ibid., 66.

25. Campion, "Director's Commentary," *Sweetie*.

26. Strauss, "Tart Family Ties in *Sweetie*."

27. Williamson, "The New Filmmakers," 9.

28. Stiles, "Jane Campion," 7.

29. Campion, "Director's Commentary," *Sweetie*.

30. Doland, "Female Film Directors Lacking at Cannes."

31. McDougall, *Theaters of the Mind*, 12.

32. Ibid., 13.

33. Feinstein, "The Jane Mutiny."

34. Dekker, "A Man of the Stage," 10.

35. Gaitanos, *Nola Millar*, 324.

36. Ciment, "Two Interviews with Jane Campion," 44.

37. Forsberg, "'Sweetie' Isn't Sugary," 15.

38. Hawker, "Jane Campion," 21.

39. Campion, "Director's Commentary," *Sweetie*.

40. Ibid.

41. Ibid. Campion reveals that she was only able to finish the shooting of the film because of the generosity of Anna Campion, who flew back from England to New Zealand to be with their mother—which is why Jane Campion dedicated the film to her sister.

4. "HOW PAINFUL IT IS TO HAVE A FAMILY MEMBER WITH A PROBLEM LIKE THAT"

1. This sister-mother substitution in *Peel* has even led some viewers, mistakenly, to assume that the sister *is* the mother.

2. Williams, "A Light on the Dark Secrets of Depression," 174.

3. See Margolis, "The Campions Indulge in *The Audition*," 39–52.

4. Ibid.

5. Ibid.

6. Ibid.

7. Campion, Introduction to *An Angel at My Table*, x.

8. Ibid.

9. Campion, "Director's Commentary," *An Angel at My Table*.

10. Campion, Introduction to *An Angel at My Table*, xi.

11. Edith Campion, Personal Papers, MS-Papers-6360-119, Alexander Turnbull Library.

12. Campion, Introduction to *An Angel at My Table*, xi.

13. Ibid.

14. Bollas, *Hysteria*, 120.

15. "Ma vie et mon cinéma se répondent même si ma vie est beaucoup moins intense. Je vis à travers mes films et, si on se réfère à eux, je m'épanouis sur le tard." Attali, "La leçon érotique de Jane Campion."

16. Campion, "Director's Commentary," *An Angel at My Table*.

17. Ciment, "Red Wigs of Autobiography," 67.

18. For the process of selection involved in the adaptation of the screenplay, see the detailed account given by Jones, "I can really see myself in her story."

19. Cordaiy, "Jane Campion Interviewed," 84. See also Jones, *An Angel at My Table*.

20. Jones, *An Angel at My Table*, 2.

21. Jones, "I can really see myself in her story."

22. Jane Campion has revealed that her mother attempted suicide during the final weeks of the shooting of *Sweetie*. It was only the return of Anna Campion to be with their mother during her recovery that had allowed Jane Campion to complete the movie. Campion, "Director's Commentary," *Sweetie*.

23. Letter from Tim Curnow, Janet Frame's agent, to Bridget Ikin, 3 February 1988. I acknowledge my debt to Pamela Gordon, Janet Frame's niece, for providing me with this information.

24. Campion, "Director's Commentary," *An Angel at My Table*.

25. "J'ai grandi à la ville, mais mes parents ont déménagé à la campagne quand j'avais 13 ans. Ma mère montait beaucoup à cheval, nous donc aussi. C'est comme ça que j'ai eu une jument." Colmant, "Jane et Janet."

26. Ikin and Lowndes, "The Making of *An Angel at My Table*."

27. Campion, "Director's Commentary," *An Angel at My Table*.

28. Ibid.

29. Campion, "Director's Commentary," *Sweetie*.

30. Campion, "Director's Commentary," *An Angel at My Table*.

31. Ikin and Lowndes, "The Making of *An Angel at My Table*."

32. Campion, "Director's Commentary," *An Angel at My Table*.

33. "Dans les premiers temps, quand j'étais à la fac, j'étais assez malheureuse, très seule. Je n'arrivais pas a m'insérer

dans un groupe, en fait, je suis assez tordue et ça m'a pris un certain temps pour trouver des gens qui partageaient mon sens d'humour. Je venais d'une école pour filles." Colmant, "Jane et Janet."

34. Campion, "Director's Commentary," *An Angel at My Table.*

35. Ibid.

36. "Je me suis beaucoup identifiée avec Janet quand elle parle de son inspiration et de sa relation avec sa muse. Moi, j'ai toujours personnalisée cette muse, depuis que je suis enfant, sous les traits d'un homme. J'avais le sentiment, très fort, que cette personne était à mes côtés pour m'aider et pour me donner des idées. Tout ça, c'est fini, maintenant." Colmant, "Jane et Janet."

37. Campion, "Director's Commentary," *An Angel at My Table.*

38. Urban, "Campion: Cannes She Do It?" 18.

39. Frame, *An Autobiography,* 434.

40. Ibid., 9.

41. See Jones, "I can really see myself in her story."

42. Jones, *An Angel at My Table,* 92.

43. Campion, "Director's Commentary," *An Angel at My Table.*

44. Hessey, "Campion Goes Out on a Limb—Again," 28.

45. I am referring to the novelization of *The Piano,* written with the assistance of Kate Pullinger; *Holy Smoke,* co-written with her sister, Anna; and the short story "Big Shell," published in *Rolling Stone.*

46. Bilbrough, "*The Piano,*" 123.

47. Reported by Simpson, "She Calls the Shots."

5. TRAUMAS OF SEPARATION AND THE ENCOUNTER WITH THE PHALLIC OTHER

1. "Oscar Doubts over Campion's *Piano.*"

2. I have written at length on the influence of Jane Mander's novel on Campion's film in Fox, "Puritanism and the Erotics of Transgression."

3. Furler, "Structure Is Essential," 91.

4. Ibid.

5. Bilbrough, "*The Piano,*" 123. Anna Campion also attests to Edith Campion's romanticism: "Passion was my mother's big number, as is reflected in *The Piano.*" Falsetto, *Personal Visions,* 46.

6. Barber, "Playing It Low-Key," 143.

7. Mander, *The Story of a New Zealand River,* 30.

8. Quoted in Macklin, "Campion's Award-winning Screenplay."

9. Ibid.

10. Bourguignon and Ciment, "Interview with Jane Campion," 101. See also Campion, "Interview."

11. Bourguignon and Ciment, "Interview with Jane Campion."

12. Ibid.

13. "La compréhension du désir était plus une obsession quand j'avais vingt ou trente ans. . . . 'La Leçon de piano' fut pour moi l'occasion d'étudier cette force comme un chercheur étudie l'organisme. Si vous voulez, j'ai mis sous mon microscope l'embryon du désir, de la curiosité et de l'érotisme, puis j'ai observé ces trois éléments se transformer en amour." d'Yvoire, "Vertige de 'amour.'"

14. Polan, *Jane Campion,* 14, 28, 35. See also Richard Allen, "Female Sexuality, Creativity, and Desire in *The Piano,*" 44–63.

15. McHugh, *Jane Campion,* 81–83.

16. Radner, *Neo-Feminist Cinema,* esp. chap. 1.

17. See chapter 4.

18. This outcome caused consternation on the part of those who had approached her to direct *The River,* given that the original project had to be abandoned when Campion's film was made, and the grant of nearly $100,000 from the New Zealand Film Commission to develop a screenplay had to be written off. Further bad feeling

was created when residual similarities between the film and Mander's novel led to allegations of plagiarism in 2000, prompting acrimonious exchanges in the Australian and New Zealand media. On the plagiarism issue, see McGregor, *Story of a New Zealand Writer*, 125–27; Paul, *Her Side of the Story*, 75–101; Frey, "The Purloined *Piano*?"; Hardy, "The Last Patriarch"; "Fight-back over Piano Claims"; and Macklin, "Creative Effort Went into Film."

19. As early as October 1993, Jane Campion had become indignantly sensitive to insinuations that she had "cheated," even though she did concede that "there are certain genre similarities" between *The Piano* and *The Story of a New Zealand River*. See Witchel, "Return of the Native," 17. Later (unwisely), she would claim that she had not been influenced by the novel in writing the screenplay; the evidence, however, proved conclusively that she had both known and used it, and Campion subsequently did admit through her lawyer that she had read the novel.

20. I wish to record my debt here to Richard O'Neill-Dean, a practicing psychoanalyst in Dunedin, who gave a thought-provoking paper, "Interpreting *The Piano* as a Dream," on this topic at the Jane Campion research colloquium held at the University of Otago, 6–9 December 2006. I have adopted certain of the ideas presented in that paper and will acknowledge them specifically as they occur.

21. Jane Campion displays these pages of her workbook during the interview on *The Piano* that was released with *La leçon de piano*. Campion, "Interview."

22. Ibid.

23. See chapter 4.

24. See chapter 2.

25. Campion, "Director's Commentary," *An Angel at My Table*.

26. Feldvoss, "Jane Campion," 99.

27. Campion, "Interview."

28. Bourguignon and Ciment, "Interview with Jane Campion," 106.

29. Campion, *The Piano*, 17.

30. Campion and Pullinger, *The Piano: A Novel*, 18.

31. Ibid., 19.

32. Ibid., 19–20.

33. Ibid.

34. Ibid., 33–34.

35. Ibid., 34.

36. Ibid., 207.

37. Pullinger, "Her Assignment."

38. On the closeness of Campion's collaboration with Kate Pullinger, see Verhoeven, *Jane Campion:*

> One notable media interview, with Campion's co-author Kate Pullinger, does provide quite a lot of detail about the process of preparing *The Piano: A Novel*, claiming that Pullinger was treated by Campion as "more like a scriptwriter than a novelist," in other words, that she was subject to strict directions and timelines and that she was not personally afforded the status befitting an "auteur." (67)

39. I acknowledge a debt to Richard O'Neill-Dean for drawing attention to the presence of this phallic image in the shadow play.

40. I am indebted to Richard O'Neill-Dean for this suggestion.

41. A suggestion made by Richard O'Neill-Dean.

42. Campion, "Interview."

43. Feldvoss, "Jane Campion," 99.

44. d'Yvoire, "Vertige de 'amour.'"

45. Campion, "Interview."

46. Ibid.

47. Bourguignon and Ciment, "Interview with Jane Campion."

48. McDougall, *Theaters of the Mind*, 266.

49. Ibid., 268.

50. Ibid., 279.

51. See discussion and note 57, below.

52. See Jacobs, "Playing Jane Campion's *Piano*," esp. 775.

53. Bourguignon and Ciment, "Interview with Jane Campion," 102.

54. Williams, "A Light on the Dark Secrets of Depression," 175.

55. Campion, *The Piano*, 121.

56. Ibid., 123.

57. Campion, "Interview."

58. Ibid.

59. Ibid.

60. Cantwell, "Jane Campion's Lunatic Women," 152.

6. THE MISFORTUNES OF AN HEIRESS

1. Gillett, "Lips and Fingers."

2. Vivian Sobchak, "What My Fingers Knew: The Cinesthetic Subject; or, Vision in the Flesh," in her *Carnal Thoughts*, 53–84. Cited by Polan, *Jane Campion*, 23.

3. See the introduction.

4. Campion, "Interview."

5. "The Making of *The Portrait of a Lady*."

6. Franke, "Jane Campion," 206.

7. Edith Campion, "5 inward correspondence and papers—Jane Campion," MS-Group-0405, no. 24, "The Reef—Fourth Draft," MS-Papers-6360-111, Alexander Turnbull Library.

8. Edith Campion, MS-Papers-6360-062 and MS-Papers-6360-063, respectively, Alexander Turnbull Library.

9. Anna Campion, personal correspondence with the author, 6 August 2008.

10. Anna Campion describes the subject matter of *Broken Skin* as "really my mother and me." Falsetto, *Personal Visions*, 50. For an argument that *The Piano* explores issues pertaining to Edith Campion and her relationship with Jane, see above, chapter 5.

11. Wharton, *The Reef*, 19.

12. Faery, "Wharton's *Reef*," 80.

13. For a discussion of cinematic adaptations of Wharton's novels, see Boswell, *Edith Wharton on Film*.

14. "Production Notes," press kit for *The Portrait of a Lady* (a Gramercy Pictures release), 19, Margaret Herrick Library.

15. "The Making of *The Portrait of a Lady*."

16. James, *The Portrait of a Lady*, 86, 96.

17. Ibid., 104.

18. Edel, *Henry James*, 262.

19. Feinstein, "Heroine Chic."

20. James, *Portrait of a Lady*, 87.

21. See the introduction.

22. James, *Portrait of a Lady*, 308.

23. See the introduction.

24. James, *Portrait of a Lady*, 367.

25. Ibid., 571.

26. Franke, "Jane Campion," 206–207.

27. James, *Portrait of a Lady*, 412.

28. Ibid., 568.

29. Campion, *A Place to Pass Through*, 153.

30. Jones, *The Portrait of a Lady: Screenplay*, 68.

31. Ibid., vi.

32. McHugh, *Jane Campion*, 94.

33. [J]'ai toujours été intriguée par la pouvoir des pulsions romantiques. Je suis quelqu'un qui est souvent tombée amoureuse et à chaque fois, j'ai adoré ça. Quand cela m'arrivait, j'avais l'impression d'être totalement revitalisée. Je me sentais non seulement amoureuse d'une personne, mais de la vie toute entière. C'était un sentiment très très fort qui m'envahissait littéralement. (d'Yvoire, "Vertige de 'amour,'" 82–86)

34. James, *Portrait of a Lady*, 357.

35. Ciment, "A Voyage to Discover Herself," 177.

36. Ibid., 180–81.

37. James, *Portrait of a Lady*, 583.

38. Ibid., 636.

39. See Dapkus, "Sloughing Off the Burdens."

40. Jones, *The Portrait of a Lady: Screenplay*, viii.

41. Ciment, "A Voyage to Discover Herself," 180.

42. Abramowitz, "Jane Campion," 186.

43. James, *Portrait of a Lady*, 360.

44. See Ciment, "A Voyage to Discover Herself," 180; and Abramowitz, "Jane Campion," 187.

45. Habegger, *Henry James*, 159.

46. Abramowitz, "Jane Campion," 187.

47. James, *Portrait of a Lady*, 634, 635.

48. Ibid., 636.

49. Edel, *Henry James*, 259.

50. See Radner, "In extremis."

51. See Gordon, "Portraits Perversely Framed," 16.

52. Ozick, "What Only Words, Not Film, Can Portray."

53. Denby, "Lady Stuck."

7. EXACTING REVENGE ON "CUNT MEN"

1. Fraser, "Portrait of the Director."

2. See, e.g., Martin, "Losing the Way," esp. 95.

3. Samson, "Jane Campion's Cult Fiction."

4. For an illuminating essay on this topic, see Hardy, "Jane Campion and the Moral Occult."

5. See the introduction.

6. McHugh, *Jane Campion*, 102.

7. Pryor, "Sister Act."

8. Baillie, "Critical Smokescreen."

9. Witchel, "Return of the Native," esp. 18.

10. Landrot, "La ligue des Campions."

11. "J'ai commencé à developper dans ma tête l'idée d'un film sur la spiritualité à notre époque, en essayant d'y introduire la séduction, la complexité, les malentendus, ainsi que le côté terre à terre qui, selon moi, sont liés à tout voyage spirituel." Ciment, "Jane Campion."

12. Bourguignon and Ciment, "Interview with Jane Campion," 104.

13. Lewis, "Wholly Jane."

14. Campion, "Big Shell." See also Verhoeven, *Jane Campion*, 58.

15. Bourguignon and Ciment, "Interview with Jane Campion," 112.

16. Ostria and Jousse, "The Piano," 132.

17. Roach, "Campion Takes on Spielberg," 173.

18. "J'avais été passionée, en le lisant, de voir les tentatives d'Isherwood de devenir moine avant qu'il n'ya renoncé car le voeu de chasteté était trop difficile pour lui! Ce qu'il voulait avant tout dans ce monde, c'était l'intimité et l'amour." Ciment, "Jane Campion."

19. "Le problème est que je n'ai jamais réussi à avoir un scénario qui me satisfasse vraiment, magré plusieurs tentatives faites par des écrivains" (ibid.).

20. Lewis, "Wholly Jane."

21. "Je voyais tout ce qui sortait [in the 1970s]. 'Le dernier tango à Paris' et 'Le conformiste' de Bertolucci, que j'adore." d'Yvoire, "Vertige de 'amour.'"

22. *Le Figaroscope*, 24 November 1999.

23. Samson, "Jane Campion's Cult Fiction," 9.

24. Kahr, *Sex and the Psyche*, 291.

25. Ibid., 175.

26. Ibid., 394.

27. Ibid., 423.

28. Ibid., 225.

29. Campion and Campion, *Holy Smoke*, 21, 23.

30. "Leurs séances de travail pour l'écriture de *Holy Smoke* ont frôlé la thérapie familiale." Landrot, "La ligue des Campions."

31. See the introduction.

32. Feinstein, "The Jane Mutiny."

33. See, e.g., the case study of "Esme," in Kahr, *Sex and the Psyche*, 304.

34. Campion, "Big Shell," 75.

35. Ibid., 76.

36. Campion and Campion, *Holy Smoke*, 76.

37. Ibid., 77.

38. Andrew, "Sects Appeal."

39. Ibid.

40. Campion and Campion, *Holy Smoke*, 99–101.

41. Ibid., 101.

42. See above, chapter 1.

43. Campion and Campion, *Holy Smoke*, 191.

44. See McHugh, *Jane Campion*, 113.

45. Pierre et Gilles (Pierre Commoy and Gilles Blanchard) are French photographers who produce highly stylized photographs often featuring images from popular culture and religion. The similarity of the vision scenes in *Holy Smoke* to the visual imagery of Pierre et Gilles was first pointed out by Muriel Andrin in "Her-land."

46. Murphy, "Jane Campion's Passage to India," 32.

47. Campion and Campion, *Holy Smoke*, 3.

48. Ibid., 142–43.

49. Ibid., 128.

50. Ibid., 130.

51. Taubin, "Jane and Anna Campion."

52. Murphy, "Jane Campion's Passage to India."

53. Campion and Campion, *Holy Smoke*, 19.

54. Ibid.

55. Ibid., 169.

56. Ibid., 171.

57. Taubin, "Jane and Anna Campion."

58. Campion and Campion, *Holy Smoke*, 82–83.

59. Ibid., 86.

60. Ibid., 191–92.

61. Ibid., 187.

62. Miramax press kit for *Holy Smoke*, 20, Margaret Herrick Library.

63. Campion and Campion, *Holy Smoke*, 188–89.

64. "Ruth," or "routhe," in older English means "pity."

65. Campion and Campion, *Holy Smoke*, 208–210.

66. Ibid., 216–17.

67. Ibid., 230.

8. "THAT WHICH TERRIFIES AND ATTRACTS SIMULTANEOUSLY"

1. Campion, "Director's Commentary," *In the Cut* (uncut director's edition).

2. Tucker, "Review of *In the Cut* (1995)."

3. Thometz, "The Book as Aphrodisiac."

4. Cantwell, "Jane Campion's Lunatic Women," 157.

5. Simpson, "She Calls the Shots," 30.

6. Sidey, "Jane's Addiction," 232.

7. Taubin, "Jane and Anna Campion."

8. "Des cinq versions écrites avec Jane Campion, elle note: 'C'est son historire maintenant, plus la mienne, et c'est bien comme ça. Qu'elle ait changé la fin, je peux le comprendre, elle est plus optimiste que moi. La fin devait lui resembler.'" In other comments, Moore was less enthusiastic about Campion's changes: "We made a mistake with the end [of the movie]. She [Frannie] should have died— although Jane Campion, the director, when I mention this to her says—she's had to say this many times to me, 'Yes but we would not have been given the $15 million if she had died at the end.' So what do you want?" Agnès, "Interview with Susanna Moore"; and Birnbaum, "Susanna Moore."

9. Birnbaum, "Susanna Moore."

10. Moore, *In the Cut*, 120.

11. Ibid., 180.

12. Taubin, "Jane and Anna Campion."

13. Ibid.

14. McHugh, *Jane Campion*, 126.

15. Ibid.

16. "Frannie effectue un voyage où l'on doit combattre son ombre, ses démons, ses peurs, pour avoir une chance de redemption." Frois, "Jane Campion l'effrontée."

17. Campion and Moore, *In the Cut* (script), Margaret Herrick Library, directions for "Credit Sequence."

18. Ibid.

19. See chapter 3.

20. Campion and Moore, *In the Cut,* scene 85.

21. This passage occurs, but in a slightly less elaborated form, in Susanna Moore's novel (143).

22. Campion and Moore, *In the Cut,* scene 27.

23. Campion, "Director's Commentary," *Sweetie.*

24. Moore, *In the Cut,* 28.

25. Ibid., 29.

26. Ibid., 65.

27. Campion, "Director's Commentary," *In the Cut* (uncut director's edition).

28. Campion and Moore, *In the Cut,* scene 6.

29. Moore, *In the Cut,* 57.

30. Ibid., 120.

31. "Simplement, elle a connu de grandes déceptions, et elle n'a jamais trouvé dans les relations avec des hommes ce qu'elle en attendait. C'est un personnage qui s'est retiré du monde." Colombani, "Jane Campion, réalisatrice."

32. Ibid.

33. Campion, "Director's Commentary," *In the Cut* (uncut director's edition).

34. "Sa rencontre avec Malloy (Mark Ruffalo) la perturbe: voilà un homme sincère, direct. Cela bouleverse ses attentes romantiques, il n'a pas de discours sentimental. Il est imprévisible. Et il a une confiance totale sur le plan physique, ce qui la terrorise et l'attire à la fois." Colombani, "Jane Campion, réalisatrice."

35. Campion and Moore, *In the Cut,* scene 32.

36. "Production Notes," press kit for *In the Cut* (Screen Gems and Pathé), 8, Margaret Herrick Library.

37. Ide, "Review of *In the Cut.*"

38. Campion, "Director's Commentary," *In the Cut* (uncut director's edition).

39. Ibid.

40. "Ma vie et mon cinéma se répondent même si ma vie est beaucoup moins intense. Je vis à travers mes films et, si on se réfère à eux, je m'épanouis sur le tard." Glanerie, "L'Amérique est puritaine et pornographique."

41. Campion, "Director's Commentary," *In the Cut* (uncut director's edition).

42. Campion and Moore, *In the Cut,* scene 99.

43. Simpson, "She Calls the Shots," 30.

44. Campion, "Director's Commentary," *In the Cut* (uncut director's edition).

45. Ibid.

46. Sidey, "Jane's Addiction," 230–32, esp. 232.

47. Cantwell, "Jane Campion's Lunatic Women," 161–62.

9. LIGHTING A LAMP

1. "Jane Campion on Jane Campion," in Verhoeven, *Jane Campion,* 195.

2. Ibid., 195–96.

3. "My daughter Alice who is 13 . . . is very passionate and quick speaking, so whenever I got to a point when I thought 'what would Fanny do about this?', I thought what would Alice do about it, and that really helped me out. She was a kind of muse for me." "Production Story," press kit for *Bright Star,* Cannes Film Festival, May 2009, Margaret Herrick Library.

4. Colmant, "Jane et Janet."

5. Speaking of Edith, Campion confirmed that "she believes in love and its redemptive power. She is extremely romantic." Bilbrough, "*The Piano,*" 123.

6. At the time of this writing (July 2009), *Bright Star* had not been released for general viewing. It was shown in competition at the Cannes Film Festival in May 2009, and was received with great critical acclaim. I was fortunate enough to see the film at a unique screening in the Auckland International Film Festival on 9 July 2009, upon which the discussion in this chapter is based. There is plenty more

to be said about this magnificent film which, visually, is one of the most beautiful cinematic artifacts ever made.

7. "Jane Campion Q&A: Female First," 18 February 2010, http://www.femalefirst.co.uk/movies/Jane+Campion-8234.html (accessed 13 March 2010).

8. Anne Thompson, "Ten Questions for *Bright Star*'s Jane Campion: 'I've Never Made a Crap Film,'" *IndieWIRE Blog Network*, 10 December 2009, http://blogs.indiewire.com/thompsononhollywood/2009/12/10/ten_questions_for_bright_stars_j (accessed 13 March 2010).

9. Motion, *Keats*, 474.

10. I acknowledge my debt to Jane Campion for providing me with a copy of this poem by her mother.

11. Noyes, *English Romantic Poetry and Prose*, 1138.

12. "Director's Notes," press kit, *Bright Star*, Margaret Herrick Library.

CONCLUSION

1. On "metonymy," see Metz, "Metaphor/Metonymy; or, The Imaginary Referent," in his *The Imaginary Signifier*, 149–203.

2. See Metz, *The Imaginary Signifier*, 237.

3. Silverman, *Acoustic Mirror*, 212.

4. An example is the use of a double mirror in *In the Cut* as a means of contrasting the reflections of Frannie and her half sister, Pauline.

5. "Cinethemes" is a neologism used by Richard O'Neill-Dean in a paper describing symbolic motifs in *The Piano*: "Interpreting *The Piano* as a Dream." He used the term again in "Interpreting *In the Cut* as a Dream," a paper presented at the University of Otago, July 2008.

6. I acknowledge my debt to Richard O'Neill-Dean for first drawing attention to many of these cinethemes.

7. "I've only started to realize how common my motifs are to myself." "Jane

Campion on Jane Campion," in Verhoeven, *Jane Campion*, 190.

8. I use the term "focalization" in the sense proposed by Genette, that is, as a narrative technique of "situated focus," in which the "field" is restricted, through a selection of narrative information, to indicate who within the narrative is perceiving the action. See Genette, *Narrative Discourse Revisited*, 74.

9. See Polan, *Jane Campion*, 26–27.

10. Flaumenbaum, *Femme désirée*, 139.

11. Silverman, *Acoustic Mirror*, 216. See also Laplanche and Pontalis, *Language of Psycho-Analysis*, 317.

12. Silverman, *Acoustic Mirror*, 215.

13. Flaumenbaum, *Femme désirée*, 153–54.

14. Hartmann, *Ego Psychology*, 76.

15. Stern, *Interpersonal World*, 257.

16. Ibid., 263.

17. Silverman, *Acoustic Mirror*, 233.

18. Winnicott, "Location of Cultural Experience" (1967), 8.

19. Ibid., 4–5.

20. Bollas, "The Aesthetic Moment," 43, 46.

21. Bollas, *Being a Character*, 17, 13.

22. Ibid., 4, 17.

23. Ibid., 15.

24. Ibid., 30.

25. See Bollas, "The Aesthetic Moment," 40–48.

26. Kahr, *Sex and the Psyche*, 311–36.

27. Ibid., 335.

28. For a consideration of the connection between trauma and creativity, see McDougall et al., *L'artiste et le psychanalyste*, especially the essay by McDougall, "L'artiste et le psychanalyste," 11–34.

29. Gillain, "Script of Delinquency," 152.

30. Ibid., 149.

31. See de Baecque and Toubiana, *Truffaut*.

32. Tobias, "Interview with Tsai Ming-liang."

33. Spoto, *Dark Side of Genius*, 263.

34. Ibid., 151.

35. Ibid., 395.

36. See Bellour, "Hitchcock the Enunciator."

37. Ciment and Niogret, "Interview with Steven Soderbergh," 17–18.

38. Ibid., 18.

39. Ibid., 20.

40. Ciment, Perez, and Tailleur, "Interview with Roman Polanski," 36.

41. Bazin, "De la politique des auteurs," 24.

42. Andrew, "The Unauthorized Auteur Today," 78.

43. Ibid., 81. See also Verhoeven, *Jane Campion,* for further comment on the forces outside the individual director that help to construct the image of the auteur.

44. Jane Campion, personal conversation with the author, 11 September 2008. Elsewhere, Campion has said that she couldn't allow an audience to leave the cinema with such a nihilistic impression as the original ending of Moore's novel would have imparted—a classic instance of the contradictory opinions to which she is prone on occasions, and to which she has admitted.

45. This useful Latin phrase was first formulated by St. Augustine in *De Trinitate* (6.6), and subsequently reiterated by philosophers like Thomas Aquinas (*Summa Theologica,* 1.76.8, and *Summa contra Gentiles,* 2.72) and Giordano Bruno (*Theses de Magia,* 9).

46. Well, what led me to write it was, really my own life. You know, I've been writing movies since I'm . . . 29. And I'm 54 now. And I found this is what interested me at this point in my life. You know, just like when I wrote *Private Benjamin,* when I was young, about a woman going off on her own, and not getting married. All those things seemed so vital to me then. This is a story that seemed vital to the life I lead now, that's all. ("Q and A with Nancy Meyers")

Works Cited

Abramowitz, Rachel. "Jane Campion." *Premiere Magazine*, 1996. Reprinted in Wexman, *Jane Campion*, 186–91.

Agnès, Catherine Poirier. "Interview with Susanna Moore." *Libération*, 28 May 2003.

Allen, Richard. "Female Sexuality, Creativity, and Desire in *The Piano*." In *Piano Lessons: Approaches to the Piano*, ed. Felicity Coombs and Suzanne Gemmell, 44–63. London: Libbey, 1999.

Andrew, Dudley. "The Unauthorized Auteur Today." In *Film Theory Goes to the Movies*, ed. Jim Collins, Hilary Radner, and Ava Preacher Collins, 77–85. New York: Routledge, 1993.

Andrew, Geoff. "Sects Appeal." *Time Out* (London), 22–29 March 2000.

Andrin, Muriel. "Her-land: Jane Campion's Cinema; or, Another Poetic of the Inner Sense." In Radner, Fox, and Bessière, *Jane Campion*, 27–36.

Astruc, Alexandre. "Naissance d'une novelle avant-garde: La caméra-stylo." *Écran Français* 144 (1948). Reprinted in *The New Wave*, ed. Peter Graham, 17–23. London: Secker and Warburg, 1969.

Attali, Danielle. "La leçon érotique de Jane Campion." *Journal du Dimanche*, 14 December 2003.

Baillie, Russell. "Critical Smokescreen." *New Zealand Herald*, 19 December 1999, E10.

Barber, Lynden. "Angel with an Eccentric Eye." *Sydney Morning Herald*, 8 September 1990. Reprinted in Wexman, *Jane Campion*, 57–61.

———. "Playing It Low-Key." *Sydney Morning Herald*, 3 August 1993. Reprinted in Wexman, *Jane Campion*, 142–45.

Barthes, Roland. "The Death of the Author." Reprinted in *Image/Music/Text*, by Roland Barthes, 142–48. New York: Hill and Wang, 1977.

Bazin, André. "De la politique des auteurs." In Grant, *Auteurs and Authorship*, 19–28.

Bellour, Raymond. *The Analysis of Film*. Edited by Constance Penley. Bloomington: Indiana University Press, 2000.

———. "Hitchcock the Enunciator." Translated by Bertrand Augst and Hilary Radner. *Camera Obscura* 2 (Fall 1977): 66–91. Reprinted in Bellour, *The Analysis of Film*, 217–37.

Bilbrough, Miro. "The Piano." *Cinema Papers* (Melbourne), May 1993. Reprinted in Wexman, *Jane Campion*, 113–23.

Birnbaum, Robert. "Susanna Moore." *Morning News*, 25 September 2007.

Bollas, Christopher. "The Aesthetic Moment and the Search for Transformation." In *Transitional Objects and Potential Spaces: Literary Uses of D. W. Winnicott,* ed. Peter L. Rudnytsky, 40–49. New York: Columbia University Press, 1993.

———. *Being a Character: Psychoanalysis and Self Experience.* London: Routledge, 1992.

———. *Hysteria.* New York: Routledge, 2000.

———. *The Shadow of the Object: Psychoanalysis of the Unthought Known.* New York: Columbia University Press, 1987.

Bordwell, David, and Kristin Thompson. *Film Art: An Introduction.* 7th ed. New York: McGraw-Hill, 2003.

Boswell, Parley Ann. *Edith Wharton on Film.* Carbondale: Southern Illinois University Press, 2007.

Bourguignon, Thomas, and Michel Ciment. "Interview with Jane Campion: More Barbarian than Aesthete." *Positif,* June 1993. Reprinted in Wexman, *Jane Campion,* 101–112.

Bradshaw, John. *Family Secrets: The Path to Self-Acceptance and Reunion.* New York: Bantam, 1995.

Campion, Anna, and Jane Campion. *Holy Smoke: A Novel.* New York: Hyperion, 1999.

Campion, Edith. "Matador." *Landfall* 142 (June 1982): 153–56.

———. Papers. Alexander Turnbull Library, Wellington, N.Z.

———. *A Place to Pass Through and Other Stories.* Wellington, N.Z.: Reed, 1977.

———. "Rider Waits." *Islands* 1, no. 1 (July 1984): 63–69.

———. "To Black Cat." *Islands* 8, no. 3 (October 1980): 238.

Campion, Edith, and Frank Sargeson. *Tandem: The Chain, Edith Campion; Frank Sargeson, En Route.* Wellington, N.Z.: Reed, 1979.

Campion, Jane. "Big Shell." *Rolling Stone* 426 (1988): 74–76.

———. "Director's Commentary." *An Angel at My Table.* DVD. Directed by Jane Campion. Irvington, N.Y.: Criterion Collection, 2005.

———. "Director's Commentary." *In the Cut.* DVD. Directed by Jane Campion. Culver City, Calif.: Sony Pictures, 2004.

———. "Director's Commentary." *In the Cut,* uncut director's edition. DVD. Directed by Jane Campion. Culver City, Calif.: Columbia TriStar Home Entertainment, 2004.

———. "Director's Commentary." *Sweetie.* DVD. Directed by Jane Campion. Irvington, N.Y.: Criterion Collection, 2006.

———. "Interview." *La leçon de piano.* DVD. Directed by Jane Campion. Paris: TF1 Video, 2003.

———. Introduction to *An Angel at My Table,* by Janet Frame. London: Virago, 2008.

———. *The Piano.* London: Bloomsbury, 1993.

Campion, Jane, and Susanna Moore. *In the Cut* (script). Margaret Herrick Library, Los Angeles, Calif.

Campion, Jane, and Kate Pullinger. *The Piano: A Novel.* London: Bloomsbury, 1994.

Canby, Vincent. "'Sweetie,' a Wry Comedy by New Australian Director." *New York Times,* 6 October 1989.

Cantwell, Mary. "Jane Campion's Lunatic Women." *New York Times Magazine,* 19 September 1993. Reprinted in Wexman, *Jane Campion,* 153–63.

Caughie, John, ed. *Theories of Authorship: A Reader.* London: British Film Institute, 1981.

Cheshire, Ellen. *The Pocket Essential Jane Campion.* Harpenden, England: Pocket Essentials, 2000.

Ciment, Michel. "The Function and the State of Film Criticism." In *Projections 8: Film-makers on Film-making,* ed. John Boorman and Walter Donohue, 35–42. London: Faber and Faber, 1998.

———. "Interview." *Jane Campion: Le coffret.* DVD. Issy-les-Moulineaux, France: Studio Canal, 2003.

———. "Jane Campion: Revenir à la période dans laquelle je vis." *Positif* 466 (December 1999): 17–26.

———. "The Red Wigs of Autobiography: Interview with Jane Campion." *Positif,* April 1991. Reprinted in Wexman, *Jane Campion,* 62–70.

———. "'Sweetie' la folle: Entretien avec Michel Ciment." *Jane Campion: Le coffret.* DVD. Issy-les-Moulineaux, France: Studio Canal, 2003.

———. "Two Interviews with Jane Campion." *Positif,* January 1990. Reprinted in Wexman, *Jane Campion,* 30–44.

———. "A Voyage to Discover Herself." *Positif,* December 1996. Reprinted in Wexman, *Jane Campion,* 177–85.

Ciment, Michel, and Hubert Niogret. "Interview with Steven Soderbergh: *Sex, Lies, and Videotape.*" In *Steven Soderbergh Interviews,* ed. Anthony Kaufman, 13–23. Jackson: University Press of Mississippi, 2002.

Ciment, Michel, Michel Perez, and Roger Tailleur. "Interview with Roman Polanski." In *Roman Polanski Interviews,* ed. Paul Cronin, 31–46. Jackson: University Press of Mississippi, 2005.

Colmant, Marie. "Jane et Janet, face à face." *Libération,* 24 April 1991.

Colombani, Florence. "Jane Campion, réalisatrice: 'Je voulais que le film ressemble à ceux des années 1970, de Friedkin et Scorsese.'" *Le Monde,* 17 December 2003.

Cordaiy, Hunter. "Jane Campion Interviewed." *Cinema Papers,* December 1990. Reprinted in Wexman, *Jane Campion,* 74–82.

Dapkus, Jeanne R. "Sloughing Off the Burdens: Ada's and Isabel's Parallel/Antithetical Quests for Self-Actualization in Jane Campion's Film *The Piano* and Henry James's Novel *The Portrait of a Lady.*" *Literature/Film Quarterly* 25, no. 3 (1997): 177–87.

de Baecque, Antoine, and Serge Toubiana. *Truffaut: A Biography.* Translated by Catherine Temerson. New York: Knopf, 1999.

Dekker, Diana. "Creator of Professional Theatre." *Dominion Post,* 27 September 2007, B7.

———. "A Man of the Stage." *Evening Post,* 21 August 1993, 10.

Denby, David. "Lady Stuck." *New York,* 13 January 1997, 45–46.

Doland, Angela. "Female Film Directors Lacking at Cannes." *ABC News,* 20 May 2007. http://abcnews.go.com/International/wireStory?id=3194100 (accessed 25 January 2008).

d'Yvoire, Christophe. "Vertige de 'amour.'" *Studio Magazine* (France), May 1993, 82–86.

Edel, Leon. *Henry James: A Life.* New York: Harper and Row, 1985.

Faery, Rebecca Blevins. "Wharton's *Reef:* The Inscription of Female Sexuality." In *Edith Wharton: New Critical Essays,* ed. Alfred Bendixen and Annette Zilversmit, 79–96. New York: Garland, 1992.

Falsetto, Mario. *Personal Visions: Conversations with Independent Film-makers.* London: Constable, 1999.

Feinstein, Howard. "Heroine Chic." *Vanity Fair,* December 1996, 214.

———. "The Jane Mutiny." *Guardian Unlimited,* 2 April 1999.

Feldvoss, Marli. "Jane Campion: Making Friends by Directing Films." *EPD Film,* August 1993. Reprinted in Wexman, *Jane Campion,* 96–100.

"Fight-back over *Piano* Claims." *Dominion,* 8 April 2000, 31.

Firestone, Robert W., and Joyce Catlett. *Fear of Intimacy*. Washington, D.C.: American Psychological Association, 1999.

Flaumenbaum, Danièle. *Femme désirée, femme désirante*. Paris: Payot et Rivages, 2006.

Forsberg, Myra. "'Sweetie' Isn't Sugary." *New York Times*, 14 January 1990, sec. 2, 15.

Foucault, Michel. "What Is an Author?" In *Language, Counter-Memory, Practice*, ed. Donald F. Bouchard, trans. Donald F. Bouchard and Sherry Simon, 124–27. Ithaca, N.Y.: Cornell University Press, 1977.

Fox, Alistair. "Puritanism and the Erotics of Transgression: The New Zealand Influence in Jane Campion's Thematic Imaginary." In Radner, Fox, and Bessière, *Jane Campion*, 103–22.

———. *The Ship of Dreams: Masculinity in Contemporary New Zealand Fiction*. Dunedin, N.Z.: Otago University Press, 2008.

Frame, Janet. *An Autobiography*. Auckland, N.Z.: Vintage Collectors' Edition, 1994.

———. *Faces in the Water*. New York: Braziller, 1961.

———. *Owls Do Cry*. Christchurch, N.Z.: Pegasus, 1957.

Franke, Lizzie. "Jane Campion Is Called the Best Female Director in the World. What's Female Got to Do with It?" *Guardian*, 21 February 1997. Reprinted in Wexman, *Jane Campion*, 205–9.

Fraser, Kennedy. "Portrait of the Director." *Vogue*, January 1997, 144–49.

Freud, Sigmund. *Collected Papers*. Edited by James Strachey. Vol. 5, *Miscellaneous Papers, 1888–1938*. London: Hogarth, 1950.

———. *The Standard Edition of the Complete Psychological Works of Sigmund Freud*. Vol. 16. London: Hogarth, 1974.

Frey, Hillary. "The Purloined *Piano*?" *Lingua Franca* 10, no. 6 (2000): 8–10.

Frois, Emmanuèle. "Jane Campion l'effrontée." *Le Figaro,* 17 December 2003.

Furler, Andreas. "Structure Is Essential/Absolutely Crucial/One of the Most Important Things." *Filmbulletin*, February 1993. Reprinted in Wexman, *Jane Campion*, 91–95.

Gaitanos, Sarah. *Nola Millar: A Theatrical Life*. Wellington, N.Z.: Victoria University Press, 2006.

Geertz, Clifford. "Thick Description: Toward an Interpretive Theory of Culture." In his *The Interpretation of Cultures: Selected Essays*, 3–30. New York: Basic, 1973.

Genette, Gérard. *Narrative Discourse Revisited*. Translated by Jane E. Lewin. Ithaca, N.Y.: Cornell University Press, 1988.

Gerstner, David A., and Janet Staiger, eds. *Authorship and Film*. New York: Routledge, 2003.

Gillain, Anne. *François Truffaut: Le secret perdu*. Paris: Hatier, 1991.

———. "The Script of Delinquency: François Truffaut's *Les 400 coups*." In *French Film: Texts and Contexts*, ed. Susan Hayward and Ginette Vincendeau, 142–57. London: Routledge, 2000.

Gillett, Sue. "Lips and Fingers: Jane Campion's *The Piano*." *Screen* 36, no. 3 (Autumn 1995): 286–87.

———. *Views from beyond the Mirror: The Films of Jane Campion*. St. Kilda, Australia: Australian Teachers of Media in association with Australian Film Institute, 2004.

Glanerie, Richard. "L'Amérique est puritaine et pornographique." *France Soir,* 17 December 2003.

Gordon, Rebecca M. "Portraits Perversely Framed: Jane Campion and Henry James." *Film Quarterly* 56, no. 2 (Winter 2002–2003): 14–24.

Grant, Barry Keith, ed. *Auteurs and Authorship: A Film Reader.* Malden, Mass.: Blackwell, 2008.

The Grass Is Greener: Interview with Jane Campion. TV program. Produced by Rymer Bayly Watson, 1990. New Zealand Film Archive.

Habegger, Alfred. *Henry James and the "Woman Business."* Cambridge: Cambridge University Press, 1989.

Harcourt, Peter. *A Dramatic Appearance: New Zealand Theatre 1920–1970.* Wellington, N.Z.: Methuen, 1978.

Hardy, Ann. "Jane Campion and the Moral Occult." In Radner, Fox, and Bessière, *Jane Campion,* 251–76.

———. "The Last Patriarch." *Illusions* 23 (1994): 6–13. Reprinted in *Jane Campion's "The Piano,"* ed. Harriet Margolis, 59–85. Cambridge: Cambridge University Press, 2000.

Hartmann, Heinz. *Ego Psychology and the Problem of Adaptation.* New York: International Universities Press, 1958.

Hawker, Philippa. "Jane Campion." *Cinema Papers* (Melbourne), May 1989. Reprinted in Wexman, *Jane Campion,* 20–25.

Hessey, Ruth. "Campion Goes Out on a Limb—Again." *Sydney Morning Herald,* 5 July 1989. Reprinted in Wexman, *Jane Campion,* 26–29.

Hillier, Jim. "Auteur Theory and Authorship: Auteur Structuralism and Beyond." *Film Encyclopedia.* http://www.filmreference.com/encyclopedia/Academy-Awards-Crime-Films/Auteur-Theory-and-Authorship-AUTEUR-STRUCTURALISM-AND-BEYOND.html (accessed 18 July 2008).

"*Holy Smoke:* Dernier tango dans le bush." *Le Figaroscope* (Paris), 24 November 1999.

Hoveyda, Fereydoun. "Les Taches du soleil." *Cahiers du cinéma* 110 (August 1960). Reprinted in *Cahiers du cinéma:* *The 1950s: Neo-Realism, Hollywood, New Wave,* ed. Jim Hillier, 8–9. Cambridge, Mass.: Harvard University Press, 1985.

Ide, Wendy. "Review of *In the Cut.*" *Times* (London), 24 October 2003.

Ihimaera, Witi. *The Dream Swimmer.* Auckland, N.Z.: Penguin, 1997.

———. *The Matriarch.* Auckland, N.Z.: Heinemann, 1986.

Ikin, Bridget, and Tiara Lowndes. "The Making of *An Angel at My Table.*" *An Angel at My Table.* DVD. Directed by Jane Campion. Irvington, N.Y.: Criterion Collection, 2005.

Jacobs, Carol. "Playing Jane Campion's *Piano:* Politically." *MLN* 109, no. 5 (1994): 757–85.

James, Henry. *The Portrait of a Lady.* Edited by Geoffrey Moore. London: Penguin, 2003.

Jones, Laura. *An Angel at My Table: The Screenplay from the Three Volume Autobiography of Janet Frame.* Auckland, N.Z.: Random Century, 1990.

———. *The Portrait of a Lady: Screenplay Based on the Novel by Henry James.* New York: Penguin, 1996.

Jones, Lawrence. "'I can really see myself in her story': Jane Campion's Adaptation of Janet Frame's *Autobiography.*" In Radner, Fox, and Bessière, *Jane Campion,* 77–100.

Jung, C. G. "Psychology and Religion." In *The Collected Works of C. G. Jung,* ed. Herbert Read, Michael Fordham, and Gerhard Adler. Vol. 11, *Psychology and Religion: West and East,* 3–105. London: Routledge, 1958.

Kael, Pauline. "Circles and Squares." *Film Quarterly* 16, no. 3 (Spring 1963): 12–26. Reprinted in Grant, *Auteurs and Authorship,* 46–54.

Kahr, Brett. *Sex and the Psyche: The Truth about Our Most Secret Fantasies.* London: Penguin, 2007.

Landrot, Marnie. "La ligue des Campions." *Télérama,* 24 November 1999.

Laplanche, J., and J.-B. Pontalis. *The Language of Psycho-analysis.* Translated by Donald Nicholson-Smith. New York: Norton, 1973.

Lewis, Judith. "Wholly Jane." *LA Weekly,* 27 January 2000. http://www.laweekly.com/2000-01-27/film-tv/wholly-jane (accessed 30 June 2009).

Mackenzie, Suzie. "Beloved Rivals." *Guardian Unlimited,* 5 June 1999.

———. "Campions Enjoy a Rich Friendship." *Otago Daily Times,* 2 October 1999, 70.

Macklin, Robert. "Campion's Award-winning Screenplay 'Inspired' by Novel." *Canberra Times,* 8 April 2000.

———. "Creative Effort Went into Film." *Canberra Times,* 11 April 2000.

"The Making of *The Portrait of a Lady.*" *The Portrait of a Lady.* DVD. Directed by Jane Campion. Universal City, Calif.: Universal Pictures, 2001.

Mander, Jane. *The Story of a New Zealand River.* Auckland, N.Z.: Vintage, 1999.

Margolis, Harriet. "The Campions Indulge in *The Audition.*" In Radner, Fox, and Bessière, *Jane Campion,* 39–52.

Martin, Adrian. "Losing the Way: The Decline of Jane Campion." *Landfall* 200 (2000): 89–102.

Mason, Bruce. "Richard Campion—Producer." *Landfall* 13, no. 52 (December 1959): 367–70.

Matthews, Philip. "Leaving Sequence." *Listener* (Wellington), 19 August 1995, 45.

McDougall, Joyce. *Plea for a Measure of Abnormality.* New York: Brunner/Mazel, 1992.

———. *Theaters of the Mind: Illusion and Truth on the Psychoanalytic Stage.* New York: Brunner-Routledge, 1991.

McDougall, Joyce, Jacques André, Dominique Schneider, and Dominique Suchet. *L'artiste et le psychanalyste.* Paris: Presses Universitaires de France, 2008.

McGregor, Rae. *The Story of a New Zealand Writer: Jane Mander.* Dunedin, N.Z.: University of Otago Press, 1998.

McHugh, Kathleen. *Jane Campion.* Urbana: University of Illinois Press, 2007.

McKee, Robert. *Story: Substance, Structure, Style, and the Principles of Screenwriting.* New York: Regan, 1997.

Metz, Christian. *The Imaginary Signifier: Psychoanalysis and the Cinema.* Bloomington: Indiana University Press, 1982.

Millar, Nola Leigh. "Theatre." In *An Encyclopaedia of New Zealand,* ed. A. H. McLintock. Republished as *Te Ara: The Encyclopedia of New Zealand* (updated 18 September 2007). http://www.TeAra.govt.nz/1966/T/Theatre/en (accessed 28 March 2008).

Moore, Susanna. *In the Cut.* Sydney: Picador, 2004.

Motion, Andrew. *Keats.* London: Faber and Faber, 1997.

Murphy, Kathleen. "Jane Campion's Passage to India." *Film Comment* 36, no. 1 (January–February 2000): 30–36.

Noyes, Russell, ed. *English Romantic Poetry and Prose.* New York: Oxford University Press, 1956.

O'Neill-Dean, Richard. "Interpreting *In the Cut* as a Dream." Paper presented at the University of Otago, July 2008.

———. "Interpreting *The Piano* as a Dream." Paper presented at the University of Otago, 7 December 2006.

"Oscar Doubts over Campion's *Piano.*" *Canberra Times,* 25 March 2000.

Ostria, Vincent, and Thierry Jousse. "*The Piano:* Interview with Jane Campion." *Cahiers du cinéma,* May 1993. Reprinted in Wexman, *Jane Campion,* 124–32.

Ozick, Cynthia. "What Only Words, Not Film, Can Portray." *New York Times,* 5 January 1997, H1.

Paul, Mary. *Her Side of the Story: Readings of Mander, Mansfield, & Hyde.* Dunedin, N.Z.: University of Otago Press, 1999.

Petrie, Graham. "Alternatives to Auteurs." *Film Quarterly* 26, no. 3 (Spring 1973): 27–35. Reprinted in Grant, *Auteurs and Authorship,* 110–18.

Polan, Dana. *Jane Campion.* London: British Film Institute, 2001.

Portuges, Catherine. *Screen Memories: The Hungarian Cinema of Marta Meszaros.* Bloomington: Indiana University Press, 1993.

Pryor, Ian. "Sister Act." *Press* (Christchurch, N.Z.), 19 December 1999.

Pullinger, Kate. "Her Assignment: Write a Novel of 'The Piano' and Make It Snappy!" *Observer* (London), 20 March 1994, Arts 17.

"Q and A with Nancy Meyers." *MovieFreak,* 15 March 2004. http://www.moviefreak.com/features/interviews/nancymeyers.htm (accessed 18 October 2008).

Radner, Hilary. "'In extremis': Jane Campion and the Woman's Film." In Radner, Fox, and Bessière, *Jane Campion,* 3–24.

———. *Neo-Feminist Cinema: Girly Films, Chick Flicks, and Consumer Culture.* London: Routledge, 2010.

Radner, Hilary, Alistair Fox, and Irène Bessière, eds. *Jane Campion: Cinema, Nation, Identity.* Detroit, Mich.: Wayne State University Press, 2009.

"Review of *Holy Smoke.*" *Le Figaroscope,* 24 November 1999.

Ripoche, Nicolas. "Fleurs de soufre." *Jane Campion: Le coffret.* DVD. Issy-les-Moulineaux, France: Studio Canal, 2003.

Rivette, Jacques. "Notes sur une révolution." *Cahiers du cinéma* 54 (1955). Reprinted in translation in *Cahiers du cinéma: The 1950s: Neo-Realism, Hollywood, New Wave,* ed. Jim Hillier, 94–97. Cambridge, Mass.: Harvard University Press, 1985.

Roach, Vicky. "Campion Takes on Spielberg at His Game." *Sydney Daily Telegraph,* 17 February 1994. Reprinted in Wexman, *Jane Campion,* 173–74.

Samson, Alan. "Jane Campion's Cult Fiction." *Dominion,* 14 December 1999, 9.

Sampson, Desmond. "Carry on Campion." *Sunday Star Times,* 5 December 1999.

Sargeson, Frank. "Review." *Landfall* 125 (1978): 90–91.

Sarmas, Lisa. "What Rape Is." *Arena Magazine,* no. 8 (December 1993–January 1994): 14.

Sarris, Andrew. "Notes on the Auteur Theory in 1962." *Film Culture* 29 (Winter 1962–1963): 1–8. Reprinted in Grant, *Auteurs and Authorship,* 35–45.

Sidey, Emma. "Jane's Addiction." *W,* October 2003, 230–32.

Silverman, Kaja. *The Acoustic Mirror: The Female Voice in Psychoanalysis and Cinema.* Bloomington: Indiana University Press, 1988.

———. "The Female Authorial Voice." In Silverman, *The Acoustic Mirror.* Reprinted in Wexman, *Film and Authorship,* 50–75.

Simpson, Emily. "She Calls the Shots." *Next,* March 2004, 28–31.

Sobchak, Vivian. *Carnal Thoughts: Embodiment and Moving Image Culture.* Berkeley: University of California Press, 2004.

Spoto, Donald. *The Dark Side of Genius: The Life of Alfred Hitchcock.* New York: Da Capo, 1999.

Staiger, Janet. "Authorship Approaches." In Gerstner and Staiger, *Authorship and Film,* 27–57.

Stam, Robert. *Film Theory: An Introduction.* Malden, Mass.: Blackwell, 2000.

Stam, Robert, and Toby Miller, eds. *Film and Theory: An Anthology.* Malden, Mass.: Blackwell, 2000.

Stern, Daniel N. *The Interpersonal World of the Infant: A View from Psychoanalysis and Developmental Psychology.* New York: Basic, 2000.

Stevens, Anthony. *Jung: A Very Short Introduction.* Oxford: Oxford University Press, 2001.

Stiles, Mark. "Jane Campion." *Cinema Papers* (Melbourne), December 1984. Reprinted in Wexman, *Jane Campion,* 3–8.

Strauss, Bob. "Tart Family Ties in *Sweetie.*" *San Francisco Chronicle,* 25 February 1990.

Taubin, Amy. "Jane and Anna Campion Make a Religious-Cult Classic." *Village Voice,* 24–30 November 1999.

Thometz, Kurt. "The Book as Aphrodisiac." *Private Library.* http://colophon.com/privatelibrary/interviews/moore.html (accessed 8 May 2008).

Tobias, Scott. "Interview with Tsai Mingliang." *A.V. Club,* 27 February 2002. http://www.avclub.com/articles/tsai-mingliang,13756 (accessed 29 July 2009).

Tranchant, Marie-Noëlle. "*Holy Smoke:* Jane Campion, la belle et le gourou." *Journal du Dimanche,* 21 November 1999.

Truffaut, Francois. "Une certaine tendance du cinéma français." Reprinted in translation as "A Certain Tendency of the French Cinema" in *Movies and Methods: An Anthology,* ed. Bill Nichols, 224–37. Berkeley: University of California Press, 1976.

———. *The Films in My Life.* New York: Da Capo, 1994.

Tucker, Ken. "Review of *In the Cut* (1995)." *EW,* 10 November 1995. http://www.ew.com/ew/article/0,,299463,00.html (accessed 8 May 2008).

Urban, Andrew L. "Campion: Cannes She Do It?" *Australian,* 13 April 1989. Reprinted in Wexman, *Jane Campion,* 16–19.

———. "The Contradictions of Jane Campion, Cannes Winner." *Australian,* 21 May 1986. Reprinted in Wexman, *Jane Campion,* 14–15.

Vanderheyden, Patricia Anne. "Religious Addiction: The Subtle Destruction of the Soul." *Pastoral Psychology* 47, no. 4 (March 1999): 293–302.

Vanoye, Francis. *Scénarios modèles, modèles de scénarios.* Paris: Nathan, 1991. Reprint, Paris: Armand Colin, 2005.

Verhoeven, Deb. *Jane Campion.* New York: Routledge, 2009.

Vidal, Gore. "Who Makes Movies?" *New York Review of Books,* 25 November 1976. Reprinted in Grant, *Auteurs and Authorship,* 148–57.

Wexman, Virginia Wright, ed. *Film and Authorship.* New Brunswick, N.J.: Rutgers University Press, 2003.

———. *Jane Campion: Interviews.* Jackson: University Press of Mississippi, 1999.

Wharton, Edith. *The Reef.* New York: Penguin, 1995.

Williams, Sue. "A Light on the Dark Secrets of Depression." *Australian,* 2 May 1995. Reprinted in Wexman, *Jane Campion,* 175–76.

———. "Portrait of an Artist." *Listener* (Wellington), 1 February 1999, 38.

Williamson, Kristin. "The New Filmmakers." *National Times* (Sydney), 20 June 1985. Reprinted in Wexman, *Jane Campion,* 9–10.

Wilson, Bryan R. *The Social Dimension of Sectarianism: Sects and New Religious Movements in Contemporary Society.* Oxford: Oxford University Press, 2004

Winnicott, D. W. "The Location of Cultural Experience." Reprinted in *Transitional Objects and Potential Spaces: Literary Uses of D. W. Winnicott,* ed. Peter L. Rudnytsky, 3–12. New York: Columbia University Press, 1993.

———. *The Maturational Processes and the Facilitating Environment: Studies in the Theory of Emotional Development.* London: Karnac, 1990.

Witchel, Diana. "Return of the Native."
    Listener (Wellington), 16 October 1993,
    16–20.

Wollen, Peter. "From *Signs and Meaning
    in the Cinema:* The Auteur Theory." In
    *Film Theory and Criticism: Introductory
    Readings,* 3rd ed., ed. Gerald Mast and
    Marshall Cohen, 553–62. New York:
    Oxford University Press, 1985.

———. *Signs and Meaning in the Cinema,*
    2nd ed. Bloomington: Indiana Univer-
    sity Press, 1972.

Wood, Robin. "Ideology, Genre, Auteur."
    Film Comment 13, no. 1 (January–Feb-
    ruary 1977). Reprinted in Grant, *Au-
    teurs and Authorship,* 84–92.

Yacowar, Maurice. "Hitchcock's Imagery
    and Art." Reprinted in Grant, *Auteurs
    and Authorship,* 203–21.

Filmography

FILMS BY JANE CAMPION

Feature Films

Two Friends (1986)

DIRECTOR Jane Campion
WRITER Helen Garner
CINEMATOGRAPHER Julian Penney
PRODUCERS Jane Campion,
    Jan Chapman
PRODUCTION COMPANY Australian
    Broadcasting Corporation
CAST (CHIEF CHARACTERS) Kris
    Bidenko (Kelly), Emma Coles
    (Louise), Sean Travers (Matthew),
    Kris McQuade (Louise's
    Mother), Peter Hehir (Malcolm),
    Stephen Leeder (Jim)
RUNNING TIME 76 minutes

Sweetie (1989)

DIRECTOR Jane Campion
WRITERS Jane Campion, Gerard Lee
CINEMATOGRAPHER Sally Bongers
PRODUCERS John Maynard,
    William Mckinnon
PRODUCTION COMPANIES Arenafilm,
    Australian Film Commission, New
    South Wales Film and Television Office
CAST (CHIEF CHARACTERS)
    Genevieve Lemon (Dawn), Karen
    Colston (Kay), Tom Lycos (Louis),
    Jon Darling (Gordon), Dorothy Barry

(Flo), Michael Lake (Bob), Andre Pa-
taczek (Clayton), Emma Fowler (Little
Sweetie)
RUNNING TIME 100 minutes

An Angel at My Table (1990)

DIRECTOR Jane Campion
WRITER Laura Jones
CINEMATOGRAPHER Stuart Dryburgh
PRODUCERS Bridget Ikin, Grant
    Major, John Maynard
PRODUCTION COMPANIES Hibiscus
    Films, New Zealand Film Commission,
    Television New Zealand, Australian
    Broadcasting Corporation, Channel 4
CAST (CHIEF CHARACTERS) Alexia
    Keogh (Young Janet), Karen
    Fergusson (Teenage Janet), Kerry
    Fox (Janet Frame), Iris Churn
    (Mother), Kevin J. Wilson (Father),
    William Brandt (Bernhard)
RUNNING TIME 158 minutes

The Piano (1993)

DIRECTOR Jane Campion
WRITER Jane Campion
CINEMATOGRAPHER Stuart Dryburgh
PRODUCERS Jan Chapman, Alain
    Depardieu, Mark Turnbull
PRODUCTION COMPANIES New South
    Wales Film and Television Office,
    Jan Chapman Productions, CIBY
    2000, Australian Film Commission

CAST (CHIEF CHARACTERS) Holly Hunter (Ada), Harvey Keitel (Baines), Sam Neill (Stewart), Anna Paquin (Flora), Kerry Walker (Aunt Morag), Genevieve Lemon (Nessie), Tungia Baker (Hira), Te Whatanui Skipwith (Chief Nihe), Pete Smith (Hone), Cliff Curtis (Mana)

RUNNING TIME 120 minutes

The Portrait of a Lady (1996)

DIRECTOR Jane Campion
WRITER Laura Jones
CINEMATOGRAPHER Stuart Dryburgh
PRODUCERS Monty Montgomery, Steve Golin, Ann Wingate, Mark Turnbull, Ute Leonhardt, Hedron Reshoeft
PRODUCTION COMPANIES Polygram Filmed Entertainment, Propaganda Films
CAST (CHIEF CHARACTERS) Nicole Kidman (Isabel Archer), John Malkovich (Gilbert Osmond), Barbara Hershey (Madame Serena Merle), Mary-Louise Parker (Henrietta Stackpole), Martin Donovan (Ralph Touchett), Richard E. Grant (Lord Warburton), Christian Bale (Edward Rosier), Viggo Mortensen (Caspar Goodwood), Valentina Cervi (Pansy Osmond)
RUNNING TIME 144 minutes

Holy Smoke (1999)

DIRECTOR Jane Campion
WRITERS Jane Campion, Anna Campion
CINEMATOGRAPHER Dion Beebe
PRODUCERS Bridget Ikin, Grant Major, John Maynard
PRODUCTION COMPANY Miramax International
CAST (CHIEF CHARACTERS) Kate Winslet (Ruth), Harvey Keitel (PJ Waters), Julie Hamilton (Mother), Sophie Lee (Yvonne), Tim Robertson (Father), Genevieve Lemon (Rahi)
RUNNING TIME 114 minutes

In the Cut (2003)

DIRECTOR Jane Campion
WRITERS Jane Campion, Susanna Moore
CINEMATOGRAPHER Dion Beebe
PRODUCERS Laurie Parker, Effie T. Brown, Francois Ivernel, Nicole Kidman, Ray Angelic
PRODUCTION COMPANIES Pathé Productions, Screen Gems, Pathé International, Red Turtle
CAST (CHIEF CHARACTERS) Meg Ryan (Frannie), Mark Ruffalo (Malloy), Jennifer Jason Leigh (Pauline), Nick Damici (Rodriguez), Sharrieff Pugh (Cornelius Webb), Kevin Bacon (John Graham)
RUNNING TIME 119 minutes

Bright Star (2009)

DIRECTOR Jane Campion
WRITER Jane Campion
CINEMATOGRAPHER Greig Fraser
PRODUCERS Jan Chapman, Caroline Hewitt
PRODUCTION COMPANIES BBC Films, Film Finance Corporation Australia, Pathé Renn Productions, UK Film Council, in association with Hopscotch International and NSW Film and Television Office
CAST (CHIEF CHARACTERS) Abbie Cornish (Fanny Brawne), Ben Wishaw (John Keats), Paul Schneider (Charles Armitage Brown), Kerry Fox (Mrs. Brawne), Edie Martin (Toots Brawne), Thomas Sangster (Samuel Brawne)
RUNNING TIME 119 minutes

Short Films

Tissues (1980)

DIRECTOR Jane Campion
WRITER Jane Campion
Filmed on Super 8.
Other details unavailable.

Mishaps: Seduction and Conquest (1981)
DIRECTOR Jane Campion
WRITER Jane Campion
CINEMATOGRAPHERS Sally
Bongers, Nicolette Freeman,
George Perykowski, Paul Cox
PRODUCER Jane Campion
PRODUCTION COMPANY Australian
Film, Television, and Radio School
CAST (CHIEF CHARACTERS) Deborah
Kennedy (Emma), Richard Evans
(Geoffrey), Stuart Campbell
(George Mallory's Voice)
RUNNING TIME 15 minutes

Peel—An Exercise in Discipline (1982)
DIRECTOR Jane Campion
WRITER Jane Campion
CINEMATOGRAPHER Sally Bongers
PRODUCER Ulla Ryghe
PRODUCTION COMPANY Australian
Film, Television, and Radio School
CAST (CHIEF CHARACTERS) Tim Pye
(Brother/Father), Katie Pye (Sister/
Aunt), Ben Martin (Son/Nephew)
RUNNING TIME 9 minutes

Passionless Moments (1983)
DIRECTOR Jane Campion
WRITERS Gerard Lee, assisted
by Jane Campion
CINEMATOGRAPHER Jane Campion
PRODUCERS Jane Campion, Gerard Lee
PRODUCTION COMPANY Australian
Film, Television, and Radio School
CAST (CHIEF CHARACTERS) David
Benton (Ed Tumbury), Ann Burriman
(Gwen Gilbert), Sean Callinan (Jim
Newbury), Paul Chubb (Jim Simpson),
Sue Collie (Angela Elliot), Elias
Ibrahim (Ibrahim Ibrahim), Paul
Melchert (Arnold), George Nezovic
(Gavin Metchalle), James Pride
(Lyndsay Aldridge), Yves Stenning
(Shaun), Rebecca Steweard (Julie Fry)
RUNNING TIME 13 minutes

A Girl's Own Story (1984)
DIRECTOR Jane Campion
WRITER Jane Campion
CINEMATOGRAPHER Sally Bongers
PRODUCER Patricia L'Huede
PRODUCTION COMPANY Australian
Film, Television, and Radio School
CAST (CHIEF
CHARACTERS) Gabrielle Shornegg
(Pam), Paul Chubb (Father),
Colleen Fitzpatrick (Mother),
Joanne Gabbe (Sister), Jane
Edwards (Deirdre), John Godden
(Graeme), Marina Knight (Gloria)
RUNNING TIME 27 minutes

After Hours (1984)
DIRECTOR Jane Campion
WRITER Jane Campion
CINEMATOGRAPHERS Laurie
McInnes, Michael Edols
PRODUCER Janet Bell
PRODUCTION COMPANY Women's
Film Unit of Australia
CAST (CHIEF CHARACTERS) Danielle
Pearse (Lorraine), Don Reid
(John Phillips), Anna Maria
Monticelli (Sandra Adams)
RUNNING TIME 29 minutes

The Water Diary (2006)
DIRECTOR Jane Campion
WRITER Jane Campion
CINEMATOGRAPHER Greig Fraser
PRODUCERS Marc Oberon, Lissandra
Haulica, Christopher Gill
PRODUCTION COMPANIES LDM
Productions, Big Shell Publishing
CAST (CHIEF CHARACTERS) Alice
Englert (Ziggy), Tintin Marova Kelly
(Sam), Isidore Tillers (Felicity Miles),
Harry Greenwood (Simon), Genevieve
Lemon (Pam Garner), Justine Clarke
(Mother), Russell Dykstra (Father)
RUNNING TIME 18 minutes

The Lady Bug (2007) (segment in
the collective film of 33 shorts,
*Chacun son cinéma; ou, Ce petit
coup au coeur quand la lumière
s'éteint et que le film commence*)
DIRECTOR Jane Campion
WRITER Jane Campion
CINEMATOGRAPHER Greig Fraser
CAST Erica Englert, Clayton Jacobson,
    Genevieve Lemon, Marney McQueen
RUNNING TIME 3 minutes

Other Films Cited

The Age of Innocence (Martin
    Scorsese, 1993)
Amarcord (Federico Fellini, 1973)
The American (Paul Unwin, 1998)
Annie Hall (Woody Allen, 1977)
Antoine et Colette (François
    Truffaut, 1962)
The Aspern Papers (Kirk Browning, 1989)
The Audition (Anna Campion, 1989)
Bed and Board (*Domicile conjugal*)
    (François Truffaut, 1970)
Broken Skin (Anna Campion, 1991)
The Children (Tony Palmer, 1990)
Ethan Frome (John Madden, 1993)
The Four Hundred Blows (*Les 400
    coups*) (François Truffaut, 1959)
The Golden Bowl (James Ivory, 2000)
The Haunting of Hell House
    (Mitch Marcus, 1999)
The House of Mirth (Terence Davies, 2000)
It's a Wonderful Life (Frank Capra, 1946)
Last Tango in Paris (Bernardo
    Bertolucci, 1972)
Live Flesh (*Carne trémula*)
    (Pedro Almodovar, 1997)
Loaded (Anna Campion, 1994)

Love on the Run (*L'Amour en fuite*)
    (François Truffaut, 1979)
Malice (Harold Becker, 1993)
The Man Who Knew Too Much
    (Alfred Hitchcock, 1956)
Mildred Pierce (Michael Curtiz, 1945)
Nora (Pat Murphy, 2000)
Pretty Woman (Garry Marshall, 1990)
The River (*He liu*) (Tsai Ming-liang, 1997)
Se7en (David Fincher, 1995)
Sex and the City: The Movie
    (Michael Patrick King, 2008)
Sex, Lies, and Videotape (Steven
    Soderbergh, 1989)
Shadow of a Doubt (Alfred
    Hitchcock, 1943)
Something's Gotta Give
    (Nancy Meyers, 2003)
Stolen Kisses (*Baisers volés*)
    (François Truffaut, 1968)
Strangers on a Train (Alfred
    Hitchcock, 1951)
The 39 Steps (Alfred Hitchcock, 1935)
To Each His Own Cinema (*Chacun son
    cinéma; ou, Ce petit coup au coeur
    quand la lumière s'éteint et que le film
    commence*) (Theodoros Angelopoulos,
    Olivier Assayas, and others, 2007)
The Turn of the Screw (Rusty
    Lemorande, 1992)
Vertigo (Alfred Hitchcock, 1958)
Washington Square (Agnieszka
    Holland, 1997)
The Wayward Cloud (*Tian bian yi duo
    yun*) (Tsai Ming-liang, 2005)
What Maisie Knew (*Ce que savait
    Maisie*) (Edouard Molinaro, 1995)
What Time Is It over There? (*Ni na bian
    ji dian*) (Tsai Ming-liang, 2001)
The Wings of a Dove (Iain Softley, 1997)

Index

ALISTAIR FOX is Professor of English and director of the Centre for Research on National Identity at the University of Otago. He has written extensively on humanism, politics, and reform in early modern England and, more recently, on New Zealand culture and identity, focusing on contemporary New Zealand literature and film.

This book was designed by Jamison Cockerham and set in type by Tony Brewer at Indiana University Press and printed by Sheridan Books Inc.

The text type is Arno and the display type is Warnock, both designed by Robert Slimbach and issued by Adobe Systems Incorporated.